The Complete Results & Line-ups of the Olympic Football Tournaments 1900-2004

Colin Jose

Acknowledgements

I would like to thank former FIFA Press Officers, Rene Courte and Guido Tognoni for their help in compiling this record. Also a special thanks to Norwegian historian Kare Torgrimsen for all the assistance he gave me.

British Library Cataloguing in Publication Data
A catalogue record for this book is available from the British Library

ISBN 1-86223-088-9

Copyright © 2004, SOCCER BOOKS LIMITED. (01472 696226)
72 St. Peter's Avenue, Cleethorpes, N.E. Lincolnshire, DN35 8HU, England

All rights are reserved. No part of this publication may be reproduced, stored in a retrieval system or transmitted, in any form or by any means, electronic, mechanical, photocopying, recording, or otherwise, without the prior written permission of Soccer Books Limited.

Printed by 4edge Ltd. www.4edge.co.uk

THE OLYMPIC FOOTBALL TOURNAMENT

The Olympic Football Tournament has been overshadowed in recent years by the World Cup, the European Championship, the South American championship and all the various other championships at the national team and club level. Yet in the years before World War Two, and just after, the Olympic Tournament had a much higher profile, in fact before the inception of the World Cup, it was looked upon as a sort of unofficial world championship.

In those years games played in the Olympics were considered full internationals by many countries, and in checking the record books of various nations you will find them listed as such. Yet following the 1930 World Cup many countries, particularly in Europe, relegated the games to a much lower status, and in most record books of today the Olympic Tournament rates only a very small space.

What is often overlooked about the Olympics is the number of great players who have taken part, often in the early years of their careers. For example in 1988 when Brazil reached the Final the striking partnership for Brazil was none other then Romario and Bebeto, and who today remembers that Sir Matt Busby was the British team manager in 1948!

As far as Britain in the Olympics is concerned the country is represented by one Olympic committee and not four national associations as is the case in the World Cup. Thus it is that officially Britain can field a combined team of the best players from all four countries. There are times when this has been done, 1948 for example, but on other occasions it has been an English team representing Britain. In all cases in this record the British team is listed as the United Kingdom.

Of course originally all participants in the Olympics were supposed to be amateurs, but this changed in 1984 when professionals were allowed to compete, "officially" for the first time.

Today the competition is played at the U-23 level, with three overage players permitted.

The Olympic Champions – Official Championships – Men

Year	Winners	Finalists	Venue
1900	* United Kingdom	France	Paris
1904	* Canada	United States	St. Louis
1906	* Denmark	Greece	Athens
1908	United Kingdom	Denmark	London
1912	United Kingdom	Denmark	Stockholm
1920	Belgium	Czechoslovakia	Antwerp
1924	Uruguay	Switzerland	Paris
1928	Uruguay	Argentina	Amsterdam
1932	No Competition		Los Angeles
1936	Italy	Austria	Berlin
1948	Sweden	Yugoslavia	London
1952	Hungary	Yugoslavia	Helsinki
1956	U.S.S.R.	Yugoslavia	Melbourne
1960	Yugoslavia	Denmark	Rome
1964	Hungary	Czechoslovakia	Tokyo
1968	Hungary	Bulgaria	Mexico City
1972	Poland	Hungary	Munich
1976	East Germany	Poland	Montreal
1980	Czechoslovakia	East Germany	Moscow
1984	France	Brazil	Los Angeles
1988	U.S.S.R.	Brazil	Seoul
1992	Spain	Poland	Barcelona
1996	Nigeria	Argentina	Atlanta
2000	Cameroon	Spain	Sydney
2004	Argentina	Paraguay	Athens

* The first three championships involved club teams.

The Olympic Champions – Official Championships – Women

Year	Winners	Finalists	Venue
1996	United States	China	Atlanta
2000	Norway	United States	Sydney
2004	United States	Brazil	Athens

2nd Olympiad – 1900 – Paris

The 2nd Olympiad ran in conjunction with the Paris International Exhibition of 1900 when various sporting events were held during a period from 14th May to 28th October. Among these events was a football competition and teams from the United Kingdom, France and Belgium competed. Very little is known of the competition except that the United Kingdom was represented by Upton Park Football Club of London, the French team was sponsored by the Union des Francaises des Sport Athletiques and the Belgian team was made up of students.

The squads for these games consisted of the following players:

Upton Park F.C.: J.H. Jones, Claude Buckenham, William Grosling, Alfred Chalk, T.E. Burridge, William Quash, Arthur Turner, F.G. Spackman, J. Nicholas, James Zealley, A. Haslom.

Union des Societes Francaises de Sports Athletiques: Lucien Huteau, Louis Bach, Pierre Allemane, Virgile Gaillard, Alfred Bloch, Maurice Macaire, Eugene Fraysse, Georges Garnier, A. Lambert, A. Grandjean, Fernand Canelle, R. Duparc, Gaston Peltier.

BELGIUM: Marcel Leboutte, Rene Kelecom, Ernest Moraeu, Alphonse Renier, Gustave Pelgrims, Eugene Neefs, Eric Thornton, Marius Delbecque, Hilaire Spaunoghe, Hendrik van Heuckelum, Lucien Londot.

Although only two games were played, it is assumed that the United Kingdom were pronounced champions as they beat France who, in turn, beat Belgium

20th September 1900

Venue: Paris

UNITED KINGDOM 4   (Turner, Nicholas 2, Zealey)
FRANCE 0
Half-time: Attendance: 500
Referee: Moignard (France)
U.K.: Jones, Buckenham, Gosling, Chalk, Burridge, Quash, Turner, Spackman, Nicholas, Zealley, Haslom.
FRANCE: Huteau, Bach, Allemane, Gaillard, Bloch, Macaire, Fraysse, Garnier, Lambert, Grandjean, Canelle.

23rd September 1900

Venue: Paris

FRANCE 6   (Peltier, Other scorers unknown)
BELGIUM 2   (Spanoghe, Van Heuckelum)
Attendance: 1,500
Referee: Wood (England)
FRANCE: Huteau, Bach, Allemane, Gaillard, Bloch, Macaire, Fraysse, Garnier, Lambert, Grandjean, Canelle.
BELGIUM: Leboutte, Kelcone, Moreau, Renier, Pelgrims, Van Hoorden, Thornton, Delbeque, Spaunoghe, Van Heuckelum, Londot.

3rd Olympiad – 1904 – St. Louis, Missouri

Very few nations sent teams of any sort to the 1904 Olympics in far off St. Louis. Once again the Olympics were held in conjunction with an exposition, this time the Louisiana Purchase Exposition. The main athletic events were held in September, but the football tournament, such as it was, was not held until November. Only two nations entered, Canada and the United States, who were represented by two teams. Originally the Canadians were to send two teams, but when Galt Football Club defeated the University of Toronto just before the teams were due to leave, the Toronto team opted to stay at home.

The squads for these games consisted of the following players:

Galt FC: Albert Ernest Linton, George Ducker, John Bell Gourlay, Robert George Lane, Albert Johnston, John Alexander Fraser, Otto Leopold Christman, Thomas S. Taylor, Frederick William Steep, Alexander Noble Hall, Gordon McDonald, William Twaits, Albert Henderson, Parnell Orde Gourlay.

Christian Brothers College: Louis Menges, Joseph Lydon, Thomas January, John January, Charles January, Peter Ratican, Warren Brittingham, Alexander Cudmore, Charles Bartliff, Oscar Brockmeyer, Raymond Lawler.

St. Rose School: Frank Frost, George Cooke, Henry Jameson, Joseph Brady, Martin Dooling, Dierkes, Cormic Cosgrove, O'Connell, Claude Jameson, Harry Tate, Thomas Cooke, Johnson.

Galt, as it turned out, defeated the two American teams with ease and returned home to a triumphal welcome.

16th November 1904

Venue: Francis Field in St. Louis, Missouri.

CANADA (Galt F.C.) 7   (Hall 3, McDonald 2, Steep, Taylor)

UNITED STATES (Christian Brothers College) 0

Half-time: 4-0

Referee: Paul McSweeney (St. Louis)

CANADA: Ernest Linton, George Ducker, John Gourlay, Robert Lane, Albert Johnston, John Fraser, Tom Taylor, Frederick Steep, Alexander Hall, Gordon McDonald, William Twaits.

U.S.A.: (Christian Brothers College): Menzies, T. January, Brockmeyer, H. January, P. Rattican, C. January, Cudmore, Brittingers, Barliff, Lyndon, Lawler.

17th November 1904

Venue: Francis Field in St. Louis, Missouri.

CANADA (Galt F.C.) 4   (Taylor 2, Henderson, o.g.)

UNITED STATES (St. Rose) 0

Half-time: 0-0

Referee: Paul McSweeney (St. Louis)

CANADA: Ernest Linton, George Ducker, John Gourlay, Robert Lane, Albert Johnston, Otto Christman, Tom Taylor, Frederick Steep, Alexander Hall, William Twaits, Albert Henderson.

U.S.A.: (St.Rose): G. Cook, H. Jamison, Brady, Durkes, Smith, Dooling, Cosgrove, O'Connell, C. Jamison, Tate, T. Cook.

20th November 1904

Venue: St. Louis, Missouri

**CHRISTIAN BROTHERS COLLEGE 0
ST. ROSE 0**

21st November 1904

Venue: St. Louis, Missouri

**CHRISTIAN BROTHERS COLLEGE 0
ST. ROSE 0**

23rd November 1904

Venue: St. Louis, Missouri

**CHRISTIAN BROTHERS COLLEGE 2
ST. ROSE 0**

Intermediate Olympiad – 1906 – Athens

Due to the success of the first Olympic Games held in Athens in 1896 the Greeks sought permission to hold the Games permanently in their country. However, although the IOC turned down their request they did obtain permission to hold an "Interim" Olympics to mark the tenth anniversary of the first games.

In 1906, Salonika (now known as Thessaloniki in Greece), was part of Turkey and in company with Smyrna (now called Izmir), and several other Greek speaking communities in Turkey, had its own independent Olympic committee which sent separate teams to the Olympic Games.

Thus a strange football competition ensued involving a Greek team, two teams from Turkey plus a team representing Denmark. The team from Smyrna was made up of eight Englishmen, of which five were brothers, two Frenchmen and one Greek. The Danes won 5-1 and thus qualified for the Final against the team from Athens. With Denmark leading 9-0 at half time, the Greeks dashed for their dressing room and refused to come out for the second half, thus handing the Danes the gold medal. Subsequently the Greeks were asked to play off with the Smyrna team for the silver medal and when they refused the two Turkish teams competed for the silver and bronze medals.

Semi-Finals

23rd April 1906

GREECE (Athens) 5
TURKEY (Salonika) 0

23rd April 1906

DENMARK 5
TURKEY (Smyrna) 1

Bronze Medal Game

TURKEY (Smyrna) 12
TURKEY (Salonika) 0

SMYRNA: Edwin Charnaud, Zarek Choyoumdzian, Edouard Giraud, Jacques Giraud, Henri Joly, Percy de la Fontaine, Donald Whittal, Albert Whittal, Godfrey Whittal, Herbert Whittal, Edward Whittal.

Final

24th April 1906

DENMARK 9
GREECE (Athens) 0

Half-time: 9-0

(The game was bandoned at half time, when the Greek team locked itself in the dressing room and refused to appear for the second half. As a result, Greece (Athens) were disqualified)

DENMARK: Viggo Andersen, Peter Petersen, Charles Buchwald, Parmo Ferslew, Stefan Rasmussen, Aage Andersen, Oscar Nielsen-Norland, Carl Pedersen, Holgar Frederiksen, August Lindgren, Henry Rambusch.

GREECE: P. Brionis, G. Barbaris, N. Dekavallas, G. Gerontakis, O. Josiphoglus, G. Kalafatis, F. Labranos, K. Mpotassis, G. Merkouris, S. Otkonomou, A. Pantos.

4th Olympiad – 1908 – London

Football became an official part of the Olympic Games for the first time in 1908, when the games were held in London. The United Kingdom (represented by an English team), Sweden, Netherlands, Denmark and France (represented by an "A" and a "B" team) participated. Hungary and Bohemia entered but then withdrew and as a result the Netherlands, who were to have played Hungary and France "A", who were to have played Bohemia, reached the Semi-Finals without playing a game.

England and Denmark were clearly the class of the competition each team containing many well known players of that time. The Danish team included Nils Middelboe, later to make a name for himself with Chelsea, while in the England team Vivian Woodward has long been regarded as one of the finest players of that era. Against France "A" in the semi-final Sophus Nielsen the bow legged Danish centre forward scored ten goals, a record that stands to this day.

In the Final England defeated Denmark 2-0, scoring one goal in each half, but the English papers of the day noted that the Danes were unlucky to lose by that score and with better goalkeeping the might well have won.

Total attendance for the six games was approximately 20,000 for an average of 3,333.

19th October 1908

Venue: Shepherds Bush Stadium, London.

DENMARK 9 (N. Middelboe 2, Wolffhagen 4, Bohr 2, S. Nielsen)

FRANCE (B) 0

Attendance: 2,000

Referee: Thomas Kyle (England)

DENMARK: Drescher, Buchwald, Hansen, Bohr, K. Middelboe, N. Middelboe, O. Nielsen, Lindgreen, S. Nielsen, Wolffhagen, Andersen.

FRANCE B: Desrousseaux, Verlet, Morillion, Destarac, Denis, Bilot, Filez, Mathaux, Holgart, Jenicot, Eucher.

20th October 1908

Venue: The White City Stadium, London.

UNITED KINGDOM 12 (Hawkes 2, Chapman, Berry, Woodward 2, Stapley 2, Purnell 4)

SWEDEN 1 (Bergstrom)

Half-time: 7-0 Attendance: 2,000

Referee: John T. Ibbottson (England)

U.K.: Bailey, Corbett, Smith, Hunt, Chapman, Hawkes, Berry, Woodward, Stapley, Purnell, Hardman.

SWEDEN: Bengtsson, Fjastad, Malm, Sven Olssen, Lindman, Ohlson, Almkvist, Bergstrom, Gustafsson, Sven Ohlsson, Ansen.

Semi-Finals

22nd October 1908

Venue: The White City Stadium, London.

NETHERLANDS 0
UNITED KINGDOM 4 (Stapley 3, Hardman)

Half-time: 1-0   Attendance: 6,000

Referee: John T. Howcroft (England)

NETHERLANDS: Beeuwkes, Heijting, Otten, Sol, de Korver, Mundt, Welcker, Snethlage, Reeman, Thomee, de Bruyn Kops.

U.K.: Bailey, Corbett, Smith, Hunt, Chapman, Hawkes, Berry, Woodward, Stapley, Purnell, Hardman.

22nd October 1908

Venue: Shepherds Bush Stadium, London.

DENMARK 17 (S.E. Nielsen 10, Wolffhagen 4, Lindgreen 2, N. Middelboe)
FRANCE (A) 1 (Sartorius)

Half-time: 6-1   Attendance: 1,000

Referee: Thomas P. Campbell (England)

DENMARK: Drescher, Buchwald, Hansen, Bohr, K. Middelboe, N. Middelboe, Gandil, Lindgreen, S. Nielsen, Wolffhagen, Rasmussen.

FRANCE A: Tilette, Dubly, Wibaut, Georges Bayrou, R. Schulbart, Renaux, Fenouillere, Cypres, Francois, Albert, Sartorius.

Bronze Medal Game

23rd October 1908

Venue: Shepherds Bush Stadium, London.

NETHERLANDS 2 (Snethlage, Reeman)
SWEDEN 0

Half-time: 1-0   Attendance: 1,000

Referee: John H. Pearson (England)

NETHERLANDS: Beeuwkes, Heijting, Otten, Sol, de Korver, Kok, Welcker, Snethlage, Reeman, Thomee, de Bruyn Kops.

SWEDEN: Bengtsson, Fjastad, Andersson, Olssen, Lindman, Liden, Fagrell, Bergstrom, Ohlson, Gustafsson, Ansen.

Final

24th October 1908

Venue: The White City Stadium, London.

UNITED KINGDOM 2 (Chapman, Woodward)
DENMARK 0

Half-time: 1-0   Attendance: 8,000

Referee: John Lewis (England)

U.K.: Bailey, Corbett, Smith, Hunt, Chapman, Hawkes, Berry, Woodward, Stapley, Purnell, Hardman.

DENMARK: Drescher, Buchwald, Hansen, Bohr, K. Middelboe, N. Middelboe, O. Nielsen, Lindgreen, S. Nielsen, Wolffhagen, Rasmussen.

5th Olympiad – 1912 – Stockholm

The United Kingdom and Denmark met again in the Final in 1912, and once again it was the United Kingdom who triumphed by a two goal margin, this time 4-2. However, the Danes played without their leading goalscorer Poul Nielsen, who was injured, and lost right half Charles Buchwald after only 15 minutes with a dislocated elbow, and as no substitutes were allowed played the rest of the game with ten men.

This time 12 teams took part: the Netherlands, Sweden, Austria, Germany, Denmark, Norway, France, Italy, Finland, Czarist Russia, Hungary and England. France withdrew giving Norway a bye into the Second Round.

A Consolation Tournament was introduced in 1912 to allow teams, eliminated early from the competition proper, to play more than just the one game. It was a practice that was to continue for a number of years. In one of the consolation games Germany defeated Czarist Russia 16-0 and it is reported that as a result the Czar refused to pay the players way back to Russia!

The winning team, who represented the United Kingdom, was made up entirely of English players with the exception of Thomas Burn who was a Scot.

Total attendance for the 17 games was 83,700 for an average of 4,924.

First Round

29th June 1912

Venue: Stockholm   (Result is after extra time)

NETHERLANDS 4   (Vos 2, Bouvy 2)
SWEDEN 3   (Erik Borjesson, Swenson 2)

Half-time: 2-1   Attendance: 14,000

Referee: G. Wagstaffe Simmons (England)

NETHERLANDS: Gobel, Wijnveldt, Feith, de Wolf, de Korver, Lotsy, van Breda Kolff, de Groot, ten Cate, vos, Bouvy.

SWEDEN: Borjesson, Levin, Bergstrom, Wicksell, Sandberg, Gustafsson, Myhrberg, Swensson, Borjesson, Ekroth, Ansen.

29th June 1912

Venue: The Idrottsplats, Rasunda

AUSTRIA 5   (Studnicka, Neubauer, Merz 2, Cimera)
GERMANY 1   (Jager)

Half-time: 0-1   Attendance: 2,000

Referee: Herbert James Willing (Netherlands)

AUSTRIA: Noll, Graubart, Kurpiel, Brandstatter, Braunsteiner, Cimera, Hussak, Muller, Studnicka, Merz, Neubauer.

GERMANY: Weber, Ropnack, Hollstein, Krogmann, Breunig, Bosch, Wegele, Jager, Worpitzky, Kipp, Hirsch.

29th June 1912

Venue: *The Sportplatz, Traneberg*   *(After extra time)*

ITALY 2   (Bontadini, Sardi)
FINLAND 3   (Ohman, Elno Soinio, Wiberg)

Half-time: 2-2   Attendance: 600

Referee: Hugo Meisl (Austria)

ITALY: Campelli, Binaschi, De Vecchi, De Marchi, Milano, Leone, Zuffi, Bontadini, Berardo, Sardi, Mariani. (Sub: Morelli di Popolo)

FINLAND: Syrjalainen, Holopainen, Lofgren, Lund, E. Soinio, K. Soinio, Wickstrom, Wiberg, Nyyssonen, Ohman, Niska.

Denmark, Russia, Hungary, Norway and the United Kingdom all received byes.

Second Round

30th June 1912

Venue: *The Stadium, Rasunda*

NETHERLANDS 3   (ten Cate, Vos, Bouvy)
AUSTRIA 1   (Muller)

Half-time: 3-1   Attendance: 7,000

Referee: David Philip (Scotland)

NETHERLANDS: Gobel, Winjveldt, Bouman, Fortgens, Boutmy, Lotsy, van Breda Kolff, de Groot, ten Cate, Vos, Bouvy.

AUSTRIA: Noll, Graubart, Kurpiel, Brandstatter, Braunsteiner, Cimera, Hussak, Muller, Studnicka, Merz, Neubauer.

30th June 1912

Venue: *The Idrottsplats, Rasunda*

DENMARK 7   (Olsen 3, Nielsen 2, Wolfhagen, N. Middleboe)
NORWAY 0

Half-time: 3-0   Attendance: 700

Referee: Ruben Gelbord (Sweden)

DENMARK: S. Hansen, Buchwald, H. Hansen, Lykke, N. Middleboe, Berth, Petersen, S. Nielsen, Olsen, Christoffersen, Wolffhagen.

NORWAY: Pedersen, Skou, Baastad, Johansen, Herlofson, Andersen, Reinholdt, Krefting, Endrerud, R. Maartmann, E. Maartmann.

30th June 1912

Venue: *The Sportplatz, Traneberg*

FINLAND 2   (Wiberg, Ohman)
CZARIST RUSSIA 1   (Butusov)

Half-time: 0-1   Attendance: 200

Referee: Per Sjoblom (Sweden)

FINLAND: Syrjalainen, Holopainen, Lofgren, Lund, E. Soinio, Lietola, Wickstrom, Wiberg, Nyyssonen, Ohman, Niska.

RUSSIA: Favorski, Sokolov, Markov, Akimov, Hromov, Kinin, Smirnov, A. Filippov, Butusov, Zhitarev, S. Filippov.

30th June 1912

Venue: *The Olympic Stadium, Stockholm.*

UNITED KINGDOM 7   (Walden 6, Woodward)
HUNGARY 0

Half-time: 3-0   Attendance: 8,000

Referee: Christiaan J. Groothoff (Netherlands)

U.K.: Brebner, Burn, Knight, Littlewort, Hanney, Dines, Berry, Woodward, Walden, Hoare, Sharpe.

HUNGARY: Domonkos, Rumbold, Payer, Biro, Karoly, Vago, Sebestyen, Bodnar, Pataki, Schlosser, Borbas.

Semi-Finals

2nd July 1912

Venue: *The Olympic Stadium, Stockholm.*

DENMARK 4   (Olsen 2, Jorgensen, Poul Nielsen)
NETHERLANDS 1   (Jorgensen)

Half-time: 3-0   Attendance: 6,000

Referee: Ede Herczog (Hungary)

DENMARK: S. Hansen, N. Middleboe, H. Hansen, Buchwald, Jorgensen, Berth, O. Nilsen, P. Nielsen, Olsen, S. Nielsen, Wolffhagen.

NETHERLANDS: Gobel, Wijnveldt, Bouman, Fortgens, Boutmy, Lotsy, van Breda Kolff, de Groot, ten Cate, vos, Bouvy.

2nd July 1912

Venue: *The Olympic Stadium, Stockholm.*

UNITED KINGDOM 4   (Sharpe, Woodward, Walden 2)

FINLAND 0

Half-time: 2-0   Attendance: 4,000

Referee: Ruben Gelbord (Sweden)

U.K.: Brebner, Burn, Knight, Littlewort, Stamper, Dines, Wright, Woodward, Walden, Hoare, Sharpe.

FINLAND: Syrjalainen, Holopainen, Lofgren, Lund, E. Soinio, Lietola, Wickstrom, Wiberg, Ohman, Nyyssonen, Niska.

Bronze Medal Game

4th July 1912

Venue: *The Stadium, Rasunda.*

NETHERLANDS 9   (de Groot 2, van der Sluis 2, Vos 5)

FINLAND 0

Half-time: 4-0   Attendance: 1,000

Referee: Per Sjoblom (Sweden)

NETHERLANDS: Gobel, Wijnveldt, Feith, de Wolf, Lotsy, Boutmy, van Breda Kolff, de Groot, van der Sluis, Vos, Bouvy.

FINLAND: Syrjalainen, Holopainen, Lofgren, Lund, E. Soinio, Lietola, Tanner, Wiberg, Ohman, Nyyssonen, Niska.

Final

4th July 1912

Venue: *The Olympic Stadium, Stockholm.*

UNITED KINGDOM 4   (Berry, Walden, Hoare 2)

DENMARK 2   (Olsen 2)

Half-time: 4-1   Attendance: 25,000

Referee: Christiaan J. Groothoff (Netherlands)

U.K.: Brebner, Burn, Knight, McWhirter, Littlewort, Dines, Berry, Woodward, Walden, Hoare, Sharpe.

DENMARK: S. Hansen, N. Middelboe, H. Hansen, Buchwald, Jorgensen, Berth, O. Nielsen, Thufason, Olsen, S. Nielsen, Wolffhagen.

Consolation Tournament

First Round

1st July 1912

Venue: *The Idrottsplats, Rasunda.*

GERMANY 16   (Fuchs 10, Forderer 4, Oberle, Burger)

CZARIST RUSSIA 0

Half-time: 8-0   Attendance: 2,000

Referee: Christiaan J. Groothoff (Netherlands)

GERMANY: Werner, Reese, Hempel, Burger, Glaser, Ugi, Uhle, Forderer, Fuchs, Oberle, Thiel.

RUSSIA: Favorski, Sokolov, Rimsa, Uverski, Hromov, Iakovlev, Smirnov, Jitarev, Butusov, Nikitin, S. Filippov.

1st July 1912

Venue: *The Idrottsplats, Rasunda.*

ITALY 1   (Bontadini)

SWEDEN 0

Half-time: 1-0   Attendance: 2,500

Referee: Herbert James Willing (Netherlands)

ITALY: Campelli, De Vecchi, Valle, Binaschi, Milano, Leone, Bontadini, Berardo, Sardi, Barbesino, Mariani.

SWEDEN: Borjesson, Bergstrom, Tornqvist, Wicksell, Frykman, Gustafsson, Myhrberg, Swenson, Borjesson, Dahlstrom, Ansen.

1st July 1912

Venue: *The Sportplatz, Traneberg.*

AUSTRIA 1   (Neubauer)

NORWAY 0

Half-time: 1-0   Attendance: 200

Referee: Per Sjoblom (Sweden)

AUSTRIA: Kaltenbrunner, Kurpiel, Braunsteiner, Weber, Brandstatter, Cimera, Muller, Blaha, Merz, Grundwald, Neubauer.

NORWAY: Pedeersen, Skov, Baastad, Johansen, Herlofsen, Jensen, Reinholdt, Krefting, Endrerud, R. Maartmann, E. Maartmann.

Hungary received a bye

Semi-Finals

3rd July 1912

Venue: The Idrottsplats, Rasunda.

HUNGARY 3   (Schlosser 3)
GERMANY 1   (Forderer)

Half-time: 2-0   Attendance: 2,000

Referee: Christiaan J. Groothoff (Netherlands)

HUNGARY: Domonkos, Rumbold, Payer, Vago, Szury, Blum, Sebestyen, Bodnar, Fekete, Schlosser, Borbas.

GERMANY: Werner, Ropnack, Hollstein, Krogmann, Ugi, Bosch, Wegele, Forderer, Fuchs, Hirsch, Oberle.

3rd July 1912

Venue: The Djurgarden Stadium, Stockholm.

AUSTRIA 5   (A. Muller, Grundwald 2, Hussak, Studnicka)
ITALY 1   (Berardo)

Half-time: 2-0   Attendance: 3,500

Referee: Herbert James Willing (Netherlands)

AUSTRIA: Kaltenbrunner, Braunsteiner, Graubart, Weber, Brandstatter, Cimera, Hussak, A. Muller, Studnicka, Leopold Neubauer, Grundwald.

ITALY: Campelli, De Vecchi, Valle, Binaschi, Milano, Leone, Zuffi, Bontadini, Berardo, Barbesino, Mariani.

Consolation Final

5th July 1912

Venue: The Stadium, Rasunda.

HUNGARY 3   (Bodnar, Pataki, Schlosser)
AUSTRIA 0

Half-time: 1-0   Attendance: 5,000

Referee: Herbert James Willing (Netherlands)

HUNGARY: Domonkos, Rumbold, Payer, Biro, Vago, Blum, Sebestyen, Bodnar, Pataki, Schlosser, Borbas.

AUSTRIA: Kaltenbrunner, Graubart, Kurpiel, Brandstatter, Braunsteiner, Cimera, Hussak, Alois Muller, Merz, Neubauer, Grundwald.

7th Olympiad – 1920 – Antwerp

The 6th Olympiad, scheduled for Berlin in 1916 was cancelled because of World War One.

Two new nations formed as a result of the war, Czechoslovakia and Yugoslavia met in the First Round of the 1920 competition, while for the first time there was an entry from Africa, Egypt then a British protectorate, being represented. Other entries were Norway, who surprisingly defeated the United Kingdom 3-1 in the First Round, France, Switzerland, Italy, Luxembourg, Netherlands, Greece, Sweden, Spain, Denmark and Belgium the host nation. Switzerland withdrew giving France a bye into the Second Round, while Belgium also received a bye.

The United Kingdom team defeated by Norway was made up of English players with the exception of Fred Nicholas, who was a Welshman. The team included the following players. John Mitchell (Manchester University), J.E. Payne (Casuals and Leytonstone), A.E. Knight (Portsmouth), K.R.G. Hunt (Corinthians), George Atkinson (Bishop Auckland), C.W. Harbridge (Civil Service), F.W.H. Nicholas (Old Foresters), M.T. Bunyan (Chelsea), H.M. Prince (Army), R. Sloley (Ealing and Corinthians), K.E. Hegan (Corinthians).

The leading goalscorer was Herbert Carlsson of Sweden, later to make a name for himself in the professional American Soccer League in the United States, while the famous Spanish goalkeeper Ricardo Zamora made his Olympic debut.

The Final was between Belgium and Czechoslovakia, but the Czechs walked off the field after 40 minutes in protest against the sending off of one ot their players. Belgium were winning 2-0 at the time and Czechoslovakia were disqualified. The consolation Final determined the silver (Spain) and bronze medalists (the Netherlands).

Football drew larger crowds than all the other sports although the figures pale in comparison to today's crowds. The football competition drew 63,612 fans, with track and field a distant second with 28,665. Next came swimming with 24,549 and then gymnastics with 16,795.

First Round

28th August 1920

Venue: Antwerp

CZECHOSLOVAKIA 7 (Janda 3, Vanik 3, J. Sedlacek)
YUGOSLAVIA 0

Half-time: 3-0 Attendance: 600

Referee: Raphael L. Van Praag (Netherlands)

CZECHOSLOVAKIA: Klapka, A. Hojer, Pospisil, Kolenaty, Pesek, Perner, J. Sedlacek, Janda, Pilat, Vanik, Mazal.

YUGOSLAVIA: Vrdjuka, Zupancic, Sifer, Tavcar, Cindric, Rupec, Vragovic, Dubravcic, Perska, Granec, Ruzic.

28th August 1920

Venue: Antwerp.

NORWAY 3 (Gundersen 2, Wilhelms)
UNITED KINGDOM 1 (Nicholas)

Half-time: 1-1 Attendance: 5,000

Referee: D. Johannes Mutters (Netherlands)

NORWAY: Wathne, Aulie, Skou, Wold, Halvorsen, Andersen, Paulsen, Wilhelms, Helgesen, Gundersen, Holm.

U.K.: Mitchell, Payne, Knight, Hunt, Atkinson, Harbridge, Nicholas, Bunyan, Prince, Sloley, Hegan.

28th August 1920

Venue: Ghent

ITALY 2 (Baloncieri, Brezzi)
EGYPT 1 (Daki Osman)

Half-time: 1-0   Attendance: 2,000

Referee: Paul Putz (Belgium)

ITALY: Giancone, Bruna, De Vecchi, Reynaudi, Meneghetti, Lovati, Sardi, Baloncieri, Brezzi, Santamaria, Forlivesi.

EGYPT: Kemel Taha, Mohamed El Sayd, Abdel Salam Handi, Riad Shawky, Aly Fahmy El Hassani, Gamil Osman, Tewfik Abdallah, Aly Hassan, Hussein Hegazi, Sayd Abaza, Daki Osman.

28th August 1920

Venue: Brussels

SPAIN 1 (Patricio)
DENMARK 0

Half-time: 0-0   Attendance: 3,000

Referee: Willem Eymers (Netherlands)

SPAIN: Zamora, Otero, Arrate, Samitier, Belauste, Eguiazabal, Pagaza, Sesumaga, Patricio, Pichichi, Acedo.

DENMARK: Hansen, Middleboe, Blicher, Groetham, Likke, Aaby, Danis, Rodhe, Viggo, Olsen, Andersen.

Belgium received a bye.

28th August 1920

Venue: Brussels

NETHERLANDS 3 (Groosjohan 2, Bulder)
LUXEMBOURG 0

Half-time: 1-0   Attendance: 3,000

Referee: Georges Hubrecht (Belgium)

NETHERLANDS: MacNeill, Denis, Verweij, Bosschart, Kuipers, Steeman, van Rappard, van Dort, Groosjohan, Bulder, de Natris.

LUXEMBOURG: Kruger, Schmit, Koetz, Hamilus, Ungeheuer, Schumacher, Metzler, Langers, Elter, Massard, Leesch.

Second Round

29th August 1920

Venue: Brussels

CZECHOSLOVAKIA 4 (Janda 3, Vanik)
NORWAY 0

Half-time: 2-0   Attendance: 4,000

Referee: Charles Barette (Belgium)

CZECHOSLOVAKIA: Klapka, A. Hojer, Steiner, Kolenaty, Pesek, Seifert, J. Sedlacek, Janda, Vanik, Mazal, Pilat.

NORWAY: Wathne, Aulie, Skou, Wold, Halvorsen, Andersen, Paulsen, Aas, Helgesen, Gundersen, Holm.

28th August 1920

Venue: Antwerp

SWEDEN 9 (Carlson 5, Olsson 2, Wicksell, Dahl)
GREECE 0

Half-time: 6-0   Attendance: 5,000

Referee: Charles Barette (Belgium)

SWEDEN: Zander, Lund, Hillen, Nordenskjold, Wicksell, Gustafsson, Bergstrom, Olsson, Carlson, Dahl, Sandberg.

GREECE: Fotiadis, Ghizis, Kaloudis, Ghiotis, A. Nikolidis, Pepis, Kalafatis, I. Andianopoulos, T. Nikolaidis, Hagiandreou, Doumitrou.

29th August 1920

Venue: Antwerp

FRANCE 3 (Bard 2, Boyer)
ITALY 1 (Brezzi)

Half-time: 2-1   Attendance: 10,000

Referee: Henri Christophe (Belgium)

FRANCE: Parsys, Huot, Baumann, Batmale, Petit, Hugues, Devaquez, Boyer, P. Nicholas, Bard, Dubly.

ITALY: Giacone, Bruna, De Vecchi, Sardi, Meneghetti, Lovati, Ferraris, Baloncieri, Brezzi, Santamaria, Marucco.

29th August 1920

Venue: Antwerp   *(Result is after extra time)*

NETHERLANDS 5   (Groosjohan 2, Bulder 2, de Natris)
SWEDEN 4   (Carlson 2, Olsson, Dahl)

Half-time: 2-3   Attendance: 5,000

Referee: Josef Fanta (Czechoslovakia)

NETHERLANDS: MacNeill, Denis, Verweij, Bosschart, Kuipers, Steeman, van Rappard, Bieshaar, Groosjohan, Bulder, de Natris.
SWEDEN: Zander, Lund, Hillen, Oijermark, Wicksell, Gustafsson, Bergstrom, Olsson, Carlson, Dahl, Sandberg.

29th August 1920

Venue: Antwerp

BELGIUM 3   (Coppee 3)
SPAIN 1   (Arrate)

Half-time: 1-0   Attendance: 18,000

Referee: Johannes Mutters (Netherlands)

BELGIUM: Debie, Swartenbroeks, Verbeeck, Musch, Hanse, Fierens, Van Hege, Coppee, Balyu, Nizot, Hebdin.
SPAIN: Zamora, Vallana, Arrate, Artola, Sancho, Eguiazabal, Pagaza, Pichichi, Patricio, Vasquez, Acedo.

Semi-Finals

30th August 1920

Venue: Antwerp

CZECHOSLOVAKIA 4   (Mazal 3, Steiner)
FRANCE 1   (Boyer)

Half-time: 1-0   Attendance: 12,000

Referee: Johannes Mutters (Netherlands)

CZECHOSLOVAKIA: Klapka, A. Hojer, Steiner, Kolenaty, Pesek, Seifert, J. Sedlacek, Janda, Mazal, Vanik, Placek.
FRANCE: Parsys, Huot, Baumann, Batmale, Petit, Hugues, Devaquez, Boyer, P. Nicholas, Bard, Dubly.

31st August 1920

Venue: Antwerp

BELGIUM 3   (Larnoe, Van Hege, Bragard)
NETHERLANDS 0

Half-time: 0-0   Attendance: 35,000

Referee: John Lewis (England)

BELGIUM: Debie, Swartenbroeks, Verbeeck, Musch, Hanse, Fierens, Van Hege, Coppee, Bragard, Larnoe, Bastin.
NETHERLANDS: MacNeill, Denis, Verweij, Bosschart, Kuipers, Steeman, van Rappard, Bieschaar, Groosjohan, Bulder, de Natris.

Final

2nd September 1920

Venue: Antwerp

BELGIUM 2   (Coppee, Larnoe)
CZECHOSLOVAKIA 0

Half-time: 2-0   Attendance: 35,000

Referee: John Lewis (England)

BELGIUM: Debie, Swartenbroecks, Verbeeck, Musch, Hanse, Fierens, Van Hege, Coppee, Bragard, Larnoe, Bastin.
CZECHOSLOVAKIA: Klapka, A. Hojer, Steiner, Kolenaty, Pesek, Seifert, J. Sedlacek, Janda, Pilat, Vanik, Mazal.

(Czechoslovakia walked off after 40 minutes in protest at a refereeing decision and were disqualified from the tournament)

Consolation Tournament

First Round

31st August 1920

Venue: Antwerp (*Result is after extra time*)

NORWAY 1   (A. Andersen)
ITALY 2   (Sardi, Badini II)

Half-time: 0-0   Attendance: 500
Referee: L. Fourgous (France)

NORWAY: Wathne, Aulie, Johnsen, Mohn, Halvorsen, G. Andersen, Paulsen, A. Andersen, Helgesen, Semb-Thorstvedt, Holm.
ITALY: Campelli, Rosetta, Bruna, Reynaudi, Parodi, Burlando, Roggero, Sardi, Ferraris, Badini, Forlivesi.

1st September 1920

Venue: Antwerp

SPAIN 2   (Belauste, Acedo)
SWEDEN 1   (Dahl)

Half-time: 0-1   Attendance: 1,500
Referee: Giovanni Mauro (Italy)

SPAIN: Zamora, Vallana, Arrate, Samitier, Belauste, Sabino, Pagaza, Sesumaga, Patricio, Pichichi, Acedo.
SWEDEN: Zander, Lund, Nordenskjold, Oijermark, Wicksell, Gustafsson, Bergstrom, Olsson, Carlson, Dahl, Sandberg.

Semi-Final

2nd September 1920

Venue: Antwerp

ITALY 0
SPAIN 2   (Sesumaga 2)

Half-time: 0-1   Attendance: 14,000
Referee: Paul Putz (Belgium)

ITALY: Campelli, Bruna, DeVecchi, Parodi, Menaghetti, De Nardo, De Marchi, Baloncieri, Brezzi, Badini, Marucco.
SPAIN: Zamora, Vallana, Otero, Artola, Sancho, Sabino, Moncho Gil, Pagaza, Sesumaga, Pichichi, Silverio.

Final

5th September 1920

Venue: Antwerp

SPAIN 3   (Sesumaga 2, Pichichi)
NETHERLANDS 1   (Groosjohan)

Half-time: 2-0   Attendance: 4,000
Referee: Paul Putz (Belgium)

SPAIN: Zamora, Vallana, Arrate, Samitier, Belauste, Eguiazabal, Moncho Gil, Sesumaga, Patricio, Pichichi, Acedo.
NETHERLANDS: MacNeill, Denis, Verweij, Bosschart, Kuipers, Steeman, van Rappard, van Dort, Groosjohan, von Heijden, Bulder.

8th Olympiad – 1924 – Paris

A whole new, and highly significant, element was introduced into the Olympic Football Tournament in 1924, when for the first time there was a South American entry, in the presence of Uruguay. In addition the United States, entered for the first time since 1904 when two club teams from St. Louis competed.

The American squad included eight players from Philadelphia clubs. Samuel Dalrymple and Raymond Hornberger (Disston), Irving Davis and Henry Farrell (Fairhill), and William Demko, Arthur Rudd, Andy Stradan and Herbert Wells all from Fleischer Yarn the U.S. amateur champions. Others in the squad were Aage Brix (Los Angeles A.C.), James Douglas (Newark), William Findlay (New York Galicia), Edward Hart (St. Matthews of St. Louis), Carl Johnson (Chicago Swedish-American), James Rhody (Erie A.A.) and James Holland (Scott A.A.) both from New Jersey, Fred Connor (Lynn of Massachusetts) and F. Burke Jones (Bridgeville, Pennsylvania) made up the team. The Americans opened with a win over Estonia but were outclassed by Uruguay.

In all, 22 countries (the largest so far) began the competition, but it was Uruguay who dazzled the crowds with their quickness and agility. The United Kingdom did not enter being embroiled in a dispute with FIFA over broken time payments to amateurs. However, for the first time the Republic of Ireland sent a team made up largely from three clubs: Athlone Town, St. James Gate of Dublin and Bohemians. The Athlone players were Patrick O'Reilly, John Dykes, Thomas Muldoon, Francis Ghent and Denis Hannon, while Ernest McKay, Michael Farrell and Patrick Duncan came from St. James Gate. Herbert Kerr, John Murray and John McCarthy represented Bohemians and Joseph Kendrick was playing for Brooklyn. The Irish lost 1-0 to Bulgaria and 2-1 to the Netherlands after extra time.

There was no Consolation Tournament in this Olympiad.

Among the many notable players who appeared in this tournament was Hungarian centre half Bela Guttmann, later to coach the Portuguese champions Benfica to glory in the European Cup, and Josef Eisenhoffer, like Guttmann a member of the famous Hakoah club of Vienna. The great Ricardo Zamora was in goal for Spain.

The Uruguayans, whose line up included a number of players who were to make their mark on the international scene for years to come, defeated the United States, France and the Netherlands before disposing of Switzerland in the Final by 3-0.

A total of 249,956 fans paid to see the 24 games of the Olympic Football Competition for an average of 10,415 per Game

25th May 1924

Venue: Paris

UNITED STATES 1 (Stradan)
ESTONIA 0

Half-time: 1-0

Referee: Paul Putz (Belgium)

U.S.A.: Douglas, Davis, Rudd, Burke-Jones, Hornberger, O'Connor, Findlay, Brix, Stradan, Farrell, Dalrymple.

ESTONIA: Lass, Pihlak, Silber, Rein, Kaljot, Kaarman, Vali, Paal, Ellman, Opraus, Joll.

25th May 1924

Venue: Paris

ITALY 1 (Vallana o.g.)
SPAIN 0

Half-time: 0-0   Attendance: 20,000

Referee: Marcel Slawik (France)

ITALY: De Pra, Rosetta, Caligaris, Barbieri, Burlando, Aliberti, Conti, Baloncieri, Della Valle, Magnozzi, Levratto.

SPAIN: Zamora, Vallana, Pasarin, Gamborena, Larraza, Pena, Piera, Salmitier, Monjardin, Carmelo, Chirri.

25th May 1924

Venue: Paris

SWITZERLAND 9 (Sturzenegger 4, Abegglen 3, Ramseyer, Dietrich)
LITHUANIA 0

Half-time: 4-1

Referee: A. Scamoni (Italy)

SWITZERLAND: Pulver, Reymond, Ramseyer, Oberhauder, Schmiedlin, Pollitz, Ehrenbolger, Sturzenegger, Dietrich, Abegglen, Fassler.

LITHUANIA: Darjus, Deringes, Razmas, Barsaschka, Deringues, Mikutschaurcas, Gombatschauka, Bartuchka, Balitchenia, Sabaliankas.

26th May 1924

Venue: Paris

URUGUAY 7 (Cea 2, Petrone 2, Vidal, Romano, Scarone)
YUGOSLAVIA 0

Half-time: 3-0   Attendance: 1,000

Referee: G. Vallat (France)

URUGUAY: Mazali, Nasazzi, Tomasina, Andrade, Vidal, Ghierra, S. Urdinaran, Scarone, Petrone, Cea, Romano.

YUGOSLAVIA: Vrdjuka, Vrbancic, Dasovic, Marjanovic, Rupec, Rodin, Babic, Petkovic, Perska, Vinek, Placerijano.

25th May 1924

Venue: Paris

CZECHOSLOVAKIA 5 (Sedlacek 2, Stapl, Jan Novak, Capek)
TURKEY 2 (Bekir 2)

Half-time: 3-0   Attendance: 5,000

Referee: P. Chr. Andersen (Norway)

CZECHOSLOVAKIA: Staplik, A. Hojer, F. Hojer, Krombholz, Pleticha, Mahrer, Sedlacek, Stapl, Jan Novak, Capek, Jelinek.

TURKEY: Nedim, Cafer, Ali, Kadri, Ismet dr., Nihat, Mehmet, Alaattin, Zeki, Bekir, Bedri.

26th May 1924

Venue: Paris

HUNGARY 5 (Hirzer 2, Opata 2, Eisenhoffer)
POLAND 0

Half-time: 1-0   Attendance: 3,000

Referee: Johannes Mutters (Holland)

HUNGARY: Biri, Fogl II, Mandi, Orth, Guttmann, Obitz, Braun, Eisenhoffer, Opata, Hirzer, Jeny.

POLAND: Wisniewski, Cyll, Fryc, Styczen, Cikowski, Spojda, Kuchar, Batsch, Kaluza, Reyman, Sperling.

France, Latvia, Netherlands, Romania, Ireland, Bulgaria, Luxembourg, Egypt, Sweden and Belgium all received byes.

Second Round

27th May 1924

Venue: Paris

FRANCE 7   (Crut 3, P. Nicholas 2, Boyer 2)
LATVIA 0

Half-time: 3-0   *Attendance:* 15,000
Referee: Henri Christophe (Belgium)
FRANCE: Chayrigues, Gravier, Baumann, Parachini, Domergue, Bonnardel, Devaquez, Boyer, P. Nicholas, Crut, Dubly.
LATVIA: Jurgens, Rogge, Aschmann, Stromschilk, Bosse, Sokolom, Pavlovs, Pludde, E. Barda, R. Barda, A. Barda.

27th May 1924

Venue: Paris

NETHERLANDS 6   (Pijl 4, Snouck Hurgronje, de Natris)
ROMANIA 0

Half-time: 2-0   *Attendance:* 500
Referee: F. Herren (Switzerland)
NETHERLANDS: van der Meulen, Denis, Tetzner, LeFevre, van Linge, Krom, Snouck Hurgronje, Groosjohan, Pijl, Visser, de Natris.
ROMANIA: Strock I, Bartha, Molnar, Zimmerman, Konigsberg, Kozovici, Tanzer, Guga, R. Wetzer, Bonclocat, Strock II.

28th May 1924

Venue: Paris

IRELAND 1   (Duncan)
BULGARIA 0

Half-time: 0-0   *Attendance:* 1,500
Referee: Henriot (France)
IRELAND: O"Reilly, Kerr, McCarthy, Dykes, McKay, Muldoon, Farrell, Hannon, Duncan, Kendrick, Murray.
BULGARIA: Ivanov, Hristov, Iankov, Radoev, Boianov, Mateev, D. Mutafciev, N. Mutafciev, Vladimirov, Maznikov, Iovovici.

28th May 1924

Venue: Paris   *(Result is after extra time)*

SWITZERLAND 1   (Dietrich)
CZECHOSLOVAKIA 1   (Stapl)

Half-time: 0-1   *Attendance:* 12,000
Referee: Chr. Andersen (Norway)
SWITZERLAND: Pulver, Reymond, Ramseyer, Oberhauser, Schmiedlin, Pollitz, Ehrenbolger, Sturzenegger, Dietrich, Abegglen, Bedouret.
CZECHOSLOVAKIA: Staplik, A. Hojer, Seifert, Kolenaty, Kad'a-Pesek, Cerveny, Sedlacek, Stapl, Capek, Vicek, Jelinek.

29th May 1924

Venue: Paris

URUGUAY 3   (Petrone 3)
UNITED STATES 0

Half-time: 3-0
Referee: Charles Barette (Belgium)
URUGUAY: Mazali, Nasazzi, Vidal, Arispe, Andrade, Tomasina, Naya, Scarone, Petrone, Cea, Romano.
U.S.A.: Douglas, Davis, O'Connor, Johnson, Hornberger, Burke-Jones, Findlay, Wells, Stradan, Farrell, Dalrymple.

29th May 1924

Venue: Paris

ITALY 2   (Baloncieri, Della Valle)
LUXEMBOURG 0

Half-time: 2-0   *Attendance:* 2,000
Referee: Jean Richard (France)
ITALY: De Pra, Rosetta, De Vecchi, Barbieri, Baldi, Aliberti, Conti, Baloncieri, Della Valle, Magnozzi, Levratto.
LUXEMBOURG: Bausch, Kolb, Kirsch, Feierstein, Koetz, Schumann, Weber, Weisgerber, Kieffer, Langers, Massard.

Third Round

29th May 1924

Venue: Paris

EGYPT 3 (Yaghen, Hegazi, Ali Riad)
HUNGARY 0

Half-time: 1-0   Attendance: 8,000

Referee: Luis Collina (Spain)

EGYPT: Taha, Fouad, Salem, Shawky, El Hassani, Hamdy, Ismail I, Riad, Hegazi, Yaghen, Ismail II.

HUNGARY: Biri, Fogl II, Mandi, Orth, Guttmannm, Obitz, Braun, Eisenhoffer, Opata, Hirzer, Jeny.

29th May 1924

Venue: Paris

SWEDEN 8 (Rydell 3, Kok 3, Brommesson, Kaufeldt)
BELGIUM 1 (Larnoe)

Half-time: 4-0   Attendance: 8,532

Referee: Heinrich Retschury (Austria)

SWEDEN: Lindberg, Alfredsson, Hillen, Friberg, Carlsson, Sundberg, Brommesson, Rydell, Kaufeldt, Keller, Kok.

BELGIUM: De Bie, Swartenbroeks, Verbeeck, Pelsmaeker, Fierens, Schelstraete, Van Hege, Coppee, Larnoe, Gillis, Bastin.

30th May 1924

Venue: Paris   (Replay)

SWITZERLAND 1 (Pache)
CZECHOSLOVAKIA 0

Half-time: 0-0   Attendance: 10,000

Referee: Marcel Slawick (France)

SWITZERLAND: Pulver, Reymond, Ramseyer, Oberhauser, Mengotti, Pollitz, Kramer, Sturzenegger, Pache, Abegglen, Fassler.

CZECHOSLOVAKIA: Hochmann, A. Hojer, F. Hojer, Kolenaty, Kad'a-Pesek, Mahrer, Sedlacek, Jan Novak, Josef Novak, Otto Novak, Jelinek.

1st June 1924

Venue: Paris

URUGUAY 5 (Scarone 2, Petrone 2, Romano)
FRANCE 1 (P. Nicholas)

Half-time: 2-1   Attendance: 45,000

Referee: P. Chr. Andersen (Norway)

URUGUAY: Mazzali, Nasazzi, Arispe, Andrade, Zivecchi, Guerra, Naya, Scarone, Petrone, Cea, Romano.

FRANCE: Chayrigues, Gravier, Domergue, Parachini, Batmale, Bonnardel, Devaquez, Boyer, P. Nicholas, Crut, Dubly.

1st June 1924

Venue: Paris

SWEDEN 5 (Brommesson 2, Kaufeldt 2, Rydell)
EGYPT 0

Half-time: 3-0   Attendance: 6,484

Referee: Henri Christophe (Belgium)

SWEDEN: Lindberg, Alfredsson, Hillen, Friberg, Carlsson, Sundberg, Brommesson, Rydell, Kaufeldt, Svensson, Kok.

EGYPT: Taha, Fouad, Salem, Rizkalla, El Hassani, Shawky, Ismail I, Riad, Hegazi, Yaghen, Ismail 11.

2nd June 1924

Venue: Paris

NETHERLANDS 2 (Formenoy 2)
IRELAND 1 (Ghent)

Half-time: 1-1   Attendance: 2,000

Referee: Heinrich Retschury (Austria)

NETHERLANDS: van der Meulen, Denis, Tetzner, Le Fevre, van linge, Krom, Groosjohan, Formenoy, ter Beek, Visser, de Natris.

IRELAND: O'Reilly, Kerr, McCarthy, McKay, Dykes, Muldoon, Farrell, Hannon, Duncan, Ghent, Murray.

2nd June 1924

Venue: Paris

SWITZERLAND 2 (Sturzenegger, Abegglen)
ITALY 1 (Della Valle)

Half-time: 0-0   Attendance: 12,000

Referee: Johannes Mutters (Netherlands)

SWITZERLAND: Pulver, Reymond, Ramseyer, Oberhauser, Schmiedlin, Pollitz, Ehrenbolger, Sturzenegger, Dietrich, Abegglen, Fassler.

ITALY: De Pra, Rosetta, Caligaris, Barbieri, Burlando, Aliberti, Conti, Baloncieri, Della Valle, Magnozzi, Levratto.

Semi-Finals

5th June 1924

Venue: Paris

SWITZERLAND 2 (Abegglen 2)
SWEDEN 1 (Kok)

Half-time: 1-1   Attendance: 7,448

Referee: Johannes Mutters (Netherlands)

SWITZERLAND: Pulver, Reymond, Ramseyer, Oberhauser, Schmiedlin, Pollitz, Ehrenbolger, Pache, Dietrich, Abegglen, Fassler.

SWEDEN: Lindberg, Alfredsson, Hillen, Friberg, Carlsson, Sundberg, Brommesson, Rydell, Kaufeldt, Dahl, Kok.

6th June 1924

Venue: Paris

URUGUAY 2 (Cea, Scarone)
NETHERLANDS 1 (Pilj)

Half-time: 0-1   Attendance: 40,000

Referee: G. Vallat (France)

URUGUAY: Mazali, Nasazzi, Arispe, Andrade, Vidal, Ghierra, S. Urdinaran, Scarone, Petrone, Cea, Romano.

NETHERLANDS: van der Meulen, Denis, Tetzner, Le Fevre, van linge, Krom, Snouck Hurgronje, Groosjohan, Pilj, Visser, de Natris.

Third Place Game

8th June 1924

Venue: Paris   (Result is after extra time)

SWEDEN 1 (Kaufeldt)
NETHERLANDS 1 (Le Fevre)

Half-time: 1-0   Attendance: 9,915

Referee: Heinrich Retschury (Austria)

SWEDEN: Lindberg, Hirsch, Mellgren, Lindqvist, Carlsson, Sundberg, Lundqvist, Rydell, Kaufeldt, Dahl, Kok.

NETHERLANDS: van der Meulen, Denis, Verweij, Le Fevre, Oosthoek, Horsten, Snouck Hurgronje, Vermetten, Breeuwer, Formenoy, Sigmond.

9th June 1924

Venue: Paris

SWEDEN 3 (Rydell 2, Lundqvist)
NETHERLANDS 1 (Formenoy)

Half-time: 2-1   Attendance: 40,522

Referee: Youssuf Mohamed (Egypt)

SWEDEN: Lindberg, Alfredsson, Hillen, Holmberg, Friberg, Sundberg, Lundqvist, Rydell, Kaufeldt, Keller, Kok.

NETHERLANDS: van der Meulen, Denis, Vermetten, Horsten, Krom, Oosthoek, de Natris, Visser, Le Fevre, Formenoy, Sigmond.

Final

9th June 1924

Venue: Paris

URUGUAY 3 (Petrone, Cea, Romano)
SWITZERLAND 0

Half-time: 1-0   Attendance: 40,522

Referee: Marcel Slawick (France)

URUGUAY: Mazali, Nasazzi, Arispe, Andrade, Vidal, Ghierra, Urdinaran, Scarone, Petrone, Cea, Romano.

SWITZERLAND: Pulver, Reymond, Ramseyer, Oberhauser, Schmiedlin, Pollitz, Ehrenbolger, Pache, Dietrich, Abegglen, Fassler.

9th Olympiad – 1928 – Amsterdam

Uruguay reigned again as Olympic champions in 1928 after defeating neighbours Argentina 2-1 in the Final, but only after a replay. It was an indication of things to come as two years later Uruguay were to defeat Argentina in the Final of the first World Cup.

In addition to Uruguay and Argentina another South American nation, Chile, competed in 1928, along with Mexico and the United States from North America. Once again, as in 1912 and 1920 there was a Consolation Tournament.

Included in the Argentine side which won the silver medal were Luisito Monti and Raimondo Orsi. Monti was in the Argentine side in the World Cup Final two years later and in the 1934 Final played for Italy, as did Orsi. Among the Uruguayan players who won two consecutive gold medals were goalkeeper Andres Mazali, full back Jose Nasazzi, half back Jose Andrade and forwards Hactor Scarone, Pedro Petrone and Pedro Cea.

The U.S. team was made up of players from clubs in New Jersey, Philadelphia and St. Louis. Among them was Henry C. Carroll, whose name always appears in the records as O'Carroll. Carroll's nickname was "Razzo" and somehow the "O" in Razzo ended up being added to his surname. The Americans didn't last very long being humiliated 11-2 by Argentina.

Twenty-two games were played and drew a total attendance of 246,699 for an average of 11,214 per game.

Preliminary Round

27th May 1928

Venue: Amsterdam

PORTUGAL 4   (J.M. Soares 2, Vitor Silva, Mota)
CHILE 2   (A. Saavedra, Carbonell)

Half-time: 2-2

Referee: Youssaf Mohamed (Egypt)

PORTUGAL: Roquete, Alves, Vieira, Figueiredo, A. Silva, Matos, Mota, Soares, Vitor Silva, A.S. Martins, J.M. Martins.

CHILE: Ibacache, Chaparro, Morales, Torres, Saavedra, Contreas, Schneeberger, Alfaro, Subiabre, Carbonell, Olgin.

First Round

27th May 1928

Venue: The Olympic Stadium, Amsterdam.

BELGIUM 5   (R. Braine 2, Versijp, Moeschal 2)
LUXEMBOURG 3   (Schutz, Weisberger, Theissen)

Half-time: 3-3   Attendance: 10,000

Referee: Lorenzo Martinez (Argentina)

BELGIUM: Caudron, Lavigne, Hoydonckx, P. Braine, Van Halme, Boesman, Versijp, Devos, R. Braine, Moeschal, Diddens.

LUXEMBOURG: Scharry, Kolb, Kirsch, Fischer, Feierstein, Reuter, Weber, Weisberger, Theissen, Kirpes, Schutz.

28th May 1928

Venue: The Olympic Stadium, Amsterdam.

GERMANY 4 (Hornauer, R. Hofmann 3)
SWITZERLAND 0

Half-time: 2-0   Attendance: 35,000

Referee: Willem Eymers (Netherlands)

GERMANY: Stuhlfauth, Beier, Weber, Knopfle, Kalb, Leinberger, Albrecht, Hornauer, Pottinger, R. Hofmann, L. Hofmann.

SWITZERLAND: Sechehaye, Weiler, Ramseyer, De Lavallaz, Pichler, Fassler, Tschirren, Jaggi, Dietrich, Abegglen, Bailly.

29th May 1928

Venue: Amsterdam

PORTUGAL 2 (V. Silva, A. Silva)
YUGOSLAVIA 1 (Bonacic)

Half-time: 1-1   Attendance: 15,000

Referee: Alfred Birlem (Germany)

PORTUGAL: Roquette, Alves, Vieira, Figueiredo, A. Silva, de Matos, Mota, Soares, V. Silva, dos Santos, J. Martins.

YUGOSLAVIA: Siflis, Ivkovic, Mitrovic, Arsenijevic, Premerl, Djordjevic, Bencic, Marjanovic, Bonacic, Cindric, Giler.

28th May 1928

Venue: Amsterdam

EGYPT 7 (Mokhtar 3, Zubeir, Ismail I, Ismail II, Riad)
TURKEY 1 (Alaatin)

Half-time: 2-0

Referee: Marcel Slawick (France)

EGYPT: Hamdi, Fahmy Abaza, Salem, Yacout El Soury, El Hassani, Soliman, Ismail I, Riad, Ismail II, Mokhtar, Zubeir.

TURKEY: Ulvi, Kadri, Burhan, Cevat, Nihat, Ismet., dr., Mehmet, Alaatin, Zeki, Bekir, Muslih.

30th May 1928

Venue: Amsterdam

URUGUAY 2 (Scarone, Urdinaran)
NETHERLANDS 0

Half-time: 1-0   Attendance: 27,730

Referee: Johannes Langenus (Belgium)

URUGUAY: Mazali, Nasazzi, Arispe, Andrade, Fernandez, Gestido, S. Urdinaran, Scarone, Borjas, Cea, Arremond.

NETHERLANDS: van der Meulen, Denis, van Kol, van Boxtel, Massy, van Heel, Elfring, Buitenweg, Freese, Ghering, Weber.

29th May 1928

Venue: Amsterdam

ITALY 4 (Rosetti, Levratto, Banchero, Baloncieri)
FRANCE 3 (Brouzes 2, Dauphin)

Half-time: 3-2   Attendance: 8,000

Referee: Henri Christophe (Belgium)

ITALY: De Pra, Rosetta, Caligaris, Pietroboni, Bernardini, Janni, Rivolta, Baloncieri, Banchero, Rosetti, Levratto.

FRANCE: Thepot, Wallet, Domergue, Chantrel, Dauphin, Villaplane, Dewaquez, Brouzes, P. Nicholas, Pavillard, Langiller.

30th May 1928

Venue: Amsterdam

SPAIN 7 (Yermo 4, Mariscal, Marculeta, Regueiro)
MEXICO 1 (E. Sota)

Half-time: 3-0   Attendance: 4,500

Referee: Gabor Boronkay (Hungary)

SPAIN: Jauregui, Vallana, Quincoces, Amadeo, Gamborena, Trino, Mariscal, Regueiro, Yermo, Marculeta, Kiriki.

MEXICO: Bonifacio, Garza Gutierrez, Ojeda, Hernandez, Suinaga, Cerrilla, Garces, Contreras, Sota, Carreno, Terrazas.

30th May 1928

Venue: Amsterdam

ARGENTINA 11 (Cherro 4, Tarasconi 3, Orsi 2, Ferreira, Carricaberry)
UNITED STATES 2 (O'Carroll, Deal)

Half-time: 4-0

Referee: Paul Ruoff (Switzerland)

ARGENTINA: Bossio, Bidoglio, Paternoster, Medici, Monti, Calandra, Carricaberry, Tarasconi, Ferreyra, Cherro, Orsi.

U.S.A.: Cooper, Duffy, Smith, Ryan, Lyons, Allen, Findlay, Deal, Kuntner, O'Carroll, Gallagher.

Second Round

1st June 1928

Venue: Amsterdam (Result is after extra time)

ITALY 1 (Baloncieri)
SPAIN 1 (Zaldua)

Half-time: 0-1

Referee: Domingo Lombardi (Uruguay)

ITALY: Combi, Rosetta, Caligaris, Pietroboni, Pitto, Janni, Rivolta, Baloncieri, Schiavio, Rosetti, Levratto.

SPAIN: Jauregui, Quincoces, Zaldua, Amadeo, Antero, Legarreta, Mariscal, Regueiro, Yermo, Marculeta, Kiriki.

2nd June 1928

Venue: Amsterdam

ARGENTINA 6 (Tarasconi 3, Ferreyra, Monti, Orsi)
BELGIUM 3 (R. Braine, Van Halme, Moeschal)

Half-time: 3-2   Attendance: 25,000

Referee: Achille Gama Malcher (Italy)

ARGENTINA: Bossio, Bidoglio, Paternoster, Medice, Monti, Orlandini, Carricaberry, Tarasconi, Ferreyra, Cherro, Orsi.

BELGIUM: Debie, Ruyssevelt, Hoydonckx, P. Braine, Van Halme, Boseman, Devos, Despae, R. Braine, Moeschal, Diddens.

3rd June 1928

Venue: Amsterdam

EGYPT 2 (Mokhtar 2)
PORTUGAL 1 (V. Silva)

Half-time: 1-0

Referee: Giovanni Mauro (Italy)

EGYPT: Hamdi, Fahmy Abaza, Salem, Yacout El Soury, El Hassani, Ezz el din Gamal, Ismail I, Riad, Ismail II, Mokhtar, Zubeir.

PORTUGAL: Roquette, Alves, Vieira, Figueiredo, A. Silva, Matos, Mota, Soares, Vitor Silva, A.S. Martins, J.M. Martins.

3rd June 1928

Venue: The Olympic Stadium, Amsterdam.

URUGUAY 4 (Petrone 2, Castro 2)
GERMANY 1 (R. Hofmann)

Half-time: 2-0   Attendance: 25,131

Referee: Youssef Mohammed (Egypt)

URUGUAY: Mazali, Nasazzi, Arispe, Piriz, Fernandez, Gestido, S. Urdinaran, Castro, Petrone, Cea, Campolo.

GERMANY: Stuhlfarth, Beier, Weber, Knopfle, Kalb, Leinberger, Albrecht, Hornauer, Pottinger, R. Hofmann, L. Hofmann.

Replay

4th June 1928

Venue: Amsterdam

ITALY 7 (Magnozzi, Schiavio, Baloncieri, Bernardini, Rivolta, Levratto 2)
SPAIN 1 (Yermo)

Half-time: 4-0

Referee: H.S. Boekman (Netherlands)

ITALY: Combi, Rosetta, Caligaris, Pitto, Bernardini, Janni, Rivolta, Baloncieri, Schiavio, Magnozzi, Levratto.

SPAIN: Jauregui, Quincoces, Zaldua, Amadeo, Gamborena, Trinio, Bienzobas, Cholin, Yermo, Marculeta, Robus.

Semi-Finals

6th June 1928

Venue: Amsterdam

ARGENTINA 6 (Tarrasconi 3, Ferreyra 3)
EGYPT 0

Half-time: 3-0

Referee: Pedro Escartin (Spain)

ARGENTINA: Diaz, Bidoglio, Paternoster, Medici, Monti, J. Evaristo, Carricaberry, Tarrasconi, Ferreyra, Cherro, Orsi.

EGYPT: Rostam, Fahmy Abaza, Salem, Yacout El Soury, Wl Hassani, Younis Hassan, Ismail I, Riad, Hassan Moussa, Mokhtar, Zubeir.

7th June 1928

Venue: Amsterdam

URUGUAY 3 (Cea, Campolo, Scarone)
ITALY 2 (Baloncieri, Levratto)

Half-time: 3-1

Referee: Willem Eymers (Netherlands)

URUGUAY: Mazali, Canavesi, Arispe, Andrade, Fernandez, Gestido, Urdinaran, Scarone, Petrone, Cea, Campolo.

ITALY: Combi, Rosetta, Caligaris, Pitto, Bernardini, Janni, Rivolta, Baloncieri, Schiavio, Magnozzi, Levratto.

Third Place Game

10th June 1928

Venue: Amsterdam

ITALY 11 (Schiavio 3, Baloncieri 2, Banchero 3, Magnozzi 3)
EGYPT 3 (Riad 2, Hassan)

Half-time: 6-2

Referee: Johannes L. Langenus (Belgium)

ITALY: Combi, Bellini, Caligaris, Genovesi, Bernardini, Pitto, Baloncieri, Banchero, Schiavio, Magnozzi, Levratto.

EGYPT: Hamdi, Fahmy Abaza, Shemels, Yacout El Soury, El Hassani, Younis Hassan, Ismail I, Riad, Ismail II, Hassan Moussa, Zubeir.

Final

10th June 1928

Venue: Amsterdam   *(Result is after extra time)*

URUGUAY 1 (Petrone)
ARGENTINA 1 (Ferreyra)

Half-time: 1-0   *Attendance:* 28,253

Referee: Johannes Mutters (Netherlands)

URUGUAY: Mazali, Nasazzi, Arispe, Andrade, Fernandez, Gestido, Urdinaran, Castro, Petrone, Cea, Campolo.

ARGENTINA: Bossio, Bidoglio, Paternoster, Medici, Monti, J. Evaristo, Carricaberry, Tarrasconi, Ferreyra, Gainzarain, Orsi.

Final Replay

13th June 1928

Venue: Amsterdam

URUGUAY 2 (Figueroa, Scarone)
ARGENTINA 1 (Monti)

Half-time: 1-1   *Attendance:* 28,113

Referee: Johannes Mutters (Netherlands)

URUGUAY: Mazali, Nasazzi, Arispe, Andrade, Piriz, Gestido, Arremon, Scarone, Borjas, Cea, Figueroa.

ARGENTINA: Bossio, Bidoglio, Paternoster, Medici, Monti, J. Evaristo, Carricaberry, Tarrasconi, Ferreyra, Perduca, Orsi.

Consolation Tournament

First Round

5th June 1928

Venue: Rotterdam

NETHERLANDS 3   (Ghering, Smeets, Tap)
BELGIUM 1   (P. Braine)

Half-time: 2-0   Attendance: 25,000

Referee: Achille Gama Malcher (Italy)
NETHERLANDS: van der Meulen, Denis, van Kol, Kools, van Heel, Krom, Elfring, Smeets, Tap, Ghering, Weber.
BELGIUM: Debie, Lavigne, Hoydonckx, Van Averbeke, Hellemans, Boesman, P. Braine, Bierna, R. Braine, Moeschal, Verhulst.

5th June 1928

Venue: Arnhem

CHILE 3   (Subiabre 3)
MEXICO 1   (Garcis)

Half-time: 1-1

Referee: M. Foltynski (Netherlands Antilles)
CHILE: Ibacache Pizzaro, Chaparro Esquival, Linford Pomareda, Riveros Conejeros, Torres Carrasco, Morales Salas, Arias Venegas, Subiabre Astorga, Bravo Paredes, Alfarro Saavedra, Carbonell Alfaro.
MEXICO, Bonfiglio, Garza Gutierrez, Ojeda, Cerrilla, Suinaga, Hernandez, Garcis, Contreras, E. Sota, Carreno, Terrazas.

Consolation Final

8th June 1928

Venue: Rotterdam   (Result is after extra time)

NETHERLANDS 2   (Smeets, Ghering)
CHILE 2   (Paredas)

Half-time: 0-2   Attendance: 18,000

Referee: G. Comorera (Spain)
NETHERLANDS: van der Meulen, Denis, van Kol, Kools, van Heel, Krom, Elfring, Smeets, Tap, Ghering, Weber.
CHILE: Ibacache Pizarro, Chaparro Esquivel, linford Pomereda, Riveros Conejeros, Torres Carrasco, Morales Salas, Arias Venegas, Subiabre Astorga, Bravo Paredes, Alfaro Saavedra, Carbonell Alfaro.

After drawing lots the Netherlands were declared winners.

10th Olympiad – 1932 – Los Angeles

There was no soccer competition at the Los Angeles Olympics in 1932.

11th Olympiad – 1936 – Berlin

The 1936 competition was held as the war clouds were gathering once again over Europe. It is said that there was seldom much gaiety during these Olympics and that the low point was reached when Peruvian fans rioted during the second half of extra time against Austria. During that time the Peruvians scored twice to win 4-2. However, Austria protested, the protest was upheld and the game ordered replayed. When Peru failed to show up for the replay Austria advanced to the next round and eventually to the Final where they were defeated by Italy.

This time the Uruguayans were not on hand to defend their title and Peru were the only South American nation to compete. Still, it is significant that the Peruvians were good enough to hold beaten Finalists Austria, only being eliminated by a decision made off the field.

With the British associations back in FIFA the United Kingdom re-entered Olympic competition disposing of China 2-0 in the First Round and then being beaten 5-4 by Poland in the Second Round. This time the U.K. team was made up of English, Irish and Scottish players and included the following: Haydn Hill (Yorkshire Amateurs), Guy Holmes (Ilford), Robert Fulton (Belfast Celtic), John Gardiner (Queens Park), Bernard Joy (Corinthians), John Sutcliffe (Corinthians), James Crawford, Joseph Kyle and John Dodds (Queens Park), Maurice Edelston (Wimbledon), Lester Finch (Barnet), Edgar Shearer (Corinthians), Bertram Clements and Frederick Riley (Corinthians).

The United States sent a team largely made up of players of German origin many of whom played for the Philadelphia German-Americans in the American Soccer League of the day. Charles Altemose, Robert Denton, Bill Fiedler, Fred Lutkefedder, George Nemchick, Francis Ryan, Peter Pietras James Crockett and Alfred Stoll were all from the Philadelphia club. Francis Bartkus and Frank Greinert (Brooklyn Germans) and John Olthaus (German Sports) also played for German clubs while the rest of the team was made up of Edward Begley (St. Louis Irish Village), Julius Chimielewski (Trenton Highlanders), Andrew Gajda (Boston S.C.), Ferdinand Zbikowski (Kearny Scots-Americans) and John Zywan (Castle Shannon) made up the squad.

The Italians fielded a team composed of players who were students at university and struggled to a First Round win over this surprisingly good U.S. team. The game was watched by Italian Crown Prince Umberto and the climax of a bitter struggle was reached early in the second half when with Italy leading 1-0, the German referee ordered Piccini of Italy off the field for a foul on Fiedler. The Italian refused to leave after three attempts, so the referee left him on the field and played on. In the second game Italy defeated Japan with ease 8-0. In the narrow 2-1 win over Norway, the Italians included American born Alfonso Negro in their line up. Negro went on to play in Serie A for Fiorentina and Napoli, but at the time was playing for GUF Firenze, GUF standing for Gruppo Universitario Fascista. The win took Italy to the Final where they defeated Austria by the same score.

Italian soccer strength at this time is underlined by the fact that the Italians had won the World Cup two years earlier in 1934 and were to win again in 1938. Yet only Alfredo Foni, Pietro Rava and Ugo Locatelli of this gold medal winning Olympic team played in the 1938 World Cup winning team.

The total attendance for football games at the 1936 Olympics was 484,500 for the 16 games, an average of 30,281.

First Round

3rd August 1936

Venue: The Post Stadion, Berlin.

ITALY 1 (Frossi)
UNITED STATES 0

Half-time: 0-0

Referee: C. Weingartner (Germany)

ITALY: Venturini, Foni, Rava, Baldo, Piccini, Locatelli, Frossi, Marchini, Scarabello, Biagi, Capelli.
U.S.A.: Bartkus, Greinert, Zbilowski, Crockett, Pietras, Altemose, Gajda, Nemchik, Lutkefedder, Fiedler, Ryan.

4th August 1936

Venue: Berlin

JAPAN 3 (T. Kamo, Ukon, Matsunaga)
SWEDEN 2 (Persson 2)

Half-time: 0-2   Attendance: 3,000

Referee: Wilhelm Peters (Germany)

JAPAN: Sano, Horie, Takeuchi, Tatsuhara, Oita, Kin, Matsunaga, Ukon, Kawamoto, T. Kamo, Sh.Kamo.
SWEDEN: Bergquist, Andersson, Kallstrom, Carlund, Emanuelsson, Johansson, Josefsson, Persson, Jonasson, Grahn, Hallman.

3rd August 1936

Venue: Berlin

NORWAY 4 (Martinsen 2, Brustad, Kvammen)
TURKEY 0

Half-time: 1-0

Referee: D. Scarpi

NORWAY: Johansen, Horn, Eriksen, Ulleberg, Juve, Holmberg, Hansen, Kvammen, Martinsen, Isaksen, Brustad.
TURKEY: Cihat, Yasar, Husnu, Resat, Lutfu, Ibrahim, Niyazi, Said, Hakki, Fikret, Rebii.

4th August 1936

Venue: Berlin

GERMANY 9 (Urban 3, Simetsreiter 3, Gauchel 2, Elbern)
LUXEMBOURG 0

Half-time: 2-0

Referee: Paul von Hertzka (Hungary)

GERMANY: Buchloh, Munzenberg, Ditgens, Mehl, Goldbrunner, Bernard, Elbern, Gauchel, Hohmann, Urban, Simetsreiter.
LUXEMBOURG: Hoscheid, Mousel, Majerus, Kieffer, Frisch, Fischer, Stamet, Mengel, Mart, Geib, Kemp.

5th August 1936

Venue: Berlin

AUSTRIA 3   (Steinmetz 2, Laudon)
EGYPT 1   (Kerim)

Half-time: 2-0

Referee: Jimmy Jewell (England)

AUSTRIA: E. Kainberger, Kunz, Kargl, Krenn, Wahlmuller, Hofmeister, Werginz, Laudon, Steinmetz, Kitzmuller, Fuchsberger.

EGYPT: Mansour, El Sayed, Halim, Hassanein, Yousif, El Kashef, Latif, Kerim. Taha, Mokhtar, Mahmoud.

6th August 1936

Venue: Berlin

UNITED KINGDOM 2   (Dodds, Finch)
CHINA 0

Half-time: 0-0

Referee: Helmut Fink (Germany)

U.K.: Hill, Holmes, Fulton, Gardiner, Joy, Sutcliffe, Crawford, Kyle, Dodds, Edelston, Finch. (Some records have Pettit for Sutcliffe).

CHINA: Pau Ka-ping, Lee Tin-sang, Tam Kong-pak, Chui Ah-pei, Wong Ki-leung, Chan Chan-ho, Tso Kwai-Shing, Fung King-cheung, Lee Wai-tong, Suen Kam-shuen, Ip Pak-wah.

5th August 1936

Venue: Berlin

POLAND 3   (God 2, Wodarz)
HUNGARY 0

Half-time: 2-0

Referee: Raffaele Scorzoni (Italy)

POLAND: Albanski, Martyna, Galecki, Kotlarczyk, Wasiewicz, Dytko, Piec, Scherfke, Peterek, God, Wodarz.

HUNGARY: Regi, Kovacs I, Bertha, Lagler, Bonyhai, Bohus, Kiraly, Soproni, Seidl, Kiss, Kallai.

Second Round

7th August 1936

Venue: The Momses Stadium, Berlin

ITALY 8   (Frossi 3, Biagi 4, Capelli)
JAPAN 0

Half-time: 2-0   Attendance: 10,000

Referee: Otto Olsson (Sweden)

ITALY: Venturini, Foni, Rava, Baldo, Piccini, Locatelli, Frossi, Marchini, Bertoni, Biagi, Capelli.

JAPAN: Sano, Suzuki, Takeuchi, Tatsuhara, Hita, Kin, Matsunaga, Ukon, Kawamste, T. Kamo, S. Kamo.

6th August 1936

Venue: Berlin

PERU 7   (T. Fernandes 5, Villanueva 2)
FINLAND 3   (Kanerva, Gronlund, Larvo)

Half-time: 3-1   Attendance: 2,500

Referee: C. Rinaldo Barlasina (Italy)

PERU: Valdivieso, A. Fernandez, Lavalle, Tovar, Castillo, Jordan, Alcalde, Magallanes, T. Fernandez, Villanueva, Morales. (Sub: Millos)

FINLAND: Salminen, Karjagin, Narvanen, Kanerva, Malmgren, Lahti, Weckstrom, Gustafsson, Larvo (Lindsten), Gronlund, Lehtonen.

7th August 1936

Venue: Berlin

NORWAY 2   (Isaksen 2)
GERMANY 0

Half-time: 1-0   Attendance: 55,000

Referee: Dr. A.W. Barton (England)

NORWAY: Johansen, Eriksen, Holmsen, Ulleberg, Juve, Holmberg, Frantzen, Kvammen. Martinsen, Isaksen, Brustad.

GERMANY: Jakob, Munzenberg, Ditgens, Gramlich, Goldbrunner, Bernard, Lehner, Siffling, Lenz, Urban, Simetsreiter.

8th August 1936

Venue: Berlin   *(Result is after extra time)*

PERU 4   (Villanueva 2, T. Fernandes, Alcalde)
AUSTRIA 2   (Werginz, Steinmetz)

Half-time: 0-2

Referee: Th. Kristiansen (Norway)

PERU: Valdivieso, A. Fernandez, Lavalle, Tovar, Castillo, Jordan, Magallanes, Alcalde, T. Fernandez, Villanueva, Morales. (Sub: Millos)

AUSTRIA: E. Kainberger, Kargl, Kunz, Krenn, Wahlmuller, Hofmeister, Werginz, Laudon, Steinmetz, Kitzmuller, Fuchsberger.

After a protest by Austria this match was cancelled by the jury of appeal. Peru failed to turn up for the replay which was ordered and the tie was awarded to Austria.

8th August 1936

Venue: Berlin

POLAND 5   (Wodarz 3, God, Piec, o.g.)
UNITED KINGDOM 4   (Joy 2, Shearer, Clements)

Half-time: 2-1

Referee: Rudolf Eklow (Sweden)

POLAND: Albanski, Martyna, Galecki, Kotlarczyk, Wasiewicz, Dytko, Piec, Scherfke, Peterek, God, Wodarz.

U.K.: Hill, Holmes, Fulton, Gardiner, Joy, Sutcliffe, Crawford, Shearer, Clements, Riley, Finch.

Semi-Finals

10th August 1936

Venue: The Olympic Stadium, Berlin   *(After extra time)*

ITALY 2   (Negro, Frossi)
NORWAY 1   (Brustad)

Half-time: 1-0   Attendance: 95,000

Referee: Paul von Hertzka (Hungary)

ITALY: Venturini, Foni, Rava, Baldo, Piccini, Locatelli, Frossi, Marchini, Bertoni, Biagi, Negro.

NORWAY: Johansen, Eriksen, Holmsen, Ulleberg, Juve, Holmberg, Frantzen, Kvammen, Martinsen, Isaksen, Brustad.

11th August 1936

Venue: Berlin

AUSTRIA 3   (Laudon, K. Kainberger, Mandl)
POLAND 1   (God)

Half-time: 1-0   Attendance: 82,000

Referee: Dr. A.W. Barton (England)

AUSTRIA: E. Kainberger, Kargl, Kunz, Krenn, Wahlmuller, Hofmeister, Werginz, Laudon, K. Kainberger, Fuchsberger.

POLAND: Albanski, Martyna, Galecki, Kotlarczyk, Wasiewicz, Dytko, Piec, Musielak, Peterek, God, Wodarz.

Third Place Game

13th August 1936

Venue: Berlin

NORWAY 3   (Brustad 3)
POLAND 2   (Wodarz, Peterek)

Half-time: 2-2   Attendance: 95,000

Referee: Alfred Birlem (Germany)

NORWAY: Johansen, Eriksen, Holmsen, Ulleberg, Juve, Holmberg, Monsen, Kvammern, Martinsen, Frantzen, Brustad.

POLAND: Albanski, Szczepaniak, Galecki, Gora, Cebulak, Dytko, Kisielinski, Matyas, Peterek, God, Wodarz.

Final

15th August 1936

Venue: The Olympic Stadium, Berlin   *(After extra time)*

ITALY 2   (Frossi 2)
AUSTRIA 1   (K. Kainberger)

Half-time: 0-0   Full-Time: 1-1   Attendance: 85,000

Referee: Dr. Peter Bauwens (Germany)

ITALY: Venturini, Foni, Rava, Baldo, Piccini, Locatelli, Frossi, Marchini, Bertoni, Biagi, Gabriotti.

AUSTRIA: E. Kainberger, Kargl, Kunz, Krenn, Wahlmuller, Hofmeister, Werginz, Laudon, Steinmetz, K. Kainberger, Fuchsberger.

12th Olympiad – 1948 – London

Just as the world was altered by the first World War, so the second World War had an even greater effect. The sequence of Olympics was of course interfered with by the great global conflict, and the games of 1940 and 1944 were not staged. The sequence was resumed in London in 1948 by which time most of the top players in Western Europe and in South America were professionals. Some bastions of the amateur game still remained, notably in Scandinavia where Sweden and Denmark as always could field strong teams. However, all of this was about to change as the state sponsored teams of Eastern Europe rose to prominence.

Once again the United States entered a team and once again their First Round opponents were Italy who thrashed them 9-0. Included in the American squad were Charlie Colombo, Walter Bahr, Frank Wallace, Gino Pariani and John and Ed Souza all of whom were to play in the American team that sensationally beat England in the 1950 World Cup two years later.

The 1948 Olympic Football Tournament was the last in which the United Kingdom played a serious role. Under the guidance of the great Matt Busby (later to become Sir Matt), the United Kingdom fielded a team which was good enough to reach the semi-final before being beaten by a fine team from Yugoslavia. In the game for the bronze medal the U.K. fell to a talented Danish side which had been beaten in the other semi-final by Sweden.

With Busby as the manager, the United Kingdom squad in 1948 contained the following players: Ron Simpson (Queens Park), Jack Neale (Walton and Hersham), G.T. Manning (Troedyrhiw), Douglas McBain (Queens Park), Eric Lee (Chester), Eric Fright (Bromley), Thomas Hopper (Bromley), Bob Hardisty (Bishop Auckland), Harry McIlvenny (Yorkshire Amateurs), Dennis Kelleher (Barnet), Peter Kippax (Yorkshire Amateurs), Kevin McAlinden (Belfast Celtic), Jim McColl (Queens Park), Frank Donovan (Pembroke Borough), Andrew Carmichael (Queens Park), Alan Boyd (Queens Park), A. Aitken (Queens Park), Jack Rawlings (Enfield), Bill Amor (Huntley and Palmers, Reading), J. Smith (Barry Town), D. Letham (Queens Park), D. Kelleher (Barnet), R.W. Phipps (Barnet).

The Final was played between two great teams: Sweden, the eventual winners, had players of the calibre of Gunnar Gren, Gunnar Nordahl, Henry Carlsson and Nils Liedholm, while Yugoslavia had Miodrag Jovanovic, Zlatko Cajkovski, Rajko Mitic, Stjepan Bobek and Bernard Vukas. The bronze medal winning Danes also had outstanding players in Viggo Jensen, Axel Pilmark and Carl Praest.

Preliminary Round

26th July 1948

Venue: Brighton

LUXEMBOURG 6 (Konter 2, Kremer 2, Wagner, V. Feller)

AFGHANISTAN 0

Half-time: 3-0   Attendance: 7,000

Referee: A.C. Williams (England)

LUXEMBOURG: Michaux, Pauly, Feller, Wagner, Feller, Schumacher, Gales, Kremer, Konter, Paulus, Schammel.

AFGHANISTAN: Ghafoor Assar, Gharzai, Yusufzai-Azimi, Barakzai, A. Kharot, M. Kharot, Afzai, Ghani Assar, Tajik, Yusufzai.

26th July 1948

Venue: Fratton Park, Portsmouth.

NETHERLANDS 3 (Roosenburg, Wilkes 2)

IRELAND 1 (R. Smith)

Half-time: 2-0   Attendance: 8,000

Referee: George Reader (England)

NETHERLANDS: Kraak, van Bun, Schijvenaar, Krigjh, Terlouw, de Vroet, van der Tuyn, Rijvers, Roosenburg, Wilkes, Lenstra.

IRELAND: Lawlor, Glennon, Richardson, Barry, Kavanagh, O'Grady, McDonald, McLoughlin, Cleary, O'Kelly, Smith.

31st July 1948

Venue: Arsenal Stadium, London.

UNITED KINGDOM 4 (Hardisty, McBain, Kelleher, McIlvenny)

NETHERLANDS 3 (Appel 2, Wilkes)

Half-time: 3-1   Attendance: 21,000

Referee: Valdemar Laursen (Denmark)

U.K.: Simpson, Neale, Manning, McBain, Lee Fright, Hopper, Hardisty, McIlvenny, Kelleher, Kippax.

NETHERLANDS: Kraak, van Bun, Schijvenaar, Krijgh, Terlouw, de Vroet, van der Tuyn, Rijvers, Appel, Wilkes, Lenstra.

31st July 1948

Venue: Ilford

FRANCE 2 (Courbin, Persillon)

INDIA 1 (Raman)

Half-time: 1-0

Referee: G. Dahlner (Sweden)

FRANCE: Rouxel, Rouelle, Bienvenu, Krug, Colau, Robert, Heckel, Persillon, Paluch, Strappe, Courbin.

INDIA: Varadaraj, Taj Mahomed, Manna, Basheer, Aao, Prasad, Das, Parab, Mewalall, Mohammed Ahmed Khan, Raman.

First Round

31st July 1948

Venue: Selhurst Park, London.

DENMARK 3 (Karl Aage Hansen 2, Ploeger)

EGYPT 1 (El Guindy)

Half-time: 0-0   Attendance: 12,000

Referee: S. Boardman (England)

DENMARK: Nielsen, V. Jensen, Overgaard, Pilmark, Ornvold, I. Jensen, Ploeger, K.A. Hansen, Lundberg, J. Hansen, Praest.

EGYPT: Yehia Imam, A. Hammami, A Fouad Sedky, Helmi Maati, M. Abu Habaga, Hanafy Bastan, Sayed El Dezwy, M. El Guindy, Ahmed El Mekkawi, A. Sakr, H. Madkour.

31st July 1948

Venue: Craven Cottage, Fulham, London.

YUGOSLAVIA 6 (Z. Cajkovski 2, Stankovic, Mihajlovic, Mitic, Bobek)

LUXEMBOURG 1 (Schammel)

Half-time: 0-1   Attendance: 7,000

Referee: Karel L. van der Meer (Holland)

YUGOSLAVIA: Sostaric, Brozovic, Stankovic, Zlatko Cajkovski, Jovanovic, Atanackovic, Mihajlovic, Mitic, Velfl, Bobek, Zeljko Cajkovski.

LUXEMBOURG: Michaux, Pauly, Feller, Wagner, May, Feller, Gales, Kettel, Konter, Paulus, Schammel.

2nd August 1948

Venue: White Hart Lane, London.

SWEDEN 3   (G. Nordahl 2, Rosen)
AUSTRIA 0

Half-time: 2-0   Attendance: 9,514

Referee: Willy H.E. Ling (England)

SWEDEN: Lindberg, K. Nordahl, Nilsson, Rosengren, B. Nordahl, Andersson, Rosen, Gren, G. Nordahl, Carlsson, Liedholm.

AUSTRIA: Pelikan, Kowanz, Happel, Mikolasch, Ockwirk, Joksch, Melchoir, Habitzl, Epp, Hahnemann, Kurner.

2nd August 1948

Venue: Dulwich

KOREA 5   (Song Gon Choi, Kook Chin Chung 2, Chong Ho Bai, Nam Sik Chung)
MEXICO 3   (Cardenas, Figueroa, Ruiz)

Half-time: 3-1

Referee: Leo Lemesic (Yugoslavia)

KOREA: Duk Yung Hong, Kyoo Chung Pak, Dai Chong Pak, Song Gon Choi, Kyoo Whan Kim, Byung Dai Main, Zung Whan Woo, Chong Ho Bai, Kook Chin Chung, Nam Sik Chung, Yong Sik Kim.

MEXICO, Quintero Nava, Rodriguez Ceralta, Rodriguez Novarro, Thompson Durand, Figueroa Rodriguez, Cordoba Alcaia, Gardunpo Gomez, Mercado Luna, Cardenas de la Vega, Sanchez Huerta, Ruiz Aguilar.

2nd August 1948

Venue: Griffin Park, Brentford, London.

ITALY 9   (Pernigo 4, Stellin, Turconi, Cavigioli 2, Caprile)
UNITED STATES 0

Half-time: 2-0   Attendance: 20,000

Referee: Charles De La Salle (France)

ITALY: Casari, Giovannini, Stellin, Presca, Neri, Mari, Cavigioli, Turconi, Pernigo. Cassani, Caprile.

U.S.A.: Strimel, Costa, Martin, Colombo, Ferreira, Bahr, Beckman, J.B. Souza, Bertani, McLaughlin, E. Souza.

2nd August 1948

Venue: Walthamstow

TURKEY 4   (Erol, Lefter 2, Bulend)
CHINA 0

Half-time: 1-0

Referee: Johann Beck (Austria)

TURKEY: Cihat, Murat, Vedii, dr. Huseyin, Bulend, Selahattin, Fikret, Erol, Gunduz, Lefter, Sukru.

CHINA: Chang Pan-rum, Hau Yung-sang, Nien Se-shing, Chau Man-shi, Sung Ling-sing, LauChung-sang, Ho Ying-fun, Chang King-hai, Chu Wing-keung, Chia Boon-Leong, Li Tei-fei.

Second Round

5th August 1948

Venue: Selhurst Park, London.

SWEDEN 12   (G. Nordahl 4, Carlsson 3, Rosen 2, Liedholm 2, Gren)
KOREA 0

Half-time: 4-0   Attendance: 7,110

Referee: Giuseppe Carpani (Italy)

SWEDEN: Lindberg, Leander, Nilsson, Rosengren, B. Nordahl, Andersoon, Rosen, Gren, G. Nordahl, Carlsson, Liedholm.

KOREA: Duk Yung Hong, Kyoo Chung Pak, Dai Chong pak, Song Gon Choi, Kyoo Whan Kim, Byung Dai Min, Zung Whan Woo, Chong Ho Bai, Nam Sik Chung, Yong Sik Kim, Kook Chin Chung.

5th August 1948

Venue: Arsenal Stadium, London.

DENMARK 5   (John Hansen 4, Ploeger)
ITALY 3   (Cavigioli, Caprile, Pernigo)

Half-time: 1-0   Attendance: 12,000

Referee: Bill Ling (England)

DENMARK: Nielsen, V. Jensen, Overgaard, Piilmark, Ornvold, I. Jensen, Ploeger, K.A. Hansen, Praest, J. Hansen, Seebach.

ITALY: Casari, Giovannini, Stellin, Maestrelli, Neri, Mari, Cavigioli, Turconi, Pernigo, Cassani, Caprile.

5th August 1948

Venue: Ilford

YUGOSLAVIA 3   (Z. Cajkovski, Bobek, Velfl)
TURKEY 1   (Sukru)

Half-time: 1-1   Attendance: 8,000

Referee: Victor Sdez (France)

YUGOSLAVIA: Sostaric, Brozovic, Stankovic, Zlatko Cajkovski, Jovanovic, Atanackovic, Tomasevic, Mitic, Velfl, Bobek, Zeljko Cajkoviski.

TURKEY: Cihat, Murat, Vedii, Naci, Bulent, Huseyin, K. Fikret, Erol, Gunduz, Lefter, Sukru.

5th August 1948

Venue: Craven Cottage, Fulham, London.

UNITED KINGDOM 1   (Hardisty)
FRANCE 0

Half-time: 1-0

Referee: Karel L. van der Meer (Netherlands)

U.K.: McAlindon, Neale, McColl, McBain, Lee, Fright, Donovan, Hardisty, McIlvenny, Kelleher, Kippax.

FRANCE: Rouelle, Krug, Bienvenu, Persillon, Colau, Robert, Heckel, Paluch, Hebinger, Straffe, Courbin.

Semi-Finals

10th August 1948

Venue: Wembley Stadium, London.

SWEDEN 4   (Rosen 2, Carlsson 2)
DENMARK 2   (Seebach, John Hansen)

Half-time: 4-1   Attendance: 20,000

Referee: S. Boardman (England)

SWEDEN: Lindberg, Leander, Nilsson, Rosengren, B. Nordahl, Andersson, Rosen, Gren, G. Nordahl, Carlsson, Liedholm.

DENMARK: Nielsen, V. Jensen, Overgaard, Piilmark, Ornvold, I. Jensen, Ploeger, K.A. Hansen, Praest, J. Hansen, Seebach.

11th August 1948

Venue: Wembley Stadium, London.

YUGOSLAVIA 3   (Bobek, Velfl, Mitic)
UNITED KINGDOM 1   (Donovan)

Half-time: 2-1   Attendance: 40,000

Referee: Karel L. van der Meer (Netherlands)

YUGOSLAVIA: Sostaric, Brozovic, Stankovic, Zlatko Cajkowski, Jovanovic, Atanakovic, Mihajlovic, Mitic, Velfl, Bobek, Zeljko Cajkowski.

U.K.: McAlindon, Neale, McColl, McBain, Lee, Fright, Donovan, Hardisty, McIlvenny, Kelleher, Kippax.

Third Place Game

13th August 1948

Venue: Wembley Stadium, London.

DENMARK 5   (John Hansen 2, Praest 2, Sorensen)
UNITED KINGDOM 3   (Hardisty, Aitken, Amor)

Half-time: 3-2   Attendance: 5,000

Referee: Karel L. van der Meer (Netherlands)

DENMARK: Nielsen, V. Jensen, Overgaard, Piilmark, Ornvold, I. Jensen, Ploeger, Lundberg, Praest, Hansen, Sorensen.

U.K.: Simpson, Neale, Carmichael, Hardisty, Lee, Fright, Boyd, Aitken, McIlvenny, Rawlings, Amor.

Final

13th August 1948

Venue: Wembley Stadium, London.

SWEDEN 3   (Gren 2, Gunnar Nordahl)
YUGOSLAVIA 1   (Bobek)

Half-time: 1-1   Attendance: 45,000

Referee: Bill Ling (England)

SWEDEN: Linberg, K. Nordahl, Nilsson, Rosengren, B. Nordahl, Andersson, Rosen, Gren, G. Nordahl, Carlsson, Liedholm.

YUGOSLAVIA: Lovric, Brozovic, Stankovic, Zlatko Cajkowski, Jovanovic, Atanakovic, Cimermancic, Mitic, Bobek, Zeljko Cajkowski, Vukas.

13th Olympiad – 1952 – Helsinki

The 1952 Olympics was noteable for the rise to prominence of one of the greatest national teams of all time. The "Magical Magyars", as the Hungarians were known, captured the gold medal and then went on to destroy England's full national team at Wembley Stadium a year later and then reach the World Cup Final in 1954. The names of the great players on this team are legendary: goalkeeper Gyula Grosics, right half Joszef Bozsik, and in the forward line Sandor Kocsis, Nandor Hidegkuti, Ferenc Puskas and Zoltan Czibor. The Hungarian revolution of 1956 caused the break up of this great team, many of the players going on to make their mark in other countries with other clubs.

This was the beginning of the domination of the Eastern European nations, players the rest of the world claimed were professionals in all but name and they dominated the Olympics until the 1984 competition.

As in 1948, Yugoslavia, with some outstanding players were beaten Finalists. Goalkeeper Vladimir Beara was ranked among the top in the world, players of the calibre of Zlatko Cajkowski, Rajko Mitic, Bernard Vukas and Stjepen Bobek returned for their second Final, while Branko Zebec was a great new addition at outside left.

In these Olympics the Soviet Union entered for the first time as did Brazil, while the United States were beaten in the First Round for the third time running by Italy. The United Kingdom squad beaten 5-3 by little Luxembourg was made up of the following players. E. Bennett (Southall), L. Stratton (Walthamstow Avenue), T. Stewart (Queens Park), D. Saunders (Walthamstow Avenue), Charlie Fuller (Bromley), L. Topp (Hendon), George Robb (Finchley), Bill Slater (Brentford), J. Lewis (Walthamstow Avenue), A.W. Noble (Leytonstone), J.R.E. Hardisty (Bishop Auckland), B. Brown (Pegasus), S. Charlton (Bromley), K. Yenson (Leyton), W. Hastie (Queens Park), L. Robbins (Lovells Athletic), K. McGarry (Cliftonville), W. Holmes (Blackburn Rovers), D. Grierson (Queens Park), H.A. Pawson (Pegasus). Manager: Walter Winterbottom. Trainer: J. Jennings (Northampton Town).

The United States once again played Italy but didn't fare any better losing 8-0. Three members of the US squad were in the team that that beat England in the World Cup two years earlier: Harry Keough, Charlie Colombo and Johnny Souza.

Preliminary Round

15th July 1948

Venue: Turku

HUNGARY 2   (Czibor, Kocsis)
ROMANIA 1   (Suru)

Half-time: 1-0   Attendance: 14,000

Referee: Nikolai Latichev (U.S.S.R.)

HUNGARY: Grosics, Dalnoki, Lorant, Lantos, Kovacs, Bozsik, Budai, Kocsis, Hidegkuti, Puskas, Czibor.
ROMANIA: Voinescu, Zavoda, Kovacs, Farmati, Calinoiu, Serfozo, Paraschiva, Iordache, Ozon, Petschowski, Suru.

15th July 1948

Venue: Tampere

DENMARK 2   (Poul E. Peterson, Seebach)
GREECE 1   (Emmanouilidis)

Half-time: 2-0   Attendance: 7,000

Referee: Wolff Waldemar Karni (Finland)

DENMARK: Johansen, Petersen, Nielsen, Terkelsen, Andersen, Blicher, J.W. Hansen, Petersen, J.P. Hansen, Lundberg, Seebach.
GREECE: Pentzaropoulos, Rossidis, Linoxylakis, Goulios, I. Ioannou, Poulis, Emmanouilidis, Darivas, Papagheorghiou, Bebis, Drosos.

15th July 1948

Venue: Lahti

POLAND 2   (Trampisz, Krasowka)
FRANCE 1   (Leblond)

Half-time: 1-1

Referee: Karel L. van der Meer (Netherlands)

POLAND: Stefaniszyn, Gedlak, Cebula, Banisz, Suszczyk, Mamon, Trampisz, Krasowka, Alszer, Cieslik, Wisniewski.
FRANCE: Deprez, Bochard, Eloy, Colliot, Druart, Barreau, Persillon, Leblond, Oliver, Bohee, Lefevre.

15th July 1948

Venue: Helsinki

YUGOSLAVIA 10   (Zebec 4, Mitic 3, Vukas 2, Ognjanov)
INDIA 1   (Ahmed Khan)

Half-time: 5-0   Attendance: 20,000

Referee: John Best (U.S.A.)

YUGOSLAVIA: Beara, Stankovic, Crnkovic, Cajkowski, Horvat, Boskov, Ognjanov, Mitic, Vukas, Bobek, Zebec.
INDIA: B. Anthony, Azizuddin, Ravat, Manna, Lateef, Shunmugham, Vankatesh, Sattar, Moinuddin, Ahmed Khan, J. Anthony.

16th July 1948

Venue: Tampere

ITALY 8   (Gimona 3, Pandolfini 2, Venturi, Fontanesi, A. Mariani)
UNITED STATES 0

Half-time: 3-0   Attendance: 10,000

Referee: Arthur Ellis (England)

ITALY: Bugatti, Rota, Corradi, Neri, Cade, Venturi, Mariani, Pandolfini, La Rosa, Gimona, Fontanesi.
U.S.A.: Burkhard, Schaller, Keough, Sheppell, Colombo, McHugh, Monsen, Souza, Surrock, Mendoza, Cook.

16th July 1948

Venue: Kotka

EGYPT 5   (El Mekkawi, El Dezwi 3, El Far)
CHILE 4   (Vial Blanco 2, Jara Constanzo 2)

Half-time: 2-2

Referee: John O. Nilsson (Sweden)

EGYPT: Hemueda, M.O. Mohamed, Kabil, Rashed, Bastan, Ali, S. Mohamed, El Far, El Hamoly, El Dezwi, El Mekkawi.
CHILE: Sanchez, Conley, Rojas, Placencia, Aninat, Qezada, Blanco, Becker, Herrera, Pillado, Constanzo.

16th July 1952

Venue: Lahti   (Result is after extra time)

LUXEMBOURG 5   (Roller 2, Letsch 2, Gales)
UNITED KINGDOM 3   (Robb, Lewis, Slater)

Half-time: 0-1

Referee: Vincenzo Orlandini (Italy)

LUXEMBOURG: Lahure, Wagner, Spartz, Jaminet, Reuter, Guth, Muller, Roller, Gales, Nurenberg, Letsch.

U.K.: Bennett, Stratton, Stewart, Saunders, Fuller, Topp, Robb, Slater, Lewis, Noble, Hardisty.

16th July 1948

Venue: Turku

BRAZIL 5   (Barbosa, Pinto de Faria 2, Moreira, Neto)
NETHERLANDS 1   (van Roessel)

Half-time: 3-1   Attendance: 16,000

Referee: Giorgio Bernardi (Italy)

BRAZIL: Cavalheiro, Homen Rodrigues, Waldir, Zozimo, Machado, Campos Martins, Pinto de Faria, Pessanha, Neto, Barbosa Tozzi, Moreira.

NETHERLANDS: Kraak, Odenthal, Alberts, Wiertz, Terlouw, Biesbrouck, va der Kuil, Bennaars, van Roessel, Mommers, Clavan.

16th July 1948

Venue: Kotka   (Result is after extra time)

U.S.S.R. 2   (Bobrov, Trofimov)
BULGARIA 1   (Kolev)

Half-time: 0-0   Attendance: 10,000

Referee: Istvan Zsolt (Hungary)

U.S.S.R.: Ivanov, Krijevski, Basaskin, Nirkov, Netto, Petrov, Trofimov, Teneaghin, Bobrov, Gogoberidze, A. Ilin.

BULGARIA: Sokolov, Vasillev, Manolov, Apostolov, Bojkov, Petkov, Milanov, Kolev, Panaiotov, Arghirov, Ianev.

First Round

19th July 1948

Venue: Helsinki

AUSTRIA 4   (Gollnhuber 2, Grohs, Stumpf)
FINLAND 3   (Stolpe 2, Rytkonen)

Half-time: 2-3   Attendance: 33,053

Referee: Willy H.E. Ling (England)

AUSTRIA: Nikolai, Kollmann, Krammer, Walter, Wolf, Fendler, Stumpf, Hochleitner, Grohs, Feldinger, Gollnhuber.

FINLAND: Laaksonen, Lindman, Myntti, Asikainen, Valkama, Beijar, Veihela, Rytkonen, Rikberg, Lehtovirta, Stolpe.

20th July 1948

Venue: Turku

WEST GERMANY 3   (Schroder 2, Klug)
EGYPT 1   (El Dezwi)

Half-time: 2-0

Referee: Giorgio Bernardi (Italy)

WEST GERMANY: Schonbeck, Eberle, Post, Sommerlatt, Jager, Gleixner, Mauritz, Stollenwerk, Schroder, Schafer, Klug.

EGYPT: Hemueda, M.O. Mohamed, Sedky, Ali, Bastan, Rashed, El Mekkawi, El Dezwi, El Hamoly, El Far, S. Mohamed.

20th July 1948

Venue: Kotka

BRAZIL 2   (Zozimo, Pinto de Faria)
LUXEMBOURG 1   (Gales)

Half-time: 1-0

Referee: Maryan Macancic (Yugoslavia)

BRAZIL: Cavalheiro, Homen Rodrigues, Waldir, Zozimo, Machado, Campos Martins, Pinto de Faria, Passanha, Neto, Barbosa Tozzi, Moreira.

LUXEMBOURG: Lahure, Wagner, Spartz, Jaminet, Reuter, Guth, Muller, Roller, Gales, Nurenberg, Letsch.

20th July 1948

Venue: Tampere

YUGOSLAVIA 5 (Zebec 2, Ognjanov, Mitic, Bobek)
U.S.S.R. 5 (Bobrov 3, Trofimov, A. Petrov)

Half-time: 3-0   Attendance: 17,000
Referee: Arthur E. Ellis (England)
YUGOSLAVIA: Beara, Stankovic, Crnkovic, Cajkowski, Horvat, Boskov, Ognjanov, Mitic, Vukas, Bobek, Zebec.
U.S.S.R.: Ivanov, Krizevskij, Basaskin, Nirkov, A. Petrov, Netto, Trofimov, Nikolajev, Bobrov, Marjutin, Beskov.

21st July 1948

Venue: Tampere

SWEDEN 4 (Brodd 2, Rydell, Bengtsson)
NORWAY 1 (Sorensen)

Half-time: 2-0   Attendance: 4,200
Referee: Johan Aksel Alho (Finland)
SWEDEN: Svensson, Samuelsson, Nilsson, Hansson, Gustavsson, Lindh, Bengtsson, Lofgren, Rydell, Brodd, Sandberg.
NORWAY: Blohm, Holmberg, Karlsen, Olsen, Svenssen, Spydevold, Hvidsten, Thoresen, Sorensen, Johannesen, Dahlen.

21st July 1948

Venue: Helsinki

HUNGARY 3 (P. Palotas 2, Kocsis)
ITALY 0

Half-time: 2-0   Attendance: 10,000
Referee: Karel L. van der Meer (Netherlands)
HUNGARY: Grosics, Buzansky, Lantos, Bozsik, Lorant, Zakarias, Csordas, Kocsis, Palotas, Puskas, Hidegkuti.
ITALY: Bugatti, Rota, Corradi, Neri, Azzini, Venturi, Mariani, Pandolfini, La Rosa, Gimona, Fontanesi.

21st July 1948

Venue: Turku

DENMARK 2 (Seebach, Svend Nielsen)
POLAND 0

Half-time: 1-0   Attendance: 8,000
Referee: Finn Balstad (Norway)
DENMARK: Johansen, P. Petersen, S. Nielsen, Terkelsen, Andersen, Blicher, J.W. Hansen, P.E. Petersen, J.P. Hansen, Lundberg, Seebach.
POLAND: Szymkowiak, Gedlak, Banisz, Mamon, Kaszuba, Bieniek, Sobek, Krasowka, Alszer, Cieslik, Wisniewski.

21st July 1948

Venue: Lahti

TURKEY 2 (Muzaffer, Tekin)
CURACAO 1 (Briezen)

Half-time: 1-0
Referee: Carl Fr. Jorgensen (Denmark)
TURKEY: Erdogan, Necdet, Ridvan, Mustafa, Basri, Ercument, Vasif, Tekin, Muzaffer, Yalcin, Macit.
CURACAO: Hato, de Lanoi, Canword, Matrona, Vlinder, Giribaldi, Heyliger, Brion, Briezen, Krips, Brokke.

22nd July 1948

Venue: Tampere   (Replay)

YUGOSLAVIA 3 (Mitic, Bobek, Cajkovski)
U.S.S.R. 1 (Bobrov)

Half-time: 2-1   Attendance: 17,000
Referee: Arthur Ellis (England)
YUGOSLAVIA: Beara, Stankovic, Crnkovic, Cajkovski, Horvat, Boskov, Ognjanov, Mitic, Vukas, Bobek, Zebec.
U.S.S.R.: Ivanov, Krizevskij, Basaskin, Nirkov, A. Petrov, Netto, Trofimov, Nikolajev, Bobrov, Beskov, Ckuaseli.

Second Round

23rd July 1948

Venue: Helsinki

SWEDEN 3 (Sandberg, Brodd, Rydell)
AUSTRIA 1 (Grohs)

Half-time: 0-1   Attendance: 10,000

Referee: Vincenzo Orlandini (Italy)

SWEDEN: Svensson, Samuelsson, Nilsson, Hansson, Gustavsson, Lindh, Bengtsson, Lofgren, Rydell, Brodd, Sandberg.

AUSTRIA: Nikolai, Kollmann, Krammer, Walter, Wolf, Fendler, Stumpf, Hochleitner, Grohs, Feldinger, Gollnhuber.

24th July 1948

Venue: Kotka

HUNGARY 7 (Kocsis 2, Puskas 2, Palotas, Lantos, Boszik)
TURKEY 1 (Ercument)

Half-time: 2-0   Attendance: 20,000

Referee: Wolff Waldemar Karni (Finland)

HUNGARY: Grosics, Buzansky, Lorant, Lantos, Boszik, Zakarias, Csordas, Kocsis, Palotas, Puskas, Czibor.

TURKEY: Erdogan, Necdet, Basri, Ridvan, Mustafa, Ercument, Vasif, Tekin, Kamil, Yalcin, Macit.

24th July 1948

Venue: Helsinki   (Result is after extra time)

WEST GERMANY 4 (Zeitler, Schroder 2, Klug)
BRAZIL 2 (Zozimo, Pinto de Faria)

Half-time: 0-1

Referee: Arthur E. Ellis (England)

WEST GERMANY: Schonbeck, Eberle, Jager, Sommerlatt, Schafer, Post, Hinterstocker, Stollenwerk, Zeitler, Schroder, Klug.

BRAZIL: Cavalheiro, Homen Rodrigues, Waldir, Zozimo, Machado, Campos Martins, Pessanha, Barbosa Tozzi, Pinto de Faria, Neto, Moreira.

25th July 1948

Venue: Helsinki

YUGOSLAVIA 5 (Cajkovski, Bobek, Zebec, Ognjanov, Vukas)
DENMARK 3 (Lundberg, Seebach, Jens Hansen)

Half-time: 3-0   Attendance: 10,000

Referee: Wolff Waldemar Karni (Finland)

YUGOSLAVIA: Beara, Stankovic, Crnkovic, Cajkovski, Horvat, Boskov, Ognjanov, Mitic, Vukas, Bobek, Zebec.

DENMARK: Johansen, P. Petersen, S, Nielsen, Terkelsen, Andersen, Blicher, J.W. Hansen, P.E. Petersen, J.P. Hansen, Lundberg, Seebach.

Semi-Finals

28th July 1948

Venue: Helsinki

HUNGARY 6 (Kocsis 2, Hidegkuti, Puskas, Palotas, o.g.)
SWEDEN 0

Half-time: 3-0   Attendance: 22,000

Referee: Willy H.E. Ling (England)

HUNGARY: Grosics, Buzansky, Lorant, Lantos, Boszik, Zakarias, Hidegkuti, Kocsis, Palotas, Puskas, Czibor.

SWEDEN: Svensson, Samuelsson, Nilsson, Hansson, Gustavsson, Lindh, Bengtsson, Lofgren, Rydell, Brodd, Sandberg.

29th July 1948

Venue: Helsinki

YUGOSLAVIA 3 (Mitic 2, Cajkovski)
WEST GERMANY 1 (Stollenwerk)

Half-time: 3-1   Attendance: 20,000

Referee: Wolff Waldemar Karni (Finland)

YUGOSLAVIA: Beara, Stankovic, Crnkovic, Cajkovski, Horvat, Boskov, Ognjanov, Mitic, Vukas, Bobek, Zebec.

WEST GERMANY: Schonbeck, Eberle, Jager, Sommerlatt, Schafer, Gleixner, Mauritz, Stollenwerk, Zeitler, Schroder, Ehrmann.

Bronze Medal Game

1st August 1948

Venue: Helsinki

SWEDEN 2 (Rydell, Lofgren)
WEST GERMANY 0

Half-time: 1-0   Attendance: 20,000

Referee: Vincenzo Orlandini (Italy)

SWEDEN: Svensson, Samuelsson, Nilsson, Ahlund, Gustavsson, Lindh, Bengtsson, Lofgren, Rydell, Brodd, Sandberg.

WEST GERMANY: Schonbeck, Eberle, Jager, Sommerlatt, Schafer, Post, Hinterstocker, Stollenwerk, Zeitler, Schroder, Ehrmann.

Final

2nd August 1948

Venue: Helsinki

HUNGARY 2 (Puskas, Czibor)
YUGOSLAVIA 0

Half-time: 0-0   Attendance: 60,000

Referee: Arthur E. Ellis (England)

HUNGARY: Grosics, Buzansky, Lorant, Lantos, Boszik, Zakarias, Hidegkuti, Kocsis, Palotas, Puskas, Czibor.

YUGOSLAVIA: Beara, Stankovic, Crnkovic, Cajkovski, Horvat, Boskov, Ognjanov, Mitic, Vukas, Bobek, Zebec.

14th Olympiad – 1956 – Melbourne

The first Olympiad held in the southern hemisphere was seriously affected by the events a world away in Hungary. As a result of the Hungarian revolution and the Soviet reaction to it, numerous nations withdrew and the result was the smallest football tournament in many years. Ironically the eventual winners were the Soviet Union, while Yugoslavia were beaten Finalists for the third time in a row.

Once again the United Kingdom was represented opening with a 9-0 thrashing of Thailand only to be humiliated themselves in the Second Round 6-1 by Bulgaria. The United States made the long journey to Australia only to end up on the wrong end of a 9-1 score against Yugoslavia. The British squad contained the following players. Harry Sharrett (Bishop Auckland), Mike Pinner (Pegasus), Don Stoker (Sutton), Tom Farrer (Walthamstow Avenue), Laurie Topp (Hendon), Harry Dodkins (Ilford), Jim Lewis (Chelsea), Derek Lewin (Bishop Auckland), Jack Laybourne (Corinthian Casuals), George Bromilow (Southport), Charles Twissell (Plymouth Argyle), D. Adams (Hendon, T.H. Robinson (Brentwood), J.R.E. Hardisty (Bishop Auckland), J. Coates (Kingstonian).

For the third Olympics in a row the United States suffered a humiliating defeat losing 9-1 to Yugoslavia.

The winning Soviet team had the great Lev Yashin in goal, a world class wing half in Igor Netto, a controversial but talented centre forward in Nikita Simonian and a first class winger in Anatoly Ilyin. With many of its team from 1948 and 1952 playing professionally in other countries this was a new Yugoslavia with a first class goalkeeper in Petar Radenkovic and a talented forward in Dragoslav Sekularac.

First Round

November 24, 1956

Venue: Melbourne

U.S.S.R. 2   (Isaev, Strelzov)
WEST GERMANY 1   (Habig)

Half-time: 1-0   Attendance: 20,000

Referee: R.H. Mann (England)

U.S.S.R.: Yashin, Tichenko, Bashaskin, Ogonikov, Paramonov, Netto, Tatushin, Isaev, Strelzov, V, Ivanov, Rishkin.

WEST GERMANY: Gortz, Gerdau, Hofer, K. Hoffmann, R. Hoffmann, Semmelman, Mauritz, Geiger, Zeitler, Schafer, Habig.

November 26, 1956

Venue: Melbourne

UNITED KINGDOM 9   (Laybourne 3, Bromilow 2, Twissell 2, Topp, Lewis)
THAILAND 0

Half-time: 4-0

Referee: Nikolai Latishev (U.S.S.R.)

U.K.: Sharratt, Stoker, Farrer, Topp, Prince, Dodkins, Lewis, Hardisty, Laybourne, Bromilow, Twissell.

THAILAND: Baikam, Suvannasith, Suvaree, Chutimawongse, Hayachanta, Chaiyong, Chitranukroh, Chermudhai, Milinthachinda, Luttimont, Mutugun.

November 27, 1956

Venue: Melbourne

AUSTRALIA 2 (McMillan, Loughran)
JAPAN 0

Half-time: 1-0

Referee: R. Lund (New Zealand)

AUSTRALIA: Lord, Bignell, Pettigrew, Arthur, Warren, Sander, Morrow, Loughren, Lennard, McMillan, Smith.
JAPAN: Furukawa, Hiraki, Takamori, Sato, Ozawa, Omura, Tokita, Uchino, Yaegashi, Kobayashi, Ivabuchi.

November 30, 1956

Venue: Melbourne

BULGARIA 6 (Stoyanov 3, Kolev 2, Nikolov)
UNITED KINGDOM 1 (Lewis)

Half-time: 3-1

Referee: R. Wright (Australia)

BULGARIA: Naydenov, Rakarov, Nikolov, Boshkov, Manolov, Kovatchev, Stoyanov, Dimitrov, Panayotov, Kolev, Yanev.
U.K.: Sharrett, Stoker, Farrer, Topp, Prince, Dodkins, Lewis, Lewin, Laybourne, Bromilow, Twissell.

Second Round

November 28, 1956

Venue: Melbourne

YUGOSLAVIA 9 (Veselinovic 2, Mujic 3, Antic 2, Papec, o.g.)
UNITED STATES 1 (Zerhusen)

Half-time: 5-1 Attendance: 20,000

Referee: Maurice Swain (New Zealand)

YUGOSLAVIA: Radenkovic, Koscak, Radovic, Santek, Spajic, Krstic, Sekularac, Papec, Antic, Veselinovic, Mujic.
U.S.A.: Engedahl, Conterio, Wecke, Snylyk, Keough, Dorrian, Murphy, Mendoza, Zerhusen, Monsen, Looby.

December 1, 1956

Venue: Melbourne (Replay)

U.S.S.R. 4 (Salnikov 2, Netto, V. Ivanov)
INDONESIA 0

Half-time: 3-0 Attendance: 10,000

Referee: R. Lund (New Zealand)

U.S.S.R.: Razinski, Tischenko, Babashkin, B. Kuznetsov, Maslenkin, Netto, Tatushin, Isaev, Strelzov, Salnikov, Ilyin.
INDONESIA: Saelan, Rasjid, Siregar, Yatim, Kwee, Tan, Witarsa, Ramang, Arifin, Thio, Jusron.

November 29, 1956

Venue: Melbourne

U.S.S.R. 0
INDONESIA 0

Half-time: 0-0 Attendance: 10,000

Referee: Sh. Takenokoshi (Japan)

U.S.S.R.: Yashin, Tischenko, Babashkin, B. Kuznetsov, Beta, Netto, Tatushin, Isaev, Strelzov, Salnikov, Rishkin.
INDONESIA: Saelan, Rasjid, Siregar, Yatim, Kwee, Tan, Witarsa, Phwa, Danoe, Thio, Ramang.

December 1, 1956

Venue: Melbourne

INDIA 4 (D'Souza 3, Kittu)
AUSTRALIA 2 (Morrow, Arthur)

Half-time: 2-2

Referee: Ch. H. Wensveen (Indonesia)

INDIA: Thangaraj, Azizuddin, Rahaman, Kempiah, Salaam, Noor, P.K. Banerjee, S. Banerjee, D'Souza, Kittu, Kannayan.
AUSTRALIA: Lord, Bignell, Pettigrew, Arthur, Warren, Sander, Loughran, Lennard, Morrow, McMillan, Smith.

Semi-Finals

December 4, 1956

Venue: Melbourne

YUGOSLAVIA 4 (Papec 2, Veselinovic, o.g.)
INDIA 1 (D'Souza)

Half-time: 0-0   Attendance: 25,269

Referee: Nikolai Latishev (U.S.S.R.)

YUGOSLAVIA: Vidinic, Koscak, Biogradlic, Santek, Spajic, Krstic, Mujic, Papec, Antic, Veselinovic, Liposinovic.

INDIA: Narayan, Rahaman, Lateef, Kempiah, Salaam, Noor, P.K. Banerjee, Nundy, D'Souza, Kittu, Balaraman.

December 5, 1956

Venue: Melbourne   (Result is after extra time)

U.S.S.R. 2 (Strelzov, Tatushin)
BULGARIA 1 (Kolev)

Half-time: 0-0   Attendance: 42,000

Referee: R.H. Mann (England)

U.S.S.R.: Yashin, Tischenko, Bashaskin, Ogonikov, Paramonov, Netto, Tatushin, V. Ivanov, Strelzov, Salnikov, Rishkin.

BULGARIA: Naidenov, Rakarov, Manolov, Goranov, Bojkov, Kovacev, Milanov, Dimitrov, Panaiotov, Kolev, Ianev.

Bronze Medal Game

December 7, 1956

Venue: Melbourne

BULGARIA 3 (Diev 2, Milanov)
INDIA 0

Half-time: 2-0   Attendance: 25,000

Referee: Nikolai Latyshev (U.S.S.R.)

BULGARIA: Yosifov, Rakarov, Kovatschev, Stefanov, Manolov, Stojanov, Milanov, Dimitrov, Panajotov, Kolev, Dijev.

INDIA: Subramaniam, Aziz, Lateef, Kempiah, Muhamed, Husain, Kannayan, D'Souza, Pal, Nundy, Kittu.

Final

December 8, 1956

Venue: Melbourne

U.S.S.R. 1 (Ilyin)
YUGOSLAVIA 0

Half-time: 0-0   Attendance: 102,000

Referee: R. Wright (Australia)

U.S.S.R.: Yashin, Kuznetsov, Bashashkin, Ogognikov, Maslenkin, Netto, Tatushin, Issayev, Simonian, Salnikov, Ilyin.

YUGOSLAVIA: Radenkovic, Koscak, Radovic, Santek, Spajic, Krstic, Sekularac, Papec, Antic, Veselinovic, Mujic.

15th Olympiad – 1960 – Rome

Success finally came the way of Yugoslavia in 1960, when they defeated Denmark in the Final played in Rome. Following the stunted tournament in 1956, Olympic Football entered the modern era in this tournament with 16 Finalists being divided into four groups of four teams each, the top four teams meeting in the Semi-finals. Topping the groups were Yugoslavia, Italy, Denmark and Hungary.

The games were played in Pescara, Grosseto, L'Aquila, Florence, Livorno, Naples and Rome and the Italian team contained a number of players who were later to make an impact on the wider scene of world football. At wing half was Giovanni Trapattoni, whose coaching exploits were to surpass those of his playing career, the very talented forward Gianni Rivera, one of Italy's finest defenders in Tarcisio Burgnich and another top class forward in Giacomo Bulgarelli.

A very different Hungarian team from the one that had won the gold medal eight years previously lacked the great names but still included talented players in in Dezso Novak, Florian Albert and Gyula Rakosi. Denmark, beaten in the Final by Yugoslavia, had great players in Flemming Nielsen and Harald Nielsen, while the winning Yugoslav team included a fine goalkeeper in Milutin Soskic, an outstanding full back in Fahrudin Jusufi and a dangerous winger in Borivoje Kostic.

Members of the United Kingdom squad in 1960, the final year in which a British team was entered, were: Mike Pinner (Queens Park Rangers), T. Thompson (Stockton), D.D. Holt (Queens Park), R. McKinven (St. Johnstone), L. Brown (Bishop Auckland), R.W. Sleap (Barnet), R. Brown (Barnet), P.J. Hasty (Tooting and Mitcham), H.M. Lindsay (Kingstonian), J.H. Devine (Queens Park), W. Neil (Airdrie), M.M. Greenwood (Bishop Auckland), H. Forde (Glenavon), T. Howard (Hendon), J.B. Wakefield (Corinthian Casuals), A. Coates (Evenwood Town), H.H. Barr (Ballymena United), L.G. Brown (Dulwich Hamlet), Jim Lewis (Walthamstow Avenue).

Preliminary Competition

Group One

26th August 1960

Venue: The Stadio Adriatico, Pescara.

YUGOSLAVIA 6   (Galic, Kostic 3, Knez, o.g.)
UNITED ARAB REPUBLIC 1   (Attia Raafat)

Half-time: 3-0

Referee: Reg Leafe (United Kingdom)

YUGOSLAVIA: Soskic, Durkovic, Jusufi, Zanetic, Roganovic, Perusic, Ankovic, Maravic, Knez, Galic, Kostic.

U.A.R.: Heikal Adel, Refai Mahamed, Elhamouli Alaaeldine, Elessnawi Amin, Elfanaguili Rifaat, Kottb Samir, Reda, Attia Raafat, Selim Abdou, Elgohari Mahmoud, Elsherbini Mohamed.

26th August 1960

Venue: The Stadio Municipal, Grosseto.

BULGARIA 3   (Diev 2, Christov)
TURKEY 0

Half-time: 1-0   Attendance: 3,000

Referee: Cesare Jonni (Italy)

BULGARIA: Najdenov, Rakarov, Kitov, Largov, Manolov, Kovatcev, Diev, Abadjiev, Dimitrov, N. Yakimov, Christov.

TURKEY: Gokalp, Cipiloglu, Taner, Ozyazici, Tunakozan, Tarhan, Uygun, Sensan, Yalcinkaya, Koken, Soydan.

29th August 1960

Venue: *The Stadio Municipal, L'Aquila.*

BULGARIA 2   (Yordanov, Diev)
UNITED ARAB REPUBLIC 0

Half-time: 1-0   Attendance: 3,500

Referee: Leo Helge (Denmark)

BULGARIA: Najdenov, Rakarov, Kovatchev, Dimitrov, Manolov, Largov, Diev, Abadjiev, Yordanov, Yakimov, Kolev.

U.A.R.: Koorshed Fetthi Aly, Zaki Yaken, Badawi Aly, Elhamouli Alaaeldine, Elfanaguili Rifaat, Kottb Samir, Reda, Noshi Mohamed, Selim Seleh, Elgohari Mahmoud, Elsherbini Mohamed.

1st September 1960

Venue: *The Stadio Ardenza, Livorno.*

UNITED ARAB REPUBLIC 3   (Attia Rafaat, Kottb 2)
TURKEY 3   (Tarkan, Koken, Yalcinkaya)

Half-time: 1-2

Referee: Lucien Van Nuffel (Belgium)

U.A.R.: Korshed Fetthi Aly, Zaki Yaken, Elhamouli Alaaeldine, Badawi Aly, Elfanaguili Rifaat, Kottb Samir, Elgohari Mahmoud, Nosseir Nabil, Noshi Mohamed, Attia Rafaat, Elsherbini Mohamed.

TURKEY: Kucukbay, Cipiloglu, Taner, Ozyazici, Tunakozan, Ertan, Uygun, Sensan, Yalcinkaya, Tarhan, Koken.

29th August 1960

Venue: *The Stadio Municipal, Florence.*

YUGOSLAVIA 4   (Kostic 2, Galic, Knez)
TURKEY 0

Half-time: 1-0

Referee: Vincenzo Orlandini (Italy)

YUGOSLAVIA: Soskic, Durkovic, Jusufi, Zanetic, Roganovic, Perusic, Takac, Maravic, Galic, Knez, Kostic.

TURKEY: Gokalp, Cipiloglu, Taner, Ozyazici, Tunakozan, Tarhan, Yildiz, Sensan, Yalcinkaya, Ertan, Soydan.

	P	W	D	L	F	A	Pts
YUGOSLAVIA	3	2	1	0	13	4	5
BULGARIA	3	2	1	0	8	3	5
TURKEY	3	0	1	2	3	10	1
U.A.R.	3	0	1	2	4	11	1

Yugoslavia, having the best "goal average" in the match with Bulgaria qualified for the Semi-Finals

Group 2

1st September 1960

Venue: *The Stadio Flaminio, Rome.*

YUGOSLAVIA 3   (Galic 3)
BULGARIA 3   (Kovatchev, Debarski 2)

Half-time: 0-0   Attendance: 15,000

Referee: Cesare Jonni (Italy)

YUGOSLAVIA: Soskic, Durkovic, Jusufi, Zanetic, Sombolac, Perusic, Kozlina, Maravic, Galic, Knez, Kostic.

BULGARIA: Najdenov, Rakarov, Manolov, Dimitrov, Largov, Kovatchev, Diev, Abadjiev, Christov, Yakimov, Debarski.

26th August 1960

Venue: *The Stadio Ardenza, Livorno.*

BRAZIL 4   (Gerson, China 2, Machado)
UNITED KINGDOM 3   (R. Brown 2, Lewis)

Half-time: 1-1

Referee: Josef Kandlbinder (West Germany)

BRAZIL: Martinis Cavalheiro, Claudionos, Texeira, Dias, Rubens, Dari, Da Silva Machado, Paulinho, China, Gerson, Valdir.

U.K.: Pinner, Thompson, Holt, McKinven, L. Brown, Sleap, Lewis, R. Brown, Hasty, Lindsay, Devine.

26th August 1960

Venue: *The Stadio Fuorigrotta, Naples.*

ITALY 4 (Rivera 2, Fanello, Tomeazzi)
TAIWAN 1 (Mok Chun Wah)

Half-time: 2-1

Referee: Leo Helge (Denmark)

ITALY: Alfieri, Noletti, Trebbi, Ferrini, Salvadore, Trapattoni, Rivera, Fanello, Tomeazzi, Bulgarelli, Magistrelli.

TAIWAN: Lau Sui Wah, Law Pak, Kok Kam Hung, Chan Hung, Lau Tim, Lam Seung Yee, Wong Chi Keung, Kwok Yu, Chau Moon, Yiu Chuk Yin, Mok Chun Wah.

1st September 1960

Venue: *The Stadio Municipal, in Florence*

ITALY 3 (Rossano 2, Rivera)
BRAZIL 1 (Valdir)

Half-time: 0-1

Referee: Pierre Schwinte (France)

ITALY: Alfieri, Burgnich, Trebbi, Tumburus, Salvadore, Trappatoni, Rancati, Ferrini, Fanello, Rossano, Rivera.

BRAZIL: Martins Cavalheiro, Claudionos, Teixeira, Dias, Rubens, Dari, Da Silva Machado, Paulinho, China, Gerson, Valdir.

29th August 1960

Venue: *The Stadio Flaminio, Rome.*

BRAZIL 5 (Gerson 3, Diaz 2)
TAIWAN 0

Half-time: 2-0

Referee: E. Erlih (Yugoslavia)

BRAZIL: Martins Cavalheiro, Claudionos, Jurandis, Dias, Candido, Dari, Da Silva Machado, Paulhinho, Chuiquinho, Gerson, Valdir.

TAIWAN: Lau Sui Wah, Law Pak, Kok Kam Hung, Chan Hung, Lau Tim, Lam Seung Yee, Wong Chi Keung, Lo Kwok Tai, Chau Moon, Yiu Chuk Yin, Mok Chun Wah.

1st September 1960

Venue: *The Stadio Municipal, Grosseto.*

UNITED KINGDOM 3 (R. Brown 2, Hasty)
TAIWAN 2 (Yiu Chuk Yin 2)

Half-time: 1-0

Referee: Josef Kandlbinder (West Germany)

U.K.: Pinner, Greenwood, Holt, McKinven, L. Brown, Forde, Lewis, R. Brown, Hasty, Lindsay, Howard.

TAIWAN: Lau Sui Wah, Law Pak, Kok Kam Hung, Chan Hung, Lau Tim, Wong Man Wai, Wong Chi Keung, Lam Seung Yee, Chau Moon, Yiu Chuk Yin, Mok Chun Wah.

29th August 1960

Venue: *The Stadio Flaminio, in Rome*

ITALY 2 (Rossano 2)
UNITED KINGDOM 2 (R. Brown, Hasty)

Half-time: 1-1

Referee: Lucien Van Nuffel (Belgium)

ITALY: Alfieri, Burgnich, Trebbi, Tumburus, Salvadore, Trappatoni, Rivera, Bulgarelli, Tomeazzi, Rossano, Cella.

U.K.: Pinner, Neil, Holt, McKinven, L. Brown, Sleap, Lewis, R. Brown, Hasty, Lindsay, Devine.

	P	W	D	L	F	A	Pts
ITALY	3	2	1	0	9	4	5
BRAZIL	3	2	0	1	10	6	4
U.K.	3	1	1	1	8	8	3
TAIWAN	3	0	0	3	3	12	0

Group 3

26th August 1960

Venue: The Stadio Flaminio, Rome

POLAND 6   (Pohl 5, Hachorek)
TUNISIA 1   (Kerrit)

Half-time: 3-1   Attendance: 3,000

Referee: Concetto Lo Bello (Italy)

POLAND: Szymkowiak, Pahla, Wozniak, Strzykalski, Szczepanski, Zientara, Gadecki, Brychczy, Hachorek, Pohl, Lentner.

TUNISIA: Khaled, Zguir, Taoufik, Chetali, Meddeb, Sghaier Ahmed, Moncef, Naji, Touati, Kerrit, Rouatbi Ridha.

26th August 1960

Venue: The Stadio Flaminio, Rome.

DENMARK 3   (Sorensen, H. Nielsen 2)
ARGENTINA 2   (Oleniak, Bilardo)

Half-time: 1-1

Referee: F. Liverani (Italy)

DENMARK: From, Andersen, Jensen, Hansen, C. Nielsen, F. Nielsen, Pedersen, Danielssen, H. Nielsen, Enoksen, Sorensen.

ARGENTINA: Periotti, Stauskas, Ginel, Blanco, De Ciancio, Diaz, Bilardo, Zarich, Desiderio, Oleniak, Perez.

29th August 1960

Venue: The Stadio Adriatico, Pescara.

ARGENTINA 2   (Oleniak 2)
TUNISIA 1   (Kerrit)

Half-time: 1-1

Referee: Istvan Zsolt (Hungary)

ARGENTINA: Periotti, Stauskas, Ginel, Blanco, De Ciancio, Diaz, Bilardo, Zarich, Desiderio, Oleniak, Perez.

TUNISIA: Khalled, Ridha, Sghaier Ahmed, Dhaou, Chetali, Taoufik, Naji, Meddeb, Ben Azzedine, Touati, Kerrit.

29th August 1960

Venue: The Stadio Ardenza, Livorno.

DENMARK 2   (H. Nielsen, Pedersen)
POLAND 1   (Gadecki)

Half-time: 1-1   Attendance: 3,700

Referee: Concetto Lo Bello (Italy)

DENMARK: From, Andersen, Jensen, Hansen, H.C. Nielsen, F. Nielsen, Pedersen, Danielsen, H. Nielsen, Troelsen, Sorensen.

POLAND: Szymkowiak, Pahla, Grzegorczyk, Wozniak, Strzykalski, Zientara, Gadecki, Brychczy, Hachorek, Pohl, Lentner.

1st September 1960

Venue: The Stadio Municipal, L'Aquila.

DENMARK 3   (F. Nielsen, H. Nielsen 2)
TUNISIA 1   (Cherif)

Half-time: 2-0

Referee: Julio Campanati (Italy)

DENMARK: From, Andersen, Jensen, Hansen, H.C. Nielsen, F. Nielsen, Pedersen, Troelsen, H. Nielsen, Danielsen, Sorensen.

TUNISIA: Khalled, Ridha, Dhaou, Meddeb, Mohieddine, Taoufik, Naji, Cherif, Chetali, Touati, Kerrit.

1st September 1960

Venue: The Stadio Fuorigrotta, Naples.

ARGENTINA 2   (Oleniak, Perez)
POLAND 0

Half-time: 1-0   Attendance: 10,000

Referee: S. Garan (Turkey)

ARGENTINA: Periotti, Stauskas, Ginel, Blanco, De Ciancio, Diaz, Rendo, Zarich, Bonnano, Oleniak, Perez.

POLAND: Stefaniczyn, Pahla, Wozniak, Strzykalski, Grzybowsky, Zientara, Gadecki, Brychczy, Hachorek, Pohl, Lentner.

	P	W	D	L	F	A	Pts
DENMARK	3	3	0	0	8	4	6
ARGENTINA	3	2	0	1	6	4	4
POLAND	3	1	0	2	7	5	2
TUNISIA	3	0	0	3	3	11	0

29th August 1960

Venue: The Stadio Fuorigrotta, Naples.

HUNGARY 6   (Albert 2, Dunai 2, Rakosi, Gorocs)
PERU 2   (Ramirez 2)

Half-time: 3-1

Referee: Piero Bonetto (Italy)

HUNGARY: Barago, Novak, Dalnoki, Solymosi, Varhidi, Kovacs, Pal, Gorocs, Albert, Dunai, Rakosi.
PERU: Salinas, Campos, Earl, Luna, De Guevara, Arguedas, Gallardo, Caceres, Nieri, Ramirez, Uribe.

Group 4

26th August 1960

Venue: The Stadio Municipal, L'Aquila.

HUNGARY 2   (Gorocs, Albert)
INDIA 1   (Balaraman)

Half-time: 1-0

Referee: Bahri Ben Said (Tunisia)

HUNGARY: Torok, Novak, Varhidi, Dainoki, Vileszal, Kovacs, Satori, Gorocs, Albert, Orosz, Rakosi.
INDIA: Thangaraj, Chandrasekhar, Jarnali Singh, Latif, Kempaiah, Yousuf Khan, Banerjee, Goswami, Kannan, Sunder Raj, Balaraman.

29th August 1960

Venue: The Stadio Municipal, Grosseto.

FRANCE 1   (Coincon)
INDIA 1   (Banerjee)

Half-time: 0-0

Referee: Ray Morgan (Canada)

FRANCE: Wettstein, Polonia, Bodin, Philippe, Samper, Artelesa, Stamm, Coincon, Giamarchi, Dubaele, Quedec.
INDIA: Thangaraj, Chandrasekhar, Latif, Kempaiah, Jarnali Singh, Ram Bahadur, Banerjee, Goswami, Yousuf Khan, Sunder Raj, Balaraman.

26th August 1960

Venue: The Stadio Municipal, Florence.

FRANCE 2   (Giamarchi, Quedec)
PERU 1   (Uribe)

Half-time: 0-1

Referee: E. Erlich (Yugoslavia)

FRANCE: Samoy, Gonzales, Polonia, Bordas, Artelesa, Barrato, Quedec, Coincon, Giamarchi, Ahmed, Loncle.
PERU: Salinas, Campos, Luna, De Guevara, Earl, Arguedas, Ruiz, Guzmann, Altuna, Uribe, Gallardo.

1st September 1960

Venue: The Stadio Flaminio, Rome.

HUNGARY 7   (Albert 2, Gorocs 3, Dunai 2)
FRANCE 0

Half-time: 3-0

Referee: Vincenzo Orlandini (Italy)

HUNGARY: Torok, Dudas, Dalnoki, Solymosi, Varhidi, Kovacs, Pal, Gorocs, Albert, Dunai, Rakosi.
FRANCE: Samoy, Polonia, Philippe, Baratto, Bodin, Artelesa, Stamm, Bordas, Quedec, Ahmed, Loncle.

1st September 1960

Venue: The Stadio Adriatico, Pescara.

PERU 3   (Nieri 2, Uribe)
INDIA 1   (Balaraman)

Half-time: 1-0

Referee: Iman Mahmoud (U.A.R.)

PERU: H. Campos, E. Campos, Boulanger, Carmona, Biselach, Arguedas, Ruiz, Nieri, Iwasaki, Uribe, Gallardo.

INDIA: Thangaraj, Chandrasekhar, Jarnali, Latif, Kempaiah, Ram Bahadur, Banerjee, Goswami, Yousuf Khan, Balaraman, Sunder Raj.

	P	W	D	L	F	A	Pts
HUNGARY	3	3	0	0	15	3	6
FRANCE	3	1	1	1	3	9	3
PERU	3	1	0	2	6	9	2
INDIA	3	0	1	2	3	6	1

Semi-Finals

5th September 1960

Venue: The Stadio Fuorigrotta, Naples
(After extra time)

YUGOSLAVIA 1   (Galic)
ITALY 1   (Tumburus)

Half-time: 0-0

Referee: Josef Kandlbinder (West Germany)

YUGOSLAVIA: Vidinic, Sombolac, Jusufi, Kozlina, Durkovic, Perusic, Zanetic, Matus, Galic, Knez, Kostic.

ITALY: Alfieri, Burgnich, Trebbi, Tumburus, Salvadore, Trappatoni, Rancatti, Rivera, Tomeazzi, Ferrini, Rossano.

Yugoslavia won on the toss of a coin.

6th September 1960

Venue: The Stadio Flaminio, Rome.

DENMARK 2   (H. Nielsen, F. Nielsen)
HUNGARY 0

Half-time: 1-0

Referee: Reg Leafe (United Kingdom)

DENMARK: From, Andersen, Jensen, Hansen, H.C. Nielsen, F. Nielsen, Pedersen, Troelsen, H. Nielsen, Enoksen, Sorensen.

HUNGARY: Torok, Dudas, Dalnoki, Vileszal, Varhidi, Kovacs, Orosz, Gorocs, Albert, Dunai, Rakosi.

Bronze Medal Game

9th September 1960

Venue: The Stadio Flaminio, Rome.

HUNGARY 2   (Orosz, Dunai)
ITALY 1   (Tomeazzi)

Half-time: 1-0

Referee: Reg Leafe (United Kingdom)

HUNGARY: Torok, Dudas, Dalnoki, Solymosi, Varhidi, Kovacs, Satori, Gorocs, Albert, Orosz, Dunai.

ITALY: Alfieri, Burgnich, Trebbi, Tumburus, Salvatore, Trappatoni, Cella, Rivera, Tomeazzi, Bulgarelli, Rossano.

Final

10th September 1960

Venue: The Stadio Flaminio, Rome.

YUGOSLAVIA 3   (Galic, Matus, Kostic)
DENMARK 1   (Flemming Nielsen)

Half-time: 2-0   *Attendance: 30,000*

Referee: Concetto Lo Bello (Italy)

YUGOSLAVIA: Vidinic, Roganovic, Jusufi, Perusic, Durkovic, Zanotic, Ankovic, Matus, Galic, Knez, Kostic.

DENMARK: From, Andersen, Jensen, Hansen, Hans Nilesen, Flemming Nielsen, Pedersen, Troelsen, Harald Nielsen, Enoksen, Sorensen.

16th Olympiad – 1964 – Tokyo

The Olympics were staged in Asia for the first time in 1964 and once again the football tournament was won by an eastern bloc country. Hungary, following its triumph in 1952, won its second gold medal in Tokyo defeating Czechoslovakia in the final. A third Eastern European nation, East Germany, captured the bronze. Before it was all over four countries played in a separate tournament in Osaka, similar to the Consolation Tournaments of the 1920's.

Once again 16 teams qualified for the Finals and were divided into four groups of four. However, this time instead of just the four winners competing in the Semi-finals, the top two teams from each group qualified for the Quarter-finals

This tournament was notable only for the absence of great names.

Group A

11th October 1964

Venue: The Mitsuzawa Stadium, Tokyo.

EAST GERMANY 4 (Bauchspiess, Vogel 2, Frenzel)
IRAN 0

Half-time: 3-0   Attendance: 15,000
Referee: Eunapio Gouveia (Brazil)
EAST GERMANY: Heinsch, Urbanczyk, Geisler, Pankau, Walter, Korner, Engelhardt, Bauchspiess, Frenzel, Frassdorf, Vogel.
IRAN: Asli, Amir-Asefi, Habibi, Miraz, Ghelichkhani, Arab, Latifi, Saedi, Jamali, Talebi, Khodaparest.

13th October 1964

Venue: The Komazawa Stadium, Tokyo.

EAST GERMANY 1 (Frenzel)
ROMANIA 1 (Pavlovici)

Half-time: 1-1   Attendance: 25,000
Referee: Vaclav Korelus (Czechoslovakia)
EAST GERMANY: Heinsch, Urbanczyk, Geisler, Pankau, Walter, Korner, Frassdorf, Bauchspiess, Frenzel, Noldner, Vogel.
ROMANIA: Datcu, Greavu, Nunweiler, Halmageanu, Jenei, Coe, Pircalab, Constantin, Pavlovici, Koszka, Creiniceanu.

11th October 1964

Venue: The Omiya Stadium, Tokyo.

ROMANIA 3 (Creinideanu, Pircalab, Ionescu)
MEXICO 1 (Rodriguez)

Half-time: 2-0
Referee: Yozo Yokoyama (Japan)
ROMANIA: Datcu, Greavu, Halmageanu, Petru, Nunweiler, Coe, Pircalab, Constantin, Koszka, Ionescu. Creiniceanu.
MEXICO: Calderon, Davila, Barba, Sanchez, Mena, Cisneros, Arellano, Perez, Rodriguez, Salcedo, De La Rosa.

13th October 1964

Venue: The Chichibu Stadium, Tokyo.

IRAN 1 (Nirlou)
MEXICO 1 (Davila)

Half-time: 1-1
Referee: John Stanley Wontumi (Ghana)
IRAN: Biari-Eslam, Amir-Asefi, Habibi, Arab, Mostafavi, Nirlou, Jamali, Latifi, Nourian, Esmaili, Talebi.
MEXICO: Calderon, Davila, Barba, Sanchez, Mena, Arellano, Perez, Cisneros, Rodriguez, Salcedo, De La Rosa.

15th October 1964

Venue: *The Mitsuzawa Stadium, Tokyo.*

EAST GERMANY 2   (Barthels, Noldner)
MEXICO 0

Half-time: *1-0*   Attendance: *13,000*
Referee: Gregg De Silva (Malaysia)
EAST GERMANY: Weigang, Urbanczyk, Rock, Seehaus, Walter, Unger, Barthels, Lisiewicz, Frassdorf, Noldner, Stocker.
MEXICO: Calderon, Padilla, Barba, Llorente, Mena, Davila, Cisneros, Rodriguez, Perez, Suarez, De La Rosa.

15th October 1964

Venue: *The Omiya Stadium, Tokyo.*

ROMANIA 1   (Pavlovici)
IRAN 0

Half-time: *1-0*
Referee: Miguel Comesana (Argentina)
ROMANIA: Andrei, Greavu, Ivan, Pavlovici, Nunweiler, Petescu, Avram, Constantin, Ioanescu, Koszka, Creiniceanu.
IRAN: Asli, Amir-Asefi, Habibi, Arab, Ghelichkhani, Latifi, Nourian, Nirlou, Mostafavi, Esmaili, Talebi.

	P	W	D	L	F	A	Pts
E. GERMANY	3	2	1	0	7	1	5
ROMANIA	3	2	1	0	5	2	5
MEXICO	3	0	1	2	2	6	1
IRAN	3	0	1	2	1	6	1

Group B

11th October 1964

Venue: *The National Stadium, Tokyo.*

HUNGARY 6   (Bene 6)
MOROCCO 0

Half-time: *2-0*
Referee: Duk Chun Kim (South Korea)
HUNGARY: Gelei, Novak, Ihasz, Palotai, Orban, Szepesi, Farkas, Varga, Bene, Komora, Katona.
MOROCCO: Kassou, El Mansouri, Fah Im, Nijam, Bensiffedine, Mokhtatif, Mohammed, Lamari, Morchid, Bamous, Bendayan.

13th October 1964

Venue: *The Mitsuzawa Stadium, Tokyo.*

YUGOSLAVIA 3   (Samardzic, Belin 2)
MOROCCO 1   (Bouachra)

Half-time: *2-1*
Referee: Hussein Imam (United Arab Republic)
YUGOSLAVIA: Curkovic, Fazlagic, Vujovic, Belin, Cop, Miladinovic, Samardzic, Zambata, Osim, Lemic, Dzajic.
MOROCCO: Kassou, El Mansouri, Fah Im, Nijim Bensiffedine, Mokhtatif, Bouachra, Lamari, Morchid, Bamous, Benayan.

15th October 1964

Venue: *The Komazawa Stadium, Tokyo.*

HUNGARY 6   (Csernai 4, Farkas, Bene)
YUGOSLAVIA 5   (Osim 2, Belin 2, Zambata)

Half-time: *5-4*
Referee: Genichi Fukushima (Japan)
HUNGARY: Szentmihalyi, Novak, Ihasz, Palotai, Orban, Nogradi, Farkas, Csernai, Bene, Komora, Katona.
YUGOSLAVIA: Curkovic, Fazlagic, Vujovic, Belin, Cop, Miladinovic, Samardzic, Zambata, Osim, Radovic, Dzajic.

	P	W	D	L	F	A	Pts
HUNGARY	2	2	0	0	12	5	4
YUGOSLAVIA	2	1	0	1	8	7	2
MOROCCO	2	0	0	2	1	9	0

(NORTH KOREA withdrew)

Group C

12th October 1964

Venue: The Omiya Stadium, Tokyo.

CZECHOSLOVAKIA 6 (Lichtnegl, Vojta, Mraz 2, Masny 2)
SOUTH KOREA 1 (Lee)

Half-time: 4-0

Referee: Rafael Valenzuela (Mexico)

CZECHOSLOVAKIA: Schmucker, Urban, Weiss, Picman, Vojta, Geleta, Brumovsky, Lichtnegl, Valosek, Mraz, Masny.

SOUTH KOREA: Heung Chul Ham, Jung Suk Kim, Hong Bok Kim, Sam Rak Kim, Tae Sung Cha, Hung Nam Kim, Yi Woo Lee, Yoon Jung Huh, Sang Kwan Woo, Yoon Ok Cho, Sung Dal Cho.

12th October 1964

Venue: The Komazawa Stadium, Tokyo.

BRAZIL 1 (Lopes Miranda)
UNITED ARAB REPUBLIC 1 (Shahin)

Half-time: 1-0

Referee: Rudi Glockner (East Germany)

BRAZIL: Oliveira Dias, Barro Pereira, Pereira, Vinagre, Lemos Quirino, Neto Virgilio, Miranda Lopes, Marques, Redes Filho, Soares Ribeiro, Caravetti.

U.A.R.: Korshed, Zaki, Elisnawi, Kotb, Badawi, Attia, Riad, Shahin, Ismail, Nosseir, Hassan.

14th October 1964

Venue: The Chichibu Stadium, in Tokyo.

CZECHOSLOVAKIA 5 (Vojta 2, Urban, Mraz, Cvetler)
UNITED ARAB REPUBLIC 1 (Riad)

Half-time: 3-0

Referee: Istvan Zsolt (Hungary)

CZECHOSLOVAKIA: Schmucker, Urban, Weiss, Picman, Vojta, Geleta, Brumovsky, Lichtnegl, Cvitler, Mraz, Masny.

U.A.R.: Korshed, Amin, Elisnawi, Elfanagili, Gad, Badawi, Riad, Mohamed, Ismail, Etman, Mahmoud.

14th October 1964

Venue: The Mitsuzawa Stadium, Tokyo.

BRAZIL 4 (Marques, Vinagre 2, Miranda Lopes)
SOUTH KOREA 0

Half-time: 2-0

Referee: Salih Mohamed Boukkili (Morocco)

BRAZIL: Oliveira Dias, Barros Pereira, Pereira, Vinagre, Lemos Quirino, Neto Virgilio, Miranda Lopes, Mattar Neto, Marques, Soares Ribeiro, Caravetti.

SOUTH KOREA: Heung Chul Ham, Woo Bonf Lee, Hong Bok Kim, Seung Ok Park, Jung Suk Kim, Young Bai Kim, Yi Woo Lee, Yoon Jung Huh, Tae Sung Cha, Yoon Ok Cho, Sung Dal Cho.

16th October 1964

Venue: The Omiya Stadium, Tokyo.

CZECHOSLOVAKIA 1 (Valosek)
BRAZIL 0

Half-time: 0-0

Referee: Asghar Tehrani (Iran)

CZECHOSLOVAKIA: Svajlen, Urban, Weiss, Picman, Matlak, Nepomucky, Brumovsky, Vojta, Valosek, Knebort, Masny.

BRAZIL: Oliveira Dias, Barros Pereira, Pereira, Vinagre, Lemos Quirino, Neto Virgilio, Miranda Lopes, Mattar Neto, Marques, Soares Ribeiro, Caravetti.

16th October 1964

Venue: *The Chichibu Stadium, Tokyo.*

UNITED ARAB REPUBLIC 10   (Riad 6, Mohamed, Elfanagili, Etman, Hassan)

SOUTH KOREA 0

Half-time: 3-0

Referee: Rudi Glockner (East Germany)

U.A.R.: Ahmed, Amin, Elisnawi, Elfanagili, Gad, Badawi, Riad, Mohamed, Ismail, Etman, Hassan.

SOUTH KOREA: Heung Chul Ham, Jung Suk Kim, Hong Bok Kim, Sam Rak Kim, Tae Siung Cha, Jung Nam Kim, Kyung Bok Cha, Yoon Jung Hih, Sang Kwon Woo, Yoon Ok Cho, Duk Joong Kim.

14th October 1964

Venue: *The Komazawa Stadium, Tokyo.*

JAPAN 3   (Sugiyama, Kawabuchi, Ogi)

ARGENTINA 2   (Dominguez 2)

Half-time: 0-1

Referee: Aleksandar Skoric (Yugoslavia)

JAPAN: Yokoyama, Katayama, Yamaguchi, Yaegashi, Kamata, Suzuki, Kawabuchi, Kamamoto, Ogi, Miyamoto, Sugiyama.

ARGENTINA: Cejas, Bertolotti, Sesana, Morales, Mori, Perfumo, Cabrera, Risso, Dominguez, Manfredi, Ochoa.

	P	W	D	L	F	A	Pts
CZECHOSLOV.	3	3	0	0	12	2	6
U.A.R.	3	1	1	1	12	6	3
BRAZIL	3	1	1	1	5	2	3
SOUTH KOREA	3	0	0	3	1	20	0

16th October 1964

Venue: *The Komazawa Stadium, Tokyo.*

GHANA 3   (Agyemang, Sam Acquah, Aggrey Fynn)

JAPAN 2   (Sugiyama, Yaegashi)

Half-time: 1-1

Referee: Cornel Nitescu (Romania)

GHANA: Dodoo-Ankrah, Okai, Oblitey, Sam Acquah, Addo-Odametey, Nkansah, Agyemang, Mfum, Agget Fynn, Edward Acquah, Pare.

JAPAN: Yokoyama; Katayama, Yamaguchi, Suzuki, Kami, Kamata, Miyamoto, Ogi, Yaegashi, Kamamoto, Sugiyama.

Group D

12th October 1964

Venue: *The Mitsuzawa Stadium, Tokyo.*

ARGENTINA 1   (Bulla)

GHANA 1   (Edward Acquah)

Half-time: 1-0

Referee: Menahem Ashkenazi (Israel)

ARGENTINA: Cejas, Bertolotti, Sesana, Morales, Mori, Perfumo, Cabrera, Malleo, Bulla, Manfredi, Tojo.

GHANA: Doddo-Ankrah, Sam Acquah, Oblitey, Acheampong, Addo-Odametey, Pare, Osei, Mfum, Aggrey, Edward Acquah, Salisu.

	P	W	D	L	F	A	Pts
GHANA	2	1	1	1	4	3	3
JAPAN	2	1	0	1	5	5	2
ARGENTINA	2	0	1	1	3	4	1

(ITALY withdrew)

Quarter-Finals

18th October 1964

Venue: *The Chichibu Stadium, Tokyo.*

EAST GERMANY 1 (Frenzel)
YUGOSLAVIA 0

Half-time: 1-0   Attendance: 10,000
Referee: Gregg De Silva (Malaysia)
EAST GERMANY: Heinsch, Urbanczyk, Geisler, Pankau, Walter, Korner, Frassdorf, Bauchspiess, Frenzel, Noldner, Vogel.
YUGOSLAVIA: Curjovic, Jeftic, Vujovic, Belin, Cop, Miladinovic, Takac, Zambata, Osim, Radovic, Dzajic.

18th October 1964

Venue: *The Mitsuzawa Stadium, Tokyo.*

HUNGARY 2 (Csernai 2)
ROMANIA 0

Half-time: 1-0
Referee: Menahem Ashkenazi (Israel)
HUNGARY: Gelei, Novak, Ihasz, Palotai, Orban, Nogradi, Farkas, Csernai, Bene, Komora, Katona.
ROMANIA: Datcu, Greavu, Halmageanu, Petru, Nunweiler, Georgescu, Pircalab, Constantin, Ionescu, Coe, Creiniceanu.

18th October 1964

Venue: *The Komazawa Stadium, Tokyo.*

CZECHOSLOVAKIA 4 (Brumovsky 2, Vojta, Mraz)
JAPAN 0

Half-time: 1-0
Referee: Eunapio Gouveia (Brazil)
CZECHOSLOVAKIA: Schmucker, Urban, Picman, Vojta, Weiss, Geleta, Brumovsky, Mraz, Lichtnegl, Masny, Valosek.
JAPAN: Yokoyama, Katayama, Yamaguchi, Suzuki, Ogi, Kamata, Kawabuchi, Yaegashi, Kamamoto, Miyamoto, Watanabe.

18th October 1964

Venue: *The Omiya Stadium, Tokyo.*

UNITED ARAB REPUBLIC 5 (Badawi 2, Riad, Elfanagili)
GHANA 1 (Mfum)

Half-time: 1-1
Referee: Rudi Glockner (East Germany)
U.A.R.: Ahmed, Amin, Elisnawi, Elfanagili, Gad, Elsherbini, Riad, Etman, Badawi, Ismail, Hassan.
GHANA: Dodoo-Ankrah, Sam Acquah, Oblitey, Acheampong, Addo-Odametey, Nkansah, Agyemang, Mfum, Aggrey Fynn, Pare, Salisu.

Semi-Finals

20th October 1964

Venue: *The Komazawa Stadium, Tokyo.*

CZECHOSLOVAKIA 2 (Lichtnegl, Mraz)
EAST GERMANY 1 (Noldner)

Half-time: 0-1   Attendance: 20,000
Referee: Menahem Ashkenazi (Israel)
CZECHOSLOVAKIA: Schmucker, Urban, Knesl, Vojta, Weiss, Geleta, Brumovsky, Mraz, Lichtnegl, Masny, Valosek.
EAST GERMANY: Heinsch, Urbanczyk, Geisler, Pankau, Walter, Korner, Stocker, Frassdorf, Frenzel, Noldner, Vogel.

20th October 1964

Venue: *The Chichibu Stadium, Tokyo.*

HUNGARY 6 (Bebe 4, Komora 2)
UNITED ARAB REPUBLIC 0

Half-time: 3-0
Referee: Migeul Comesana (Argentina)
HUNGARY: Szentmihalyi, Novak, Ihasz, Palotai, Orban, Nogradi, Farkas, Csernai, Bene, Komora, Katona.
U.A.R.: Ahmed, Amin, Elisnawi, Elfanagili, Gad, Elsherbini, Riad, Shahin, Badawi, Etman, Hassan.

Bronze Medal Game

23rd October 1964

Venue: The National Stadium, Tokyo.

EAST GERMANY 3   (Frenzel, Vogel, Stocker)
UNITED ARAB REPUBLIC 1   (Attia)

Half-time: 1-0   Attendance: 60,000
Referee: Yozo Yokoyama (Japan)
EAST GERMANY: Heinsch, Rock, Geisler, Pankau, Walter, Korner, Stocker, Frassdorf, Frenzel, Noldner, Vogel.
U.A.R.: Ahmed, Zaki, Elisnawi, Kotb, Attia, Elsherbini, Mohamed, Riad, Badawi, Nosseir, Etman.

Final

23rd October 1964

Venue: The National Stadium, Tokyo.

HUNGARY 2   (o.g., Bene)
CZECHOSLOVAKIA 1   (Brumovsky)

Half-time: 0-0
Referee: Menahem Ashkenazi (Israel)
HUNGARY: Szentmihalyi, Novak, Ihasz, Szepesi, Orban, Nogradi, Farkas, Csernai, Bene, Komora, Katona.
CZECHOSLOVAKIA: Schumucker, Urban, Picman, Vojta, Weiss, Geleta, Brumovsky, Mraz, Lichtnegl, Masny, Valosek.

Osaka Tournament

20th October 1964

Venue: Osaka

YUGOSLAVIA 6
JAPAN 1

Half-time: 3-0
Referee: Hussein Iman (United Arab Republic)

20th October 1964

Venue: Kyoto

ROMANIA 4
GHANA 2

Half-time: 3-2
Referee: Gregg Da Silva (Malaysia)

22nd October 1964

Venue: Osaka

ROMANIA 3
YUGOSLAVIA 0

Half-time: 0-0   Attendance: 10,000
Referee: Istvan Zsolt (Hungary)

17th Olympiad – 1968 – Mexico City

Hungary captured its third gold medal at the 1968 Olympics held in Mexico, defeating Bulgaria 4-1 in a less than memorable Final in which four players were sent off, three from Bulgaria in the first half and one Hungarian in the second.

Once again 16 teams competed in the final rounds and once again the top two teams from each group qualified for the Quarter-finals. This produced some surprises with Japan defeating France, Guatemala losing narrowly to Hungary, Mexico winning over Spain and Bulgaria squeezing by Israel on a coin toss. Japan went on to capture the bronze medal against the host nation before 105,000 fans at the Azteca Stadium.

Group A

13th October 1968

Venue: The Azteca Stadium, Mexico City

MEXICO 1   (Estrada)
COLOMBIA 0

Half-time: 1-0

Referee: Istvan Zsolt (Hungary)

MEXICO: Vargas, Alejandrez, Medina, Sanabria, Perez, Regueiro, Pulido (Basagueren), Bustos, Estrada, Pereda, Victorino.

COLOMBIA: Quintana, Hernandez, Soto, Munoz, Lopez, Pardo, Gonzales, Arango (Tamayo), Ortiz, Santa, Berdugo.

15th October 1968

Venue: The Azteca Stadium, Mexico City.

FRANCE 4   (Dit Kanyan 2, Tamboueon, o.g.)
MEXICO 1   (Victorino)

Half-time: 3-1

Referee: Erwin Hieger (Peru)

FRANCE: Lempereur-Havrez, Zix, Verhoeve-Thorez, Plante-Lenoir, Larque-Pere, Hodoul-Mouren, Horlaville-L'Hernault, Dit Kanyan, Hallet-Demantin, Ribul-Conte, Tamboueon.

MEXICO: Vargas, Alejandrez, Medina, Sanabria, Perez, Regueiro, Pulido, Bustos, Estrada (Munoz), Pereda, Victorino.

13th October 1968

Venue: The Cuauhtemoc Stadium, Puebla.

FRANCE 3   (Hallet-Delantin, Horlaville, Perrigaud)
GUINEA 1   (Camara)

Half-time: 0-0

Referee: Dr. Milivoje Gugulovic (Yugoslavia)

FRANCE: Lempereur-Navrez, Zix, Verhoeve-Thorez, Plante-Lenori, Larque-Pere, Hodoul-Mouren, Perrigaud-Parry, Horlaville-L'Hernault.

GUINEA: Morlaye Camara, Bangoura, Fofana, Conde, Sankon, N'Dongo Camara (Fod'e Camara), Diallo, Cherif, Maxine Camara, Keita, Soumah.

15th October 1968

Venue: The Cuauhtemoc Stadium, Puebla.

GUINEA 3   (Fod'e Camara 2, Mamadoua Camara)
COLOMBIA 2   (Santa, Mosquera)

Half-time: 1-0

Referee: Dimitier Rumentchev (Bulgaria)

GUINEA: Sanconra, Fofana, Conde, Sankon, Soumah, M. Camara, F. Camara, Cherif, M.M. Camara, Keita, Sano (Morlaye Camara).

COLOMBIA: Quintana, Hernandez, Soto, Munoz, Lopez, Gonzalez (Pardo), Arango, Ortiz, Berdugo, Mosquera, Santa.

17th October 1968

Venue: The Azteca Stadium, Mexico City.

MEXICO 4 (Pereda 2, Pulido 2)
GUINEA 0

Half-time: 0-0

Referee: Wanchai Suvaree (Thailand)

MEXICO: Vargas, Alejandrez, Medina, Sanabria, Perez, Regueiro, Pulido, Bustos (Munoz), Estrada (Morales), Pereda, Victorino.

GUINEA: Bangoura, Fofana, Conde, Sankon, Soumah (Dia), M.N. Camara, F. Camara (Diallo), Cherif, M.M. Camara, Keita, Sano.

17th October 1968

Venue: The Cuauhtemoc Stadium, Puebla.

COLOMBIA 2 (Tamayo, Jaramillo)
FRANCE 1 (Tamboueon)

Half-time: 2-0

Referee: Dr. Karol Galba (Czechoslovakia)

COLOMBIA: Quintana, Hernandez, Soto, Pardo, Ospina, Viafara, Escobar, Berdugo, Tamayo (Ortiz), Jaramillo (Arango), Mosquera.

FRANCE: Delhumeau-Lejars, Grava-Martini, Goueffic-Lailet, Plante-Lenoir, Laurier-Taille (Larque-Pere), Hodoul-Moruren, Horlaville-L'Hernault, Dit Kanyan, Tamboueon-Bouanou, Parmentier-Rouge (Hallet-Demantin), Delafosse-Lefebvre.

	P	W	D	L	F	A	Pts
FRANCE	3	2	0	1	8	4	4
MEXICO	3	2	0	1	6	4	4
COLOMBIA	3	1	0	2	4	5	2
GUINEA	3	1	0	2	4	9	2

Group B

14th October 1968

Venue: The Azteca Stadium, Mexico City

SPAIN 1 (Fernandez)
BRAZIL 0

Half-time: 0-0

Referee: Abraham Klein (Israel)

SPAIN: Marine Mora, Benito Rubio, Espildora, Ochoa, Piugvedal Sala, Ripolo Asensi, Rodriguez Jaen, Juan Fernandez, Garzon, Cereijo Grande (Alcaide), Plasco Ortuno.

BRAZIL: Cruz Cetulio, Ferreira Delmeida, Alves da Silva, Sebastio Silva, Dutra, Barbosa dos Santos, Ueta (De Godoy), Ferreti, Moreno, De Jesus.

14th October 1968

Venue: The Cuauhtemoc Stadium, Puebla.

JAPAN 3 (Kamamoto 3)
NIGERIA 1 (Okoye)

Half-time: 1-1

Referee: Ramon Marmol (El Salvador)

JAPAN: Yokoyama, Katayama, M. Miyamoto, Kamata, Mori, Ogi, Yaegashi (Kuwahara), T. Miyamoto, Kamamoto, Matsumoto, Sugiyama.

NIGERIA: Fregene, Iowe, Okoye, Olumomeji, Opone, Hamilton (Olayomeo), Anieke, Lawal, Broderick, Omojememe, Achochovsia.

16th October 1968

Venue: The Azteca Stadium, Mexico City.

SPAIN 3 (Ortuno, Grande 2)
NIGERIA 0

Half-time: 1-0

Referee: Augusto Robles (Guinea)

SPAIN: Mora, Rubio, Espildora, Ochoa, Sala, Asensi (Crispi), Jaen, Fernandez (Ortega), Garzon, Grande, Ortuno.

NIGERIA: Fregene, Igwe, Ofuokwu, Okpoye, Olumodeji, Opone, Anieke, Lawal, Broderick, Obojememe, Salami.

16th October 1968

Venue: *The Cuauhtemoc Stadium, Puebla.*

BRAZIL 1   (Ferreti)
JAPAN 1   (Watanabe)

Half-time: 1-0

Referee: George Lamptey (Ghana)

BRAZIL: Getulio Cruz, Ferreira Pereira, De Almeida Filho, Silva, Dutra dos Santos, Ferreti (De Mattos), Moreno, De Jesus, Deodato, De Godoy, Byron Mello.

JAPAN: Yokoyama, Katayama, Yamaguchi, Kamata, Mori, Ogi, T. Miyamato, Kuwahara (M. Miyamato), Kamamoto, Matsumoto (Watanabe), Sugiyama.

	P	W	D	L	F	A	Pts
SPAIN	3	2	1	0	4	0	5
JAPAN	3	1	2	0	4	2	4
BRAZIL	3	0	2	1	4	5	2
NIGERIA	3	0	1	2	4	9	1

Group C

18th October 1968

Venue: *The Azteca Stadium, Mexico City.*

SPAIN 0
JAPAN 0

Half-time: 0-0

Referee: Erwin Hieger (Peru)

SPAIN: Mendieta, Benito (Sala), Espildora, Ochoa, Ciaurriz, Icartua, Alfonseda, Alcaide, Barrios, Grande, Ortega.

JAPAN: Yokoyama, Katayama, Miyamoto, Yamaguchi, Kamata, Mori, Ogi, T. Miyamato (Yucuchi), Watanabe, Kamamoto, Sugiyama.

13th October 1968

Venue: *The Jalisco Stadium, Guadalajara.*

HUNGARY 4   (Menczel, Dunai, Fazekas, Sarnozi)
EL SALVADOR 0

Half-time: 1-0

Referee: Diego de Leo (Mexico)

HUNGARY: Fater, Novak, Pancsics, Menczel, Szucs, Fazekas (Kocsis), Dunai, Nagy, Nosko, Juhasz, Sarzoki (Rasti).

EL SALVADOR: Ricardo Martinez (Fernandez), Rivas, Morales, Vazquez, Flamenco (Juan Martinez), Avila, Quintanilla, Lindo, Acevedo, Gonzales, Mendez.

18th October 1968

Venue: *The Cuauhtemoc Stadium, Puebla.*

BRAZIL 3   (Ferreti, Silva, o.g.)
NIGERIA 3   (Olayombo 2, Anike)

Half-time: 3-0

Referee: Seyoum Tarekegn (Ethiopia)

BRAZIL: Cruz, Ferreira, De Almeida (Aryee), Silva, Dutra dos Santos, Ferreti, De Jesus, Deodato, De Godoy, Byron Mello, Chance.

NIGERIA: Fregene, Iowe, Olumodelji (Ofuokwu), Opone, Oshode (Salami), Olayombo, Anieke, Lawal, Broderick, Obojememe, Aryee.

13th October 1968

Venue: *The Leon Stadium, Leon.*

ISRAEL 5   (Shpigel 2, Faygenbaum 3)
GHANA 3   (Malik 2, Amosa)

Half-time: 3-2 Att:

Referee: Michel Kitabdjian (France)

ISRAEL: Bar, Bello, Rosen, Shwager, Rosenthal, Talbi, Shpigel, Faygenbaum, Shpigler, Borba, Malika-Aharon.

GHANA: Eshun, Addo, Sunday, Atuquayefio, Alhassan, Amosa, Naawii, Malik, Acquah, Kpakpo, Foley (Ahukari).

15th October 1968

Venue: The Jalisco Stadium, Guadalajara.

HUNGARY 2 (Dunai, Menczel)
GHANA 2 (Sunday, Stevens)

Half-time: 2-2

Referee: Yoshiyuki Murayama (Japan)

HUNGARY: Fater, Pancsics, Menczel, Szucs, Fazekas (Rasti), Dunai, Nagy, Keglovich, Nosko, Juhasz, Sarkozi (Kocsis).

GHANA: Eshum, Sunday, Osei, Amosa, Stevens, Bortey Naamu, Wilson, Malik, Acquah, Kpakpo, Foley.

15th October 1968

Venue: The Leon Stadium, Leon.

ISRAEL 3 (Taldi, Shpiegler, Bar)
EL SALVADOR 1 (Martinez)

Half-time: 2-0

Referee: Shakibudeen Thompson (Nigeria)

ISRAEL: Lein, Bello, Rosen, Shwager (Bar), Rosenthal, Talbi, Shpigel, Feygenbaum, Shpiegler, Druker, Borba.

EL SALVADOR: Rivas, Castro, Vasquez, Guzman, Villalta Avila, Quintanilla, Rodriguez Lindo (Azucar Urrutia), Flores Ramos (Juan Martinez), Barillas, Mendez, Fernandez.

17th October 1968

Venue: The Jalisco Stadium, Guadalajara.

HUNGARY 2 (A. Dunai 2)
ISRAEL 0

Half-time: 1-0

Referee: Arturo Yamasaki (Mexico)

HUNGARY: Fater, Novak, D. Dunai, Pancsics, Menczel, Szucs, Fazekas, A. Dunai, Nosko, Juhasz (Szalai), Rasti.

ISRAEL: Levin, Bar, Bello, Rosen, Talbi, Shpigel, Feygenbaum, Shpigler, Druker, Borba (Young), Karako (Kastro).

17th October 1968

Venue: The Leon Stadium, Leon.

EL SALVADOR 1 (Rodriguez)
GHANA 1 (Osei)

Half-time: 1-1

Referee: Mariano Medina Iglesias (Spain)

EL SALVADOR: Rivas, Castro, Vazquez, Ruano (Angel), Flamenco, Quintanilla, Rodriguez, Gonzales, Juan Martinez (Azucar), Mendez, Fernandez.

GHANA: Eshum, Sunday, Osei, Amosa, Stevens (Kusi), Bortey Naawu, Wilson, Malik, Acquah, Kpakpo, Foley.

	P	W	D	L	F	A	Pts
HUNGARY	3	2	1	0	8	2	5
ISRAEL	3	2	0	1	8	6	4
GHANA	3	0	2	1	6	8	2
EL SALVADOR	3	0	1	2	2	8	1

Group D

14th October 1968

Venue: The Jalisco Stadium, Guadalajara.

GUATEMALA 1
CZECHOSLOVAKIA 0

Half-time: 1-0

Referee: Romualdo Arppi Filho (Brazil)

GUATEMALA: Lopez, Leon de Leon, Camposeco, Montoya, Melgar, Roldan, Torres, Valdez, Pena, Stokes (Melgar), Garcia.

CZECHOSLOVAKIA: Kramerius, Vercerek, Japasek, Mutkuvic, Souska, Linhart, Strunc, Petras, Bartovic (Pajerchin), Stratil (Krnac), Kral.

14th October 1968

Venue: *The Leon Stadium, Leon.*

BULGARIA 7 (Christov 2, Guionine, Jekov, Zafirov, Donev, Ivkov)
THAILAND 0
Half-time: 1-0
Referee: Guillermo Velasquez (Colombia)
BULGARIA: Yordanov, Guerov, Christiakev, Gaidarski, Ivkov, Gueorguiev, Jekov (Zafirov), A. Christov (Yantchovski), Vassiliev, Donev, Guionine.
THAILAND: Pathipakornchai, Sanokasuwan, Sangkagowit, Pimpawatin, Unyapo, Paholpat, Sornmutnark, Sesawassi (Sangdhankichakul), Panich (Muanckasen), Nilpiron, Nukulsonpratana.

18th October 1968

Venue: *The Jalisco Stadium, Guadalajara.*

CZECHOSLOVAKIA 8 (Petras 3, Stratil 2, Herbst, Vecerek, Krnac)
THAILAND 0
Half-time: 6-0
Referee: Felipe Buergo (Mexico)
CZECHOSLOVAKIA: Kramerius, Vecerek, Jarabek, Mutkovic, Bouska, Linhart, Petras, Stratil (Krnac), Pajerchin, Kral, Herbst (Strung).
THAILAND: Pathipakornchai, Sangkasuwan, Sangkagowit, Pimpawatin, Unyapo, Sornbutnark (Vimoslate), Thongpleow, Panich, Milpirom, Sangdhamikichakul, Nukulsompratana.

16th October 1968

Venue: *The Jalisco Stadium, Guadalajara.*

CZECHOSLOVAKIA 2 (Jarabinsky, Petras)
BULGARIA 2 (Gueorguiev, Jekov)
Half-time: 2-1
Referee: E. Abel Aguilar (Mexico)
CZECHOSLOVAKIA: Kramerius (Holes), Vecerek, Mukovic, Bouska, Linhart, Petras, Boroc, Findejs (Bartovic), Pajerchin, Kral, Jarabinsky.
BULGARIA: Yordanov, Guerov, Christiakov, Ivkov, Gueorguiev, Jekev, A. Christov, K. Christov, Guionine, Dimitrov (Donev), Zafirov.

18th October 1968

Venue: *The Leon Stadium, Leon.*

BULGARIA 2 (Donev, Jekov)
GUATEMALA 1 (Lopez)
Half-time: 0-0
Referee: Raul Osiris (Mexico)
BULGARIA: Yordanov, Guerov, Christakiev, Gaidarski, Ivkov, Gueorguiev, Christov, Vassiliev (Dimitrov), Donev, Guionine, Ivanov (Jakov).
GUATEMALA: Lopez, Leon, Camposeco, Villavicencio, Montoya, Roldan, Torres, Slusher, Valdez, Pena, Garcia (Gonzalez).

16th October 1968

Venue: *The Leon Stadium, Leon.*

GUATEMALA 4 (Melgar Nelson 2, Lopez Oliva, Roldan Popol)
THAILAND 1 (Sornbutnark)
Half-time: 1-1
Referee: J.L. Faber (Guinea)
GUATEMALA: Gonzalez Lam, Lopez Oliva, Leon De Leon, Hasse Ovalle, Villavicencio, Monteya, Roldan Popol, Garcia Ramirez (Slusher Dayle), Valdez Melgar Nelson, Chacon Paredes (Clarck).
THAILAND: On-Iam, Sangkasuwan, Sangkagowit (Sangdhamkichakul), Pimpawatin, Onyapo, Paholpat, Sornbutnark, Sesawasdi (Chaiyong), Panich, Milpirom, Nukulsompratana.

	P	W	D	L	F	A	Pts
BULGARIA	3	2	1	0	11	3	5
GUATEMALA	3	2	0	1	6	3	4
CZECHOSLOV.	3	1	1	1	10	3	3
THAILAND	3	0	0	3	1	19	0

Quarter-Finals

20th October 1968

Venue: The Azteca Stadium, Mexico City

JAPAN 3 (Kamamoto 2, Watanabe)
FRANCE 1 (Tamboueon)

Half-time: 1-1

Referee: Seyoum Tarekegn (Ethiopia)

JAPAN: Yokoyama, Katayama, Miyamoto, Yamaguchi, Mori, Ogi, Miyamoto, Watanabe, Kamamoto, Sugiyama (Matsumoto), Kamata.

FRANCE: Lempereur, Zix, Verhoeve-Thorez, Plante-Lenoir (Goueffic-Lailet), Larque-Pere, Hodoul-Mouren, Horlaville L'Hernault, Dit Kanyan, Tamboueon, Hallet-Demantin, Conte-Deon.

20th October 1968

Venue: The Cuauhtemoc Stadium, Puebla.

MEXICO 2 (Morales, Pereda)
SPAIN 0

Half-time: 1-0

Referee: Dr. Milivoje Gugulovic (Yugoslavia)

MEXICO: Vargas, Alejandrez, Sanabria, Perez, Regueiro, Pulido, Pereda, Victorino (Bustos), Galindo, Munoz, Morales.

SPAIN: Marine Mora, Benito Rubio, Munoz, Ochoa, Puiovedal Sala, Ripoli Asensi, Rodriguez (Crispi), Vilela, Fito (De Francisco), Cereijo, Blasco.

20th October 1968

Venue: The Jalisco Stadium, Guadalajara.

HUNGARY 1 (Szucs)
GUATEMALA 0

Half-time: 0-0

Referee: Arturo Yamasaki (Mexico)

HUNGARY: Fater, Novak, D. Dunai, Pancsics, Menczel (Kocsis), Szucs, Fazekas, A. Dunai, Nosko, Juhasz, Rasti (Szalai).

GUATEMALA: Gonzalez Lam, Lopez Oliva (Melgar), Leon, Villavincencio, Montoya, Roldan Popol, Torres Ocamo, Slusher, Melgan Nelson, Pena Segura (Valdez), Stokes Rawn.

20th October 1968

Venue: Leon   (Result is after extra time)

BULGARIA 1 (Christakiev)
ISRAEL 1 (Faygenbaum)

Half-time: 1-0

Referee: Michel Kitabdjian (France)

BULGARIA: Yordanov, Christakiev, Gaidarski, Ivkov, Yantchovski, Christakov (Gueorguiev), Donev, Guionine (Jekov), Dimitrov, Ivanov, Zafinov.

ISRAEL: Levin, Bar, Bello, Rosen, Shwager (Borba), Rosenthal, Shpigel, Faygenbaum, Shpiegler, Young (Englander), Druker.

Bulgaria won on the toss of a coin

Semi-Finals

22nd October 1968

Venue: The Azteca Stadium, Mexico City

HUNGARY 5 (Szucs 3, Novak 2)
JAPAN 0

Half-time: 1-0

Referee: Romualdo Arppi Filho (Brazil)

HUNGARY: Fater (Szarka), Novak, D. Dunai, Pancsics, Szucs, Fazekas, Kocsis (Menczel), A. Dunai, Nagy, Nosko, Juhasz.

JAPAN: Yokoyama, Katayama, M. Miyamoto (Tomizawa), Yamaguchi, Kamata, Mori, Ogi, T. Miyamoto (Yaegashi), Watanabe, Kamamoto, Sugiyama.

22nd October 1968

Venue: The Jalisco Stadium, Guadalajara.

BULGARIA 3 (Jekov, Christov, Dimitrov)
MEXICO 2 (Morales, Pulido)

Half-time: 2-1

Referee: Seyoum Tarekegn (Ethiopia)

BULGARIA: Guerov, Christakiev, Gaidarski, Gueorguiev (Y. Dimitrov), T. Dimitrov (Zafirov), Yantchovski, Jekov, A. Christov, K. Christov, Donev, Nikolov.

MEXICO: Vargas, Alejandrez, Sanabria, Perez, Regueiro (Basaguren), Pulido, Pereda, Victorino, Sanchez, Munoz (Alvarez Crespo), Morales.

Bronze Medal Game

24th October 1968

Venue: The Azteca Stadium, Mexico City.

JAPAN 2   (Kamamoto 2)
MEXICO 0

Half-time: 2-0   Attendance: 105,000

Referee: Abraham Klein (Israel)

JAPAN: Yokoyama, Katayama, Yamaguchi, Kamata, Mori, Ogi, Miyamoto, Watanabe, Kamamoto, Matsumoto, Sugiyama.

MEXICO: Vargas, Alejandrez, Sanabria, Perez, Regueiro, Estrada (Hernandez), Pereda, Victorino (Munoz), Sanchez, Basaguren, Morales.

Final

26th October 1968

Venue: The Azteca Stadium, Mexico City.

HUNGARY 4   (A. Dunai 2, Menczel, Juhasz)
BULGARIA 1   (Dimitrov)

Half-time: 2-1   Attendance: 55,000

Referee: Diego de Leo (Mexico)

HUNGARY: Fater, Novak, Drestyak, Pancsics, Menczel, Szucs, Fazekas, A. Dunai, Nagy, Nosko, Juhasz.

BULGARIA: Yordanov, Guerov, Christiakov, Gaidarski, Ivkov, Gueorguiev, Dimitrov, Yantchovski (K. Christov), Jekov, A. Christov, Donev (Ivanov).

18th Olympiad – 1972 – Munich

Above all the 1972 Olympiad will be remembered for the raid on the Israeli compound, but in a football sense it marked the emergence of a very good Polish team with some particularly talented players. It was also noteworthy as the first time that an East German national team had played in West Germany.

Once again 16 teams qualified for the finals, but this time the top two teams from each group qualified for the Second Round rather than a sudden death quarter-final. The top teams from each of the two Second Round groups, Poland and Hungary, met in the Final

The United States qualified for the first time through the qualifying process, their other appearances coming before a qualifying competition was necessary, but with a tie against Morocco and losses to Malaysia and West Germany the U.S. failed to reach the Quarter-finals

Poland's performance in this competition led to another outstanding performance in West Germany two years later when the Poles narrowly missed reaching the World Cup Final and ended up with the bronze medal. A stand out for Poland in this competition was midfielder Kazimierz Deyna, while at centre back Jerezy Gorgon emerged as one of the world's top defenders. In attack Wlodzimierz Lubanski and Robert Gadocha ranked among the best.

Group One

27th August 1972

Venue: Munich

WEST GERMANY 3   (Kalb, Seliger, o.g.)
MALAYSIA 0

Half-time: 0-0   Attendance: 60,000

Referee: Armando Marques (Brazil)

WEST GERMANY: Wienhold, Baltes, Hollmann, E. Schmitt, Haebermann, Bitz, Seliger, Hoeness, Hammes (Kalb), Nickel, Worm (Hitzfeld).

MALAYSIA: Fook, Othman, Namat, Chandran, Aun, Zawawi, Krishnasamy, Wah (Hamzah), Salleh, Shaharudin, Ramin (Teik).

27th August 1972

Venue: Augsburg

MOROCCO 0
UNITED STATES 0

Half-time: 0-0   Attendance: 4,000

Referee: Rudi Glockner (East Germany)

MOROCCO: Hazzaz, Benkhrif, Ihardane, Lamrani, Elbakti, Yaghcha (Merzaq), Tazi, Zahraoui, Faras, Maouhoub (Elfilali), Najah.

U.S.A.: Ivanow, Bahr, Bocwinski, Demling (Trost), Stemke, Stam, Roboostoff, Seerey, Carenza, Hernandez, Salcedo.

29th August 1972

Venue: Passau

WEST GERMANY 3 (Nickel 2, Hitzfeld)
MOROCCO 0

Half-time: 2-0   Attendance: 16,000

Referee: Dogan Babacan (Turkey)

WEST GERMANY: Wienhold, Baltes, Bleidick, E. Schmitt, Haebermann, Bitz, Seliger (Hammes), Kalb, Hitzfeld, Nickel, Worm.
MOROCCO: Hazzaz, Benkhrif, Ihardane, Lamrani, Elbakti, Yaghcha (Zouita), Merzaq (Tazi), Elfilali, Faras, Maouhoub, Najah.

29th August 1972

Venue: Ingolstadt

MALAYSIA 3 (Zawawi, Salleh, Shaharudin)
UNITED STATES 0

Half-time: 1-0   Attendance: 3,000

Referee: Henry Oberg (Norway)

MALAYSIA: Fook, Othman, Namat, Chandran, Aun, Zawawi, Hamzah, Wah, Salleh, Shaharudin (Mohd), Teik.
U.S.A.: Ivanow, Bahr, Bocwinski, Demling (Hamm), Stemke, Stam, Roboostoff, Seerey. Carenza (Gay), Hernandez, Salcedo.

31st August 1972

Venue: Munich

WEST GERMANY 7 (Bitz, Hitzfeld, Seliger, Nickel 4)
UNITED STATES 0

Half-time: 2-0   Attendance: 65,000

Referee: Marco Antonio Dorantes Garcia (Mexico)

WEST GERMANY: Wienhold, Baltes (Mietz), Bleidick, E. Schmitt, Haebermann, Bitz, Hoeness, Kalb, Hitzfeld, Nickel, Worm (Seliger).
U.S.A.: Messing, Bahr, Ziaja, Hamm, Stemke, Stam, Roboostoff, Trost, Gay (Zylker), Demling, Flater (Margulis).

31st August 1972

Venue: Ingolstadt

MOROCCO 6 (Scorers not recorded)
MALAYSIA 0

Half-time: 4-0   Attendance: 2,500

Referee: Karoly Palotai (Hungary)

MOROCCO: Hazzaz, Benkhrif (Yaghcha), Ihardane, Lamrani, Elbakti, Zouita, Tazi (Jafri), Elfilali, Faras, Hadry, Najah.
MALAYSIA: Fook (Bahwandi), Othman, Namat, Chandran, Aun, Zawawi, Hamzah, Wah, Salleh, Shaharudin, Teik.

	P	W	D	L	F	A	Pts
W. GERMANY	3	3	0	0	13	0	6
MOROCCO	3	1	1	1	6	3	3
MALAYSIA	3	1	0	2	3	9	2
U.S.A.	3	0	1	2	0	10	1

Group Two

28th August 1972

Venue: Regensburg

U.S.S.R. 1 (Kolotov)
BURMA 0

Half-time: 0-0   Attendance: 6,000

Referee: Djaffar Namdar (Iran)

U.S.S.R.: Rudakov, Dzodzuashvili, Kaplichny, Kuksov, Istomin, Kolotov, Sabo, Onischenko (Blokhin), Eliseev, Yevrushikhin, Andriasian (Zanazanian).
BURMA: Aung Tin, Maung Tin Maung, Sein Tin, Nyunt Win Myo, Aye San, Maung Aye (I), Maung Aye (II), Nyunt Ye, Maung Win, Soe Than, Aung Moe Tin (Kyu Myint).

28th August 1972

Venue: Nuremberg

MEXICO 1   (Manzo)

SUDAN 0

Half-time: 1-0   Attendance: 500

Referee: Francesco Francescon (Italy)

MEXICO: Sanchez, Rico, Trejo, Alvarez, Del Campo, Alejandro Hernandez, Blanco, Reyes (Talavera), Manzo, Pena, Cuellar.

SUDAN: Mohamed Abdel Fattah, Mohsin Atta Elmannan, Gafar Mohamed Sulimann, Mahmoud Saeed Salim, Nagm El-Din Hassan, Bushara Abdel Nadif, Bushara Wahba, Mohamed El-Basheir Ahmed (Abdo Mustafa Ahmed), Abas Nasreldin Gaksa, Izz-El-Din Osman, Hasab El-Rasoul Omer.

30th August 1972

Venue: Munich

U.S.S.R. 2   (Yevrushikhin, Zanazanian)

SUDAN 1   (Abas Nasreldin)

Half-time: 2-0   Attendance: 25,000

Referee: Ferdinand Biwersi (West Germany)

U.S.S.R.: Rudakov, Dzodzuashvili, Kaplichny (Kuksov), Istomin (Lovchev), Kolotov, Sabo, Onischenko (Khurtsilava), Eliseev, Yevrushikhin, Zanazanian.

SUDAN: Mohamed Abdel Fattah, El-Sir Abdalla Mohamed (Izz-El-Din Osman), Gafar Mohamed Sulimann, Mahmoud Saeed Salim, Nagm El-Din Hassan, Bushara Abdel Nadif, Bushara Wahba, Sharafeldin Ahmed Mohammed, Abas Nasreldin Gaksa, Mustafa Abdo Ahmed, Mohsin Atta Elmannan.

30th August 1972

Venue: Nuremberg

MEXICO 1   (Cuellar)

BURMA 0

Half-time: 0-0   Attendance: 1,000

Referee: Robert Amoo Quarshie (Ghana)

MEXICO: Sanchez, Rico, Trejo, Alvarez, Del Campo, Alejandro Hernandez, Blanco, Reyes (Talavera), Manzo, Razo, Cuellar.

BURMA: Aung Tin, Maung Tin Maung, Sein Tin, Nyunt Win Myo, Aye San, Maung Aye (I), Maung Aye (II), Nyunt Ye (Maung Lay Khin), Maung Win, Soe Than, Aung Moe Tin.

1st September 1972

Venue: Regensburg

U.S.S.R. 4   (Scorers not recorded)

MEXICO 1   (Razo)

Half-time: 3-0   Attendance: 8,000

Referee: Luis Pestarino (Argentina)

U.S.S.R.: Rudakov (Puilguy), Istomin, Kaplichny (Olchansky), Khurtsilava, Lovchev, Andriansian, Kuksov, Blokhin, Semenov, Yakubik, Zanazanian.

MEXICO: Ruiz, Barba, Trejo, Alvarez (Manzo), Del Campo (Rico), Talavera, Borja, Marquez, Regalado, Razo, Alfredo Hernandez.

1st September 1972

Venue: Passau

BURMA 2   (Soe Than, Aung Moe Tin)

SUDAN 0

Half-time: 1-0   Attendance: 2,000

Referee: Marian Srodecki (Poland)

BURMA: Aung Tin, Maung Tin Maung, Sein Tin, Nyunt Win Myo, Aye San, Maung Aye (I), Maung Aye (II), Nyunt Ye, Maung Win, Soe Than, Aung Moe Tin.

SUDAN: Mohammed Abdel Fattah, El-Sir Abdalla Mohamed, Gafar Mohammed Sulimann, Mahmoud Saeed Salim, Nagm El-Din Hassan, Bushara Abdel Nadif, Bushara Wahba (Izz-El-Din Osman), Sharafeldin Ahmed Mohammed, Abas Nasreldin Gaksa, Abdo Mustafa Ahmed, Mohsin Atta Elmannan.

	P	W	D	L	F	A	Pts
U.S.S.R.	3	3	0	0	7	2	6
MEXICO	3	2	0	1	3	4	4
BURMA	3	1	0	2	2	2	2
SUDAN	3	0	0	3	1	5	0

Group Three

27th August 1972

Venue: Nuremberg

HUNGARY 5 (Kozma, Antal Dunai 3, Varadi)
IRAN 0

Half-time: 1-0   Attendance: 2,000

Referee: Guillermo Velasquez (Colombia)

HUNGARY: Geczi (Rothermel), Vepi, Pancsics, Vidats, Juhasz, Kovacs, Kocsis (Branikovics), Szucs, Kozma, Antal Dunai, Varadi.

IRAN: Mansour Rashidi, Ebrahim Ashtiyani, Akbar Kargarjam, Jafar Ashraf Kashani, Parviz Ghelichkhani, Ali Parvin, Ali Jabbari (Gholam Vafakhah), Magid Halvaei, Mohamed Sadeghi, Safar Iranpak, Asghar Sharafi.

27th August 1972

Venue: Passau

DENMARK 3 (Rontved, Simonsen 2)
BRAZIL 2 (Dirceu, Ze Carlos)

Half-time: 1-0   Attendance: 10,000

Referee: Pavel Kazakov (U.S.S.R.)

DENMARK: Therkildsen, Ahlberg, Rontved, Andresen, J. Rasmussen, H.A. Hansen, Bak, H.E. Hansen (Ziegler), J. Hansen, Nygaard, Simonsen.

BRAZIL: Nielsen, Tereza, Frederico, Osmar, Celso, Rubens, Angelio, (Falcao), Dirceu, Pedrinho (Ze Carlos), Washington, Manoel.

29th August 1972

Venue: Munich

HUNGARY 2 (Juhasz, Antal Dunai)
BRAZIL 2 (Pedrinho, Dirceu)

Half-time: 1-0   Attendance: 50,000

Referee: William J. Mullan (Scotland)

HUNGARY: Geczi, Vepi, Pancsics, Vidats (Balint), Juhasz, Kovacs, Kocsis, Szucs, Kozma, Antal Dunai, Varadi.

BRAZIL: Nielsen, Tereza, Omar, Abel, Celso (Bolivar), Falcao, Rubens, Dirceu, Pedrinho, Washington (Ze Carlos), Manoel.

29th August 1972

Venue: Augsberg

DENMARK 4 (Nygaard, Simonsen, H.A. Hansen 2)
IRAN 0

Half-time: 3-0   Attendance: 3,500

Referee: Abdelkrim Ziani (Morocco)

DENMARK: Therkioldsen, Ahlberg, Rontved, Andresen, J. Rasmussen (Pedersen), H.A. Hansen, Bak, H.E. Hansen (Ziegler), J. Hansen, Nygaard, Simonsen.

IRAN: Mansour Rashidi, Ebrahim Ashtiyani, Akbar Kargarjam, Mehdi Monajati (Mahmoud Khordbeen), Parviz Ghelichkhani, Ali Parvin, Gholam Vafakah, Magid Halvaei, Mohammed Sadeghi, Safar Iranpak, Javad Ghorab

31st August 1972

Venue: Augsberg

HUNGARY 2 (Ede Dunai 2)
DENMARK 0

Half-time: 1-0   Attendance: 8,500

Referee: Oei Poh Hwa (Malaysia)

HUNGARY: Geczi, Vepi, Pancsics, Szucs, Juhasz, Balint, Kocsics (Ku), Ede Dunai, Kozma (Toth), Antal Dunai, Varadi.

DENMARK: Therkildsen, Ahlberg, Rontved, Andresen, J. Rasmussen, H.A. Hansen, Bak, H.E. Hansen, J. Hansen, Nygaard, Simonsen.

31st August 1972

Venue: Regensberg

IRAN 1 (Halvaei)
BRAZIL 0

Half-time: 0-0   Attendance: 2,200

Referee: Gerhard Schulenburg (West Germany)

IRAN: Mansour Rashidi, Ebrahim Ashtiyani, Akbar Kargarjam, Jafar Ashraf Kashani, Parviz Ghelichkhani, Ali Parvin, Gholam Vafakhah, Magid Halvaei, Mahmoud Khordbeen, Safar Iranpak (Alireza Azizi), Mehdi Lari Lavasani.

BRAZIL: Nielsen, Tereza, Chinoca, Abel, Bolivar, Falcao (Angelio), Rubens, Dirceu, Oliveira (Washington), Ze Carlos, Manoel.

	P	W	D	L	F	A	Pts
HUNGARY	3	2	1	0	9	2	5
DENMARK	3	2	0	1	7	4	4
IRAN	3	1	0	2	1	9	2
BRAZIL	3	0	1	2	4	6	1

Group Four

28th August 1972

Venue: Munich

EAST GERMANY 4 (Sparwasser, Kreische 2, Streich)

GHANA 0

Half-time: 2-0 Attendance: 40,000

Referee: Michael Wuertz (U.S.A.)

EAST GERMANY: Croy, Zapf, Kurbjuweit (Irmscher), Weise, Watzlich, Pommerenke, Bransch, Kreische, Sparwasser, P. Ducke, Streich (Schulenberg).

GHANA: Essel Mensah, Armah Akuetteh, Oliver Acquah, Alex Mingle, John Eshun, Malik Jabir, Ibrahim Sunday Osei Kofi (Peter Lamptey), Taw Sam, Abukari Garibah, Kwasi Owusu.

28th August 1972

Venue: Ingolstadt

POLAND 5 (Deyna 2, Gadocha 3)

COLOMBIA 1 (Moron)

Half-time: 3-0 Attendance: 4,000

Referee: Ahmed Gindil Salih (Sudan)

POLAND: Kostka, Symanowski, Gorgon, Cmikiewicz, Anczok, Szoltysik (Kraska), Deyna, Maszczyk, Kmiecik, Lubanski, Gadocha.

COLOMBIA: Antonio Rivas, Guette, Moncada, Orlando Rivas, Calle, Gonzales (Espinosa), Palacios, Diaz (Torres), Santamaria, Lugo, Moron.

30th August 1972

Venue: Passau

EAST GERMANY 6 (Sparwasser, Kreische, Streich 3, Ducke, Vogel)

COLOMBIA 1 (Espinosa)

Half-time: 4-1 Attendance: 4,500

Referee: Abdelkader Aouissi (Algeria)

EAST GERMANY: Croy, Zapf, Weise, Kurbjuweit, Watzlich, Pommerenke (Irmscher), Bransch, Kreische, Sparwasser, P. Ducke (Vogel), Streich.

COLOMBIA: Antonio Rivas, Guette, Moncada, Orlando Rivas, Calle, Palacios, Diaz, Lugo (Torres), Moron, Espinosa, Reyes (Revellon).

30th August 1972

Venue: Regensburg

POLAND 4 (Deyna, Lubanski, Gadocha 2)

GHANA 0

Half-time: 1-0 Attendance: 2,200

Referee: Kan-Chee Lee (Hong Kong)

POLAND: Kostka, Symanowski, Gorgon, Cmikiewicz, Anczok, Maszczyk, Deyna, Kraska, Kmiecik (Marks), Lubanski, Gadocha.

GHANA: Essel Mensah, Edward Boye (Clifford Odame), Oliver Acquah, Alex Mingle, John Eshun, Joe Ghartey, Malik Jabir, Ibrahim Sunday, Peter Lamptey, Taw Sam, Abukari Garibah.

1st September 1972

Venue: Nuremberg

POLAND 2 (Gorgon 2)

EAST GERMANY 1 (Streich)

Half-time: 1-0 Attendance: 10,000

Referee: Werner Winsemann (Canada)

POLAND: Kostka, Symanowski, Ostafinski (Szymczak), Gorgon, Anczok, Kraska, Cmikiewicz, Deyna, Gut, Lubanski, Gadocha.

EAST GERMANY: Croy, Kurbjuweit (Pommerenke), Zapf, Weise, Watzlich (Vogel), Irmscher, Kreische, Bransch, Sparwasser, P. Ducke, Streich.

1st September 1972

Venue: Munich

COLOMBIA 3 (Moron, Torres, Montano)
GHANA 1 (Scorer not recorded)

Half-time: 0-0   Attendance: 25,000

Referee: Kurt Tschenscher (West Germany)

COLOMBIA: Quintero, Moncada, Reyes, Orlando Rivas, Revellon, Espinoza, Palacios, Santamaria (Lugo), Diaz (Montano), Moron, Torres.

GHANA: Henry France, Armah Akuetteh (Edward Boye), John Eshun, Clifford Odame, Alex Mingle, Malik Jabir, Ibrahim Sunday, Osei Kofi (Peter Lamptey), Taw Sam, Abukari Garibah, Kwasi Owusu.

3rd September 1972

Venue: Passau

HUNGARY 2 (Antal Dunai, Toth)
EAST GERMANY 0

Half-time: 0-0   Attendance: 8,500

Referee: Armando Marques (Brazil)

HUNGARY: Geczi, Vepi, Pancsics, Szucs, Juhasz, Balint, Kocsis (Ku), Ede Dunai, Toth, Antal Dunai, Varadi (Branikovics)

EAST GERMANY: Croy, Zapf, Ganzera, Weise, Bransch, Seguin, Pommerenke (Irmscher), Kreische, Sparwasser, P. Ducke (Vogel), Streich.

	P	W	D	L	F	A	Pts
POLAND	3	3	0	0	11	2	6
E. GERMANY	3	2	0	1	11	3	4
COLOMBIA	3	1	0	2	4	12	2
GHANA	3	0	0	3	1	11	0

Second Round

Group A

3rd September 1972

Venue: Nuremberg

WEST GERMANY 1 (Hitzfeld)
MEXICO 1 (Cuellar)

Half-time: 1-0   Attendance: 40,000

Referee: Oei Poh Hwa (Malaysia)

WEST GERMANY: Wienhold, Baltes, Bleidick, E. Schmitt, Haebermann, Bitz, Hoeness, Kalb (Kaltz), Hitzfeld, Nickel, Seliger (Worm).

MEXICO: Sanchez, Rico, Trejo, Alvarez, Del Campo, Alejandro Hernandez, Blanco, Pena, Manzo, Razo, Cuellar.

5th September 1972

Venue: Ingolstadt

EAST GERMANY 7 (Sparwasser 3, Kreische, Streich, Ganzera, Hafner)
MEXICO 0

Half-time: 2-0   Attendance: 5,500

Referee: Djaffar Namdar (Iran)

EAST GERMANY: Croy, Zapf, Ganzera, Weise, Bransch, Pommerenke, Seguin (Hafner), Kreische, Sparwasser, P. Ducke (Schulenberg), Streich.

MEXICO: Sanchez, Rico, Trejo, Alvarez, Del Campo, Alejandro Hernandez, Blanco, Pena, Manzo, Razo, Cuellar.

6th September 1972

Venue: Munich

HUNGARY 4 (Antal Dunai, Ku 2, Ede Dunai)
WEST GERMANY 1 (Hitzfeld)

Half-time: 2-1   Attendance: 70,000

Referee: Luis Pestarino (Argentina)

HUNGARY: Geczi, Vepi, Pancsics, Szucs, Juhasz, Balint, Ku, Ede Dunai, Toth, Antal Dunai, Branikovics.

WEST GERMANY: Wienhold, Baltes, Hollmann, E. Schmitt, Haebermann, Bitz (Seliger), Hoeness, Kalb, Hitzfeld, Nickel, Wunder (Worm).

8th September 1972

Venue: Regensberg

HUNGARY 2   (Antal Dunai, Kocsis)
MEXICO 0

Half-time: 1-0   Attendance: 2,500

Referee: Kan-Chee Lee (Hong Kong)

HUNGARY: Geczi, Vepi, Pancsics, Szucs, Juhasz, Balint, Ku (Kocsis), Ede Dunai, Toth, Antal Dunai (Varadi), Branikovics.

MEXICO: Sanchez, Rico, Trejo, Alvarez, Del Campo, Alejandro Hernandez, Blanco, Pena, Manzo, Razo, Cuellar.

8th September 1972

Venue: Munich

EAST GERMANY 3   (Pommerenke, Streich, Vogel)
WEST GERMANY 2   (Hitzfeld, Hoeness)

Half-time: 1-1   Attendance: 80,000

Referee: William J. Mullan (Scotland)

EAST GERMANY: Croy, Zapf, Weise, Ganzera, Bransch, Pommerenke, Seguin, Kreische, Sparwasser, P. Ducke, Streich (Vogel).

WEST GERMANY: Bradler, Baltes, Hollmann (Seliger), E. Schmitt, Haebermann, Bitz, Hoeness, Kalb, Hitzfeld, Nickel, Wunder (Worm).

	P	W	D	L	F	A	Pts
HUNGARY	3	3	0	0	8	1	5
E. GERMANY	3	2	0	1	10	4	4
W. GERMANY	3	0	1	2	4	8	1
MEXICO	3	0	1	2	1	10	1

Group B

3rd September 1972

Venue: Munich

U.S.S.R. 3   (Kolotov, Eliseev, Semenov)
MOROCCO 0

Half-time: 2-0   Attendance: 55,000

Referee: Guillermo Velasquez (Colombia)

U.S.S.R.: Rudakov, Dzodzuashvili (Istomin), Kaplichny, Khurtsilava, Lovchev, Kolotov, Sabo, Blokhin, Semenov (Eliseev) Yevrushikhin, Zanazanian.

MOROCCO: Hazzaz, Benkhrif, Ihardane, Lamrani, Elbakhti, Zahraoui (Yaghcha), Hadry, Faras, Elfilali, Maouhoub (Tazi), Najah.

3rd September 1972

Venue: Regensberg

DENMARK 1   (H.A. Hansen)
POLAND 1   (Deyna)

Half-time: 1-1   Attendance: 4,000

Referee: Abdelkader Aouissi (Algeria)

DENMARK: Therkildsen, Ahlberg, Rontved, Andresen, J. Rasmussen, H.A. Hansen, Bak, M. Rasmussen, J. Hansen, Nygaard, Simonsen.

POLAND: Kostka, Symanowski, Gorgon, Cmikiewicz, Anczok, Szoltysik (Gut), Deyna, Maszczyk, Marks (Lato), Lubanski, Gadocha.

5th September 1972

Venue: Passau

DENMARK 3   (Bak 2, Prinzlau)
MOROCCO 1   (Merzaq)

Half-time: 0-0   Attendance: 3,100

Referee: Werner Winsemann (Canada)

DENMARK: Therkildsen, Ahlberg, Rontved, Andresen, J. Rasmussen, H.A. Hansen (Prinzlau), Bak, Ziegler, J. Hansen, Nygaard, Simonsen (M. Rasmussen).

MOROCCO: Hazzaz, Benkhrif, Ihardane, Yaghcha (Zaghrari), Elbakti, Zahraoui, Tazi (Zouita), Maouhoub, Merzaq, Elfilali, Najah.

5th September 1972

Venue: Augsburg

POLAND 2 (Deyna, Szoltysik)
U.S.S.R. 1 (Blokhin)

Half-time: 0-1 *Attendance:* 5,000

Referee: Henry Oberg (Norway)

POLAND: Kostka, Symanowski, Ostafinski, Gorgon (Kraska), Anczok, Gut (Szoltysik), Cmikiewicz, Maszczyk, Deyna, Lubanski, Gadocha.

U.S.S.R.: Rudakov, Dzodzuashvili, Kaplichny, Khurtsilava, Lovchev, Kolotov, Sabo, Blokhin, Semenov (Onischenko), Yevrushikhin, Zanazanian (Kuksov).

8th September 1972

Venue: Nuremberg

POLAND 5 (Deyna 2, Lubanski, Gadocha, Kmiecik)
MOROCCO 0

Half-time: 3-0 *Attendance:* 500

Referee: Francesco Francescon (Italy)

POLAND: Kostka, Symanowski, Gorgon, Ostafinski, Anczok, Cmikiewicz (Maszczyk), Deyna, Kraska (Szoltysik), Kmiecik, Lubanski, Gadocha.

MOROCCO: Hazzaz (Belkorchi), Benkhrif, Ihardane, Lamrani, Elbakti, Yaghcha, Zahraoui, Tazi (Maouhoub), Faras, Elfilali, Merzaq.

8th September 1972

Venue: Augsburg

U.S.S.R. 4 (Kolotov, Blokhin, Sabo, Semenov)
DENMARK 0

Half-time: 2-0 *Attendance:* 4,000

Referee: Dogan Babacan (Turkey)

U.S.S.R.: Pilguy, Istomin, Kaplichny, Khurtsilava, Lovchev, Kolotov, Sabo, Kuksov, Semenov (Andriansian), Yevrushikhin, Blokhin (Olchansky).

DENMARK: Therkildsen, Ahlberg, Rontved, Andresen, J. Rasmussen, H.A. Hansen, Bak, M. Rasmussen, J. Hansen, Nygaard (H.E. Hansen), Simonsen (Prinzlau).

	P	W	D	L	F	A	Pts
POLAND	3	2	1	0	8	2	5
U.S.S.R.	3	2	0	1	8	2	4
DENMARK	3	1	1	1	4	6	3
MOROCCO	3	0	0	3	1	11	0

Bronze Medal Game

10th September 1972

Venue: Munich

EAST GERMANY 2 (Kreische, Vogel)
U.S.S.R. 2 (Blokhin, Khurtsilava)

Half-time: 1-1 *Attendance:* 80,000

Referee: Armando Marques (Brazil)

EAST GERMANY: Croy, Zapf, Weise, Bransch, Ganzera (Kurbjuweit), Pommerenke, Seguin (Vogel), Kreische, Sparwasser, Ducke, Streich.

U.S.S.R.: Rudakov, Istomin, Kaplichny, Khurtsilava, Lovchev, Kolotov, Olchansky, Blokhin, Semenov (Andriasian), Yevrushikin, Zanazanian.

Final

10th September 1972

Venue: Munich

POLAND 2 (Deyna 2)
HUNGARY 1 (Varadi)

Half-time: 0-1 *Attendance:* 30,000

Referee: Kurt Tschenscher (West Germany)

POLAND: Kostka, Gut, Gorgon, Cmikiewicz, Anczok, Szoltysik, Kraska, Deyna (Szymczak), Maszczyk, Lubanski, Gadocha.

HUNGARY: Geczi, Vepi, Pancsics, Szucs, Juhasz, Balint, Ku (Kocsis), Ede Dunai, Kozma, Antal Dunai (Toth), Varadi.

19th Olympiad – 1976 – Montreal

Politics reared its ugly head again when the Olympics came to Canada for the first time in 1976. This time it was the policies of South Africa's apartheid government that caused the problem, which led to a boycott on the part of the African nations. As this happened at the last minute there was no time to replace the three nations that dropped out of the football tournament, thus reducing the competition to 13 teams.

Poland, of course, were the favourites and they reached the Final once again but this time were defeated by a fine East German team. Canada, the host nation were in the finals for the first time since the competition in St. Louis in 1904 and faced the powerful Soviet team at the Olympic Stadium. With two goals early in the game it seemed as if the Soviets would run up a large score, but Canada came back in the second half and when Jimmy Douglas scored late in the game the Soviets were reeling. In the dying minutes Canada had a shot kicked off the line.

Representing Canada were Jack Brand (Toronto Metros-Croatia), Tino Lettieri (Quebec), Gary Ayre (New Westminster Blues), Kevin Grant (Hamilton Croatia), Tony Lawrence (Toronto White Eagles), Ray Telford (Nanaimo City), Mike McLenaghen (Vancouver Pegasus), Robin Megraw (Toronto First Portuguese), Jimmy Douglas (St. Catharines Heidelberg), Bob Bolitho (London Boxing Club, Victoria), Wes McLeod (Coquitlam Blue Mountain), John McGrane (Simon Fraser University), Carl Rose (Toronto Emerald), Ken Whitehead (Simon Fraser University), John Connor (New Westminster Blues), Jim McLoughlin.

Due to the boycott Canada had but one other game, this against North Korea in Toronto, which they lost and were thus eliminated. Meanwhile Brazil, so dominant in the World Cup, were making an impression in the Olympics for the first time while France had a young Michel Platini in its line up. The Spanish team was coached by Ladislav Kubala.

In the Quarter-finals, which had reverted to a sudden death competition, Brazil easily beat Israel, the Soviet Union narrowly defeated Iran while East Germany and Poland easily disposed of France and North Korea respectively. The semi-final between East Germany and the Soviet Union was a dour affair while Poland defeated the popular Brazilians in Toronto.

East Germany took a surprising early lead in the Final thanks to two goalkeeping errors by Polish goalkeeper Jan Tomaszewski and the Poles never recovered. The winning East German team included some very experienced players in goalkeeper Jurgen Croy, defenders Konrad Weise, Lothar Kurbjuweit, and Gerd Kische, while left winger Martin Hoffmann was a major factor in the East German victory. The Poles still had Kazimierz Deyna in midfield and an outstanding winger in Gregorz Lato, but for the Final Jerzy Gorgon failed a last minute fitness test and this might well have tipped the balance in East Germany's favour.

The total overall attendance for the 23 games was 647,683 for an average of 26,421. However, the Montreal average attendance in the Olympic stadium was 44,207.

Group A

18th July 1976

Venue: The Varsity Stadium in Toronto, Ontario.

BRAZIL 0
EAST GERMANY 0

Half-time: 0-0   Attendance: 21,643

Referee: John Paterson (Scotland)

BRAZIL: Carlos, Mauro, Tecao (Edval, 28), Edinho, Chico Fraga, Batista, Erivelto, Junior, Rosemiro, Jarbas, Santos (Marinho, 77).

EAST GERMANY: Croy, Weber, Weise, Kische, Kurbjuweit, Lauck, Hafner, Dorner, Heidler, Riediger (Riedel), Lowe (Hoffmann).

	P	W	D	L	F	A	Pts
BRAZIL	2	1	1	0	2	1	3
E. GERMANY	2	1	1	0	1	0	3
SPAIN	2	0	0	2	1	3	0

20th July 1976

Venue: The Olympic Stadium in Montreal, Quebec.

BRAZIL 2   (Rosemiro 7, Chico Fraga 47)
SPAIN 1   (Idigoras 14)

Half-time: 1-1   Attendance: 38,123

Referee: Paul Schiller (Austria)

BRAZIL: Carlos, Rosemiro (Mauro, 19), Edval, Edinho, Chico Fraga, Batista, Erivelto, Alberto, Marinho, Jarbas (Julinho, 82), Santos.

SPAIN: Arconada, Olmo, I. San Jose (Sanchez, 84), Camus, F. San Jose, Saura, Bermejo, Vitoria (Mir, 45), Juanito, Idigoras, Vigo.

22nd July 1976

Venue: The Olympic Stadium in Montreal, Quebec.

EAST GERMANY 1   (Dorner 45)
SPAIN 0

Half-time: 0-0   Attendance: 36,198

Referee: Werner Winsemann (Canada)

EAST GERMANY: Croy, Weber (Schade, 76), Dorner, Weise, Kurbjuweit, Kische, Lauck, Heidler, Hafner, Lowe, Hoffmann.

SPAIN: Arconada, Pulido, I. San Jose, Camus (Sanchez, 22), Suarez (Castillo, 61), Suara, Olmo, Vitoria, Juanito, Idigoras, Vigo.

Group B

19th July 1976

Venue: Lansdowne Road in Ottawa, Ontario.

FRANCE 4   (Schaer 14, Baronchelli 33, Rubio 78, Amisse 90)
MEXICO 1   (Sanchez 81)

Half-time: 2-0   Attendance: 14,286

Referee: Angel Coerezza (Argentina)

FRANCE: Larrieu, Battiston, Chazottes, Stassievich, Meynieu, Fernandez, Platini, Rubio, Baronchelli, Schaer, Amisse.

MEXICO: Regalado, Lopezmalo, Viveros, Rergis, De la Rosa, Caballero, Garcia (Marquez, 45), Sanchez, Tapia, Rangel, Cosio (Toribio, 45).

19th July 1976

Venue: The Varsity Stadium in Toronto, Ontario.

ISRAEL 0
GUATEMALA 0

Half-time: 0-0   Attendance: 9,500

Referee: Vladimir Rudnev (U.S.S.R.)

ISRAEL: Vissoker, Ben Dor, Leventhal, Bar, Lev, Nimni (Gal, 30), Shani, Shum (Cohen, 85), Oz, Peretz, Damti.

GUATEMALA: Piccinini, Gomez, C. Monterroso, Wellman, Rivera, Bolanos, B. Monterroso (Fion, 63), Hurtarte, Sanchez, Pennat (Sandoval, 45), Morales.

21st July 1976

Venue: The Olympic Stadium in Montreal, Quebec.

MEXICO 2   (Rangel 19, 44)
ISRAEL 2   (Oz 51, Shum 55)

Half-time: 2-0   Attendance: 36,569

Referee: Alberto Michelotti (Italy)

MEXICO: Regalado, Lopezmalo, Viveros, Rergis, De la Rosa, Caballero, Marquez, Sanchez, Tapia (Navarette, 60), Rangel, Cosio (Toribio, 45).

ISRAEL: Vissoker, Ben Dor, Levanthal, Bar, Lev, Nimni, Shani, Shum, Oz, Peretz (Nachness, 78), Damti.

23rd July 1976

Venue: The Olympic Stadium in Montreal, Quebec.

FRANCE 1   (Platini, 80)
ISRAEL 1   (Peretz, 75)

Half-time: 0-0   Attendance: 33,639

Referee: Ramon Barreto (Uruguay)

FRANCE: Larrieu, Battiston, Chazottes, Potteri, Strassievich, Fernandez, Platini, Rubio, Amisse, Rouyer, Schaer.

ISRAEL: Vissoker, Ben Dor, Leventhal, Bar, Nimni, Shani, Shum, Cohen, Peretz, Tourk, Damti.

21st July 1976

Venue: The Stadium in Sherbrooke, Quebec.

FRANCE 4   (Platini 7, 86, Amisse 41, Schaer 82)
GUATEMALA 1   (Fion 58)

Half-time: 2-0   Attendance: 3,163

Referee: Jafar Namdar (Iran)

FRANCE: Larrieu, Battiston, Chazottes, Pottier, Stassievich, Fernandez, Platini, Rubio, Baronchelli (Pecout, 71), Schaer, Amisse (Rouyer, 45).

GUATEMALA: Piccinini, Gomes, C. Monterroso, Wellman, Rivera, Bolanos, B. Monterroso, Hurtarte, Sanchez (Pennant, 76), Fio (MacDonald, 82), Morales.

	P	W	D	L	F	A	Pts
FRANCE	3	2	1	0	9	3	5
ISRAEL	3	0	3	0	3	3	3
GUATEMALA	3	0	2	1	2	5	2
MEXICO	3	0	2	1	4	7	2

Group C

23rd July 1976

Venue: The Stadium in Sherbrooke, Quebec.

MEXICO 1   (Rangel 36)
GUATEMALA 1   (own goal 8)

Half-time: 1-1   Attendance: 4,118

Referee: Marian Kuston (Poland)

MEXICO: Regalado, Carillo, Garcia, Rergis (Hernandez, 23), De la Rosa, Caballero, Marquez, Sanchez, Tapia (Toribio, 69), Rangel, Cosio.

GUATEMALA: Garcia, Gomez, C. Monterroso, Wellman, Rivera, Bolanos, Villavicencio (B. Monterroso, 64), MacDonald, Pennat, Fion, Sandoval (Morales, 79).

18th July 1976

Venue: The Olympic Stadium in Montreal, Quebec.

POLAND 0
CUBA 0

Half-time: 0-0   Attendance: 29,417

Referee: Abraham Klein (Israel)

POLAND: Tomaszewski, Symanowski, Gorgon, Zmuda, Wawrowski, Kasperczak (Maszczyk, 45), Deyna, Cmikiewicz, Lato, Szarmach, Kmiecik.

CUBA: Reinoso, Rivero, Holmaza, Elejalde, Garces, Masso, Delgado, Bonora, Roldan, Hernandez (Pereira, 68), Farinas.

20th July 1976

Venue: Lansdowne Park in Ottawa, Ontario.

IRAN 1   (Mazloomi, 28)
CUBA 0

Half-time: 1-0   Attendance: 11,324

Referee: Adolf Prokop (East Germany)

IRAN: Hejazi, Nazavi, Zolfoqalnassab, Abdollahi, Eskandarian (Nayebagha, 45), Parvin, Qelichkhani, Ghassempour, Rowshan, Mazloomi (Jahani, 84), Khorshidi.

CUBA: Reinoso, Rivero, Holmaza, Elejalde, Garces, Masso, Delgado, Bonora, Roldan, Hernandez (Cepero, 73), Farinas.

22nd July 1976

Venue: The Olympic Stadium in Montreal, Quebec.

POLAND 3   (Szarmach 48, 75, Deyna 51)
IRAN 2   (Parvin 6, Rowshan 79)

Half-time: 0-1   Attendance: 32,309

Referee: Arnaldo Coelho (Brazil)

POLAND: Tomaszewski, Symanowski, Gorgon, Zmuda, Wawrowski, Maszczyk, Deyna, Cmikiewicz, Lato, Szarmach, Kmiecik (Beniger).

IRAN: Hejazi, Nazavi, Zolfoqalnassab, Abdollahi, Eskandarian, Parvin, Qelichkhani, Ghassempor, Rowshan, Mazloomi (Jahani, 53), Khorshidi.

	P	W	D	L	F	A	Pts
POLAND	2	1	1	0	3	2	3
IRAN	2	1	0	1	3	3	2
CUBA	2	0	1	1	0	1	1

Group D

19th July 1976

Venue: The Olympic Stadium in Montreal, Quebec.

U.S.S.R. 2   (Onischenko 8, 11)
CANADA 1   (Douglas 88)

Half-time: 2-0   Attendance: 34,320

Referee: Robert Helies (France)

U.S.S.R.: Astapovsky, Konkov, Troshkin, Reshko, Matvienko, Kolotov, Veremeev (Fomenko, 45), Buriak, Minaev, Onischenko (Feodorov, 73), Blokhin.

CANADA: Brand, Ayre, Lawrence, Grant, Telford, Megraw, Douglas, Bolitho (McLenaghen, 76), McLeod, Connor, McGrane (Rose, 63).

21st July 1976

Venue: The Varsity Stadium in Toronto, Ontario.

NORTH KOREA 3   (Se Uk An 18, Song Nam Hong 66, 80)
CANADA 1   (Douglas 51)

Half-time: 0-1   Attendance: 12,638

Referee: Marco Antonio Dorantes Garcia (Mexico)

NORTH KOREA: In Chol Jin, Gil Wan An, Mu Gil Kim, Jong Min Kim, Jong Hun Pak, Dong Chan Myong, Song Nam Hong, Jong Sok Cha, Song Guk Yang, Se Uk An, Hi Yon Li (Il Nam Kim, 59).

CANADA: Brand, Ayre, Grant, Lawrence, Telford (McLenaghen, 53), Megraw, Douglas, Bolitho, McLeod, McGrane (Whitehead, 78), Connor.

23rd July 1976

Venue: Lansdowne Park in Ottawa, Ontario.

U.S.S.R. 3   (Kolotov 76, Veremeev 81, Blokhin, 89)
NORTH KOREA 0

Half-time: 0-0   Attendance: 15,233

Referee: Emilio Guruceta-Muro (Spain)

U.S.S.R.: Astapovsky, Konkov (Fomenko, 12), Troshkin, Reshko, Matvienko, Kolotov, Veremeev, Buriak (Feodorov, 65), Minaev, Onischenko, Blokhin.

NORTH KOREA: Kyong Won Pak, Gil Wan An, Mu Gil Kim, Jong Min Kim, Jong Hun Pak, Dongchan Myong (Jong U Ma, 81), Song Nam Hong, Jong Sok Cha, Song Guk Yang, Se Uk An, Hi Young Li (Il Nam Kim, 64).

	P	W	D	L	F	A	Pts
U.S.S.R.	2	2	0	0	5	1	4
N. KOREA	2	1	0	1	3	4	2
CANADA	2	0	0	2	2	5	0

Quarter-Finals

25th July 1976

Venue: The Varsity Stadium in Toronto, Ontario.

BRAZIL 4   (Jarbas 56, 74, Erivelto 72, Junior 88)

ISRAEL 1   (Peretz 80)

Half-time: 0-0   Attendance: 18,601

Referee: Karoly Palotai (Hungary)

BRAZIL: Carlos (Ze Carlos, 77), Mauro, Tecao, Edinho, Chicao Fraga, Batista, Erivelto, Alberto, Junior, Jarbas (Eudes, 74), Santos.

ISRAEL: Vissoker, Levanthal, Bar (Nachness, 52), Ben Dor, Nimni, Shani (Tourk, 26), Shum, Cohen, Oz, Peretz, Damti.

25th July 1976

Venue: The Stadium in Sherbrooke, Quebec.

U.S.S.R. 2   (Minaev 40, Zvagintsev 67)

IRAN 1   (Qelichkhani 82 pen)

Half-time: 1-0   Attendance: 5,855

Referee: Guillermo Velasquez (Colombia)

U.S.S.R.: Astopovsky, Troshkin, Fomenko, Zvgintsev, Matvienko, Kolotov, Buriak, Minaev, Nazarenko (Veremeev, 62), Feodorov, Blokhin (Onischenko, 73).

IRAN: Hejazi, Nazavi, Zolfoqalnassab, Mirfakhrai, Eskandarian, Parvin, Qelichkhani, Ghassempor, Rowshan, Nourai (Mazloomi, 67), Jahani.

25th July 1976

Venue: Lansdowne Park in Ottawa, Ontario.

EAST GERMANY 4   (Lowe 27, Dorner 60, 68 pen, Riediger 76)

FRANCE 0

Half-time: 1-0   Attendance: 20.083

Referee: Alberto Michelotti (Italy)

EAST GERMANY: Croy (Grapenthin, 80), Schade, Dorner, Weise, Kurbjuweit, Kische, Lauck, Heidler, Hafner, Loew (Riediger, 76), Hoffmann.

FRANCE: Larrieu, Meynieu, Chazottes, Pottier, Stassievitch, Fernandez, Platini, Rubio, Amisse (Pecout, 66), Rouyer, Schaer (Couge, 66).

25th July 1976

Venue: The Olympic Stadium in Montreal, Quebec.

POLAND 5   (Szarmach 13, 49, Lato 59, 79, Symanowski 64)

NORTH KOREA 0

Half-time: 1-0   Attendance: 46,855

Referee: Paul Schiller (Austria)

POLAND: Tomaszewski, Symanowski, Gorgon, Zmuda, Wawrowski (Rudy, 64), Maszczyk (Ogaza, 69), Kasperczak, Cmiliewicz, Lato, Deyna, Szarmach.

NORTH KOREA: In Chol Jin, Il Nam Kim, Jong Min Kim, Mu Gil Kim (Gwangsok Kim, 21), Song Nam Hong, Jong Hun Pak, Se Uk An, Hi Yon Li, Dongchan Myong (Jong U Ma, 47), Song Guk Yang.

Semi-Finals

27th July 1976

Venue: The Olympic Stadium in Montreal, Quebec.

EAST GERMANY 2   (Dorner 59, Kurbjuweit 66)

U.S.S.R. 1   (Kolotov 84)

Half-time: 0-0   Attendance: 57,182

Referee: Marco Antonio Dorantes Garcia (Mexico)

EAST GERMANY: Croy, Hafner, Kische, Weise, Kurbjuweit, Heidler, Dorner, Lauck, Schade, Lowe, Hoffmann.

U.S.S.R.: Astapovsky, Troshkin, Zvagintsev (Fomenko, 71), Reshko, Matvienko, Kolotov, Veremeev, Buriak, Minaev, Onischenko (Feodorov, 71), Blokhin.

27th July 1976

Venue: *The Varsity Stadium in Toronto, Ontario.*

POLAND 2 (Szarmach 51, 82)

BRAZIL 0

Half-time: 0-0   Attendance: 21,743

Referee: John Paterson (Scotland)

POLAND: Tomaszewski, Symanowski, Gorgon, Zmuda, Wawrowski, Maszczyk, Kasperczak, Cmikiewicz (Kmiecik, 28), Lato, Deyna, Szarmach.

BRAZIL: Carlos, Rosemiro (Marinho, 61), Tecao, Edinho, Junior, Batista, Erivelto, Alberto, Marinho, Jarba (Eudes, 77), Julinho.

Final

31st July 1976

Venue: *The Olympic Stadium in Montreal, Quebec.*

EAST GERMANY 3 (Schade 7, Hoffmann 14, Hafner 84)

POLAND 1 (Lato 59)

Half-time: 2-0   Attendance: 71,617

Referee: Ramon Barreto (Uruguay)

EAST GERMANY: Croy, Lauck, Weise, Dorner, Kurbjuweit, Kische, Schade, Riediger (Bransch, 86), Hafner, Lowe (Grobner, 68), Hoffmann.

POLAND: Tomaszewski (Mowlik, 19), Symanowski, Wieczorek, Zmuda, Wawrowski, Maszczyk, Deyna, Kasperczak, Lato, Szarmach, Kmiecik.

Bronze Medal Game

29th July 1976

Venue: *The Olympic Stadiumm in Montreal, Quebec.*

U.S.S.R. 2 (Onischenko 5, Nazarenko 49)

BRAZIL 0

Half-time: 1-0   Attendance: 55,647

Referee: Abraham Klein (Israel)

U.S.S.R.: Astapovsky, Zvagintsev, Troshkin, Fomenko, Reshko, Matvienko, Kolotov, Buriak, Minaev, Onischenko (Nazarenko, 40), Blokhin.

BRAZIL: Carlos, Mauro, Tecao, Edinho, Junior, Batista, Erivelto, Alberto (Rosemiro, 56), Marinho, Jarbas (Eudes, 63), Julinho.

20th Olympiad – 1980 – Moscow

The 1980 Olympic Games saw a number of nations withdraw as a result of the Soviet invasion of Afghanistan, among them the United States, whose football team had qualified for the finals.

The overall result of the withdrawals was that the Eastern European nations found themselves facing relatively weak opposition. The host nation, the Soviet Union, found itself in a group with Cuba, Venezuela and Zambia. Czechoslovakia were in a group with Kuwait, Colombia and Nigeria, East Germany was opposed by Algeria, Spain and Syria, while Yugoslavia faced Iraq, Finland and Costa Rica.

Groups A and B were played in Moscow and Leningrad, while groups C and D were played in Kiev and Minsk.

Naturally, the four strong nations reached the Semi-finals where East Germany upset the Soviet Union and Czechoslovakia defeated Yugoslavia. In the Final played in Moscow, Czechoslovakia triumphed 1-0 over an East German side that did not contain one player from the team that had won the gold medal in Montreal in 1976.

Record crowds watched the games in the Soviet Union with a total attendance of 1,821,624.

Group A

20th July 1980

Venue: *The Loujniki Stadium, Moscow.*

U.S.S.R. 4   (Andreev 3, Tcherenkov 25, Gavrilov 34, Oganesyan 51)
VENEZUELA 0

Half-time: *3-0*

Referee: Franz Wohrer (Austria)

U.S.S.R.: Dasaev, Sulakvelidze, Tchivadze, Khidiatullin, Romantsev, Shavio, Andreev, Bessonov, Gavrilov (Oganesyan, 37), Tcherenkov (Prokopenko, 63), Gazzaev.

VENEZUELA: E. Sanchez, Aguirre, Campos, Acosta, Cichero (Carrero, 56), Elie, Pena (Castillo, 66), A. Sanchez, Anor, Carvajal, Vidal.

20th July 1980

Venue: *The Kirov Stadium, Leningrad.*

CUBA 1   (Roldan 58)
ZAMBIA 0

Half-time: *0-0*

Referee: Marjan Raus (Yugoslavia)

CUBA: Madera, Lopez, Sanchez, Dreke, Roldan (Povea, 90), Lara, Nunez, Pereira (Espinosa, 80), Delgado, Masso, Loredo.

ZAMBIA: Mwape, Muke, Kalambo, Sinkala, Katumba, Katebe, Simwals, Banda, Chola, Chitalu, Kaimana.

22nd July 1980

Venue: *The Loujniki Stadium, Moscow.*

U.S.S.R. 3   (Khidiatullin 9, 51, Tcherenkov 87)
ZAMBIA 1   (Chitalu 13)

Half-time: 1-1

Referee: Marwan Arafat (Syria)

U.S.S.R.: Dasaev, Sulakvelidze, Tchivadze, Khidiatullin, Romantsev, Andreev, Bessonov, Gazzaev, Baltachia, Prokopenko, Tchelebadze (Tcherenkov, 63).

ZAMBIA: Mwape, Muke, Kalambo, Sinkala, Katumba, Katebe, Simwals, Banda, Chola, Chitalu, Kaimana.

24th July 1980

Venue: *The Kirov Stadium, Leningrad.*

VENEZUELA 2   (Zubizarreta 86, Elie 90)
ZAMBIA 1   (Chitalu 73)

Half-time: 0-0

Referee: Luis Siles Calderon (Costa Rica)

VENEZUELA; E. Sanchez, Pereira (Aguirre, 75), Elie, Acosta, Campos, A. Sanchez, Carrero, Anor, Carvajal, Zubizarreta, Pena (Castillo, 64).

ZAMBIA: Mwape, Muke, Kalambo, Sinkala, Katumba, Katebe, Simwals, Banda, Kashimoto (Tembo, 63), Chitalu, Kaimana.

22nd July 1980

Venue: *The Kirov Stadium, Leningrad.*

CUBA 2   (Dreke 49, Hernandez 71)
VENEZUELA 1   (Zubizarreta 68)

Half-time: 0-0

Referee: Emilio Guruceta-Muro (Spain)

CUBA: Madera, Lopez, Loredo, Dreke, Sanchez, Delgado, Masso, Lara, Roldan, Nunez, Hernandez (Povea, 81).

VENEZUELA: E. Sanchez, Aguirre, Vidal, Acosta, Campos, A. Sanchez (Castillo, 54), Elie, Carero, Anor (Febles, 70), Carvajal, Zubizarreta.

	P	W	D	L	F	A	Pts
U.S.S.R.	3	3	0	0	15	1	6
CUBA	3	2	0	1	3	9	4
VENEZUELA	3	1	0	2	3	7	2
ZAMBIA	3	0	0	3	2	6	0

Group B

24th July 1980

Venue: *The Dynamo Stadium, Moscow.*

U.S.S.R. 8   (Andreev 8, 27, 44, Romantsev 20, Shavlo 43, Tcherenkov 55, Gavrilov 75, Bessonov 77)
CUBA 0

Half-time: 5-0

Referee: Robert Valentine (Scotland)

U.S.S.R.: Dasaev (Pilguj, 64), Sulakvelidze, Tchivadze, Khidiatullin, Romantsev, Shavlo, Andreev, Bessonov, Gavrilov, Tcherenkov, Gazzaev (Nikulin, 46).

CUBA: Madera, Sanchez, Dreke, Espinosa, Roldan, Povea, Lara, Nunez, Masso (Lopez, 24, Frometa, 80), Loredo, Hernandez.

21st July 1980

Venue: *The Kirov Stadium, Leningrad.*

CZECHOSLOVAKIA 3   (Pokluda 14, Berger 18, Vizek 85)
COLOMBIA 0

Half-time: 2-0

Referee: Belaid Lacarne (Algeria)

CZECHOSLOVAKIA: Seman, Macela, Mazurea, Radimec, Rygel, Rott, Berger, Stambacher, Vizek, Pokluda, Licka (Svoboda, 69).

COLOMBIA: Valencia, Gonzalez, Romero, Viafara, Porras, Hernandez, R. Garcia (Fiorillo, 24), Sarmiento, Peluffo (A. Garcia, 58), G. Garcia, Cardona.

21st July 1980

Venue: *The Dynamo Stadium, Moscow.*

KUWAIT 3 (Aldaakhil 16, 25, 40)
NIGERIA 1 (o.g.)

Half-time: 2-1

Referee: Klaus Scheurell (East Germany)

KUWAIT: Altarabullsi, Mubarek, Alqabendi, Almubarek, Alhouti, Marzouq, Albuloushi, Sultan (Alhaddad, 86), Bohamad, Alshemmari, Aldaakhil.

NIGERIA: Ogedegbe, Okpalla, Boateng, Bamidele, Okey (Orlando, 19), Mohamed, Owolabi, Lawal, Ameisimaka, Osuigwe, Kadiri (Atuegbu, 46).

23rd July 1980

Venue: *The Kirov Stadium, Leningrad.*

CZECHOSLOVAKIA 1 (Vizek 25)
NIGERIA 1 (Nwosu 84)

Half-time: 1-0

Referee: Enrique Labo Revoredo (Peru)

CZECHOSLOVAKIA: Seman, Macela, Radimec, Vizek, Berger, Svoboda, Pokluda, Licka (Vaclavicek, 65), Sreiner, Stambacher, Kunzo.

NIGERIA: Ogedegbe, Adiele, Boateng, Bamidele, Orlando, Okpalla, Atuegbu (Mohamed, 46), Odgebami (Lawal 46), Nwosu, Osigwe, Ameisimaka.

23rd July 1980

Venue: *The Dynamo Stadium, Moscow.*

COLOMBIA 1 (Molinares 73)
KUWAIT 1 (Sultan 64)

Half-time: 0-0

Referee: Anders Mattsson (Finland)

COLOMBIA: Rios, Gonzalez, Romero, Viafara, Porras, Sarmiento, Peluffo (Viloria, 42), A. Garcia (Molinares, 69), Cardona, G. Garcia, Fiorillo.

KUWAIT: Altarabulsi, Alshemmari, Mubarek, Alqabendi, Almubarek, Alhouti, Albuloushi, Bohamad, Sultan, Marzouq, Aldaakhil.

25th July 1980

Venue: *The Kirov Stadium, Leningrad.*

CZECHOSLOVAKIA 0
KUWAIT 0

Half-time: 0-0

Referee: Riccardo Lattanzi (Italy)

CZECHOSLOVAKIA: Seman, Macela, Mazura, Radimec, Nemec, Vizek, Berger, Pokluda (Stambacher, 68), Licka, Rott, Kunzo.

KUWAIT: Altarabulsi, Mubarek, Alhashash, Alshemmari, Almubarek, Albuloushi (N. Mubarek, 46), Alhouti, Hasan (Alsuwayed, 46), Bohamad, Sultan, Aldaakhil.

25th July 1980

Venue: *The Dynamo Stadium, Moscow.*

COLOMBIA 1 (Cardona 55)
NIGERIA 0

Half-time: 0-0

Referee: Salim Naji Al-Hachami (Iraq)

COLOMBIA: Rios, Gonzalez, Viafara, Romero, Viloria, Sarmiento, Porras, Cardona (Peluffo, 89), G. Garcia, Molinares, Perez (A. Garcia, 59).

NIGERIA: Ogedegbe, Adiele, Boateng, Bamidele, Orlando, Okpalla, Atuegbu, Nwosu, Lawal, Osuigwe, Mohamed.

	P	W	D	L	F	A	Pts
CZECHOSLOV.	3	1	2	0	4	1	4
KUWAIT	3	1	2	0	4	2	4
COLOMBIA	3	1	1	1	2	4	3
NIGERIA	3	0	1	2	2	5	1

Group C

20th July 1980

Venue: The Republican Stadium, Kiev.

EAST GERMANY 1 (Kuhn 49)
SPAIN 1 (M. Alonso, 50)

Half-time: 0-0   Attendance: 100,000
Referee: Ulf Eriksson (Sweden)
EAST GERMANY: Rudwaleit, Ullrich, Hause, Baum, Schnuphase, Terletzki (Liebers, 82), Steinbach, Bahringer (Peter, 72), Kuhn, Trieloff, Netz.
SPAIN: Buyo, Urquiaga, De Andres, Ramos, J. Alonso, Gajate, M. Alonso (Ortega, 90), Munoz, Rincon, Lopez (Guerri, 74), Gonzalez.

20th July 1980

Venue: The Dinamo Stadium, Minsk.

ALGERIA 3 (Belloumi 36, Madjer 48, Merzekane 73)
SYRIA 0

Half-time: 1-0
Referee: Vojtech Christov (Czechoslovakia)
ALGERIA: Amara, Merzekane (Derouaz, 79), Larbes, Guendouz, Kheddia, Mahyouz, Madjer, Fergani, Bansaoula, Belloumi (Menad, 79), Assad.
SYRIA: Beirakdar, Chit, Dahman, Asfahani, Mahallame, Hadna, Jazaeri, Abdulkader (Haouache, 80), Mardikian, Hojeir, Madrati.

20th July 1980

Venue: The Republican Stadium, Kiev.

EAST GERMANY 1 (Terletzki 61)
ALGERIA 0

Half-time: 0-0   Attendance: 70,000
Referee: Romualdo Arppi Filho (Brazil)
EAST GERMANY: Rudwaleit, Trieloff, Uhlig, Hause, Ullrich, Schnuphase, Terletzki, Steinbach, Bahringer, Kouhn (Liebers, 87), Peter.
ALGERIA: Amara, Merzekane, Larbes, Guendouz, Mahyouz (Derouaz, 83), Kheddis, Madjer (Menad, 78), Fergani, Bensaoula, Belloumi, Assad.

22nd July 1980

Venue: The Dinamo Stadium, Minsk.

SPAIN 0
SYRIA 0

Half-time: 0-0
Referee: Jose Castro Lozada (Venezuela)
SPAIN: J. Alonso, M. Alonso, De Andres, Gajate, Gonzalez (Zuniga, 81), Lopez, Munoz, Ramos, Rincon (Ortega, 65), Rodriguez, Urquiaga.
SYRIA: Beirakdar, Chit, Dahman, Mahallame, Hadna, Jazaeri, Abdulkadar, Mardikian, Hojeir, Madrati, Shana (Assassa, 86).

24th July 1980

Venue: The Republican Stadium, Kiev.

EAST GERMANY 5 (Hause 6, Netz 25, 45, Peter 75, Terletzki 82)
SYRIA 0

Half-time: 3-0   Attendance: 80,000
Referee: Guillermo Velazquez Ramirez (Colombia)
EAST GERMANY: Hause, Baum, Schnuphase, Terletzki, Steinbach (Liebers, 46), Bahringer (Peter, 67), Kuhn, Trieloff, Muller, Jakubowski, Netz.
SYRIA: Beirakdar, Chit, Dahman, Asfahani, Mahallame, Hadna, Abdulkadar, Mardikian, Hojeir (Aref, 46), Haouache, Assassa (Shana, 73).

24th July 1980

Venue: The Dinamo Stadium, Minsk.

SPAIN 1 (Rincon 38)
ALGERIA 1 (Belloumi 63)

Half-time: 1-0
Referee: Eldar Azim-Zade (U.S.S.R.)
SPAIN: Buyo, Urquiaga, De Andres, Gajate, Ramos (Felipe, 66), Lopez, J. Alonso, Munoz, M. Alonso, Rincon, Gonzalez (Ortega, 66).
ALGERIA: Amara, Derouaz, Merzekane, Larbes, Guendouz, Mahyouz (Belloumi, 51), Madjer, Fergani, Bensaoula, Ghrib, Assad.

	P	W	D	L	F	A	Pts
E. GERMANY	3	2	1	0	7	1	5
ALGERIA	3	1	1	1	4	2	4
SPAIN	3	0	3	0	2	2	3
SYRIA	3	0	1	2	0	8	1

Group D

21st July 1980

Venue: The Dinamo Stadium, Minsk.

YUGOSLAVIA 2 (Secerbegovic 56, Sestic 58)
FINLAND 0

Half-time: 0-0

Referee: Lamberto Rubio Vazquez (Mexico)

YUGOSLAVIA: Pantevic, Zoran Vujovic, Jovin, Matievic, Primorac, Klincarski, Zlatko Vujovic, Sestic, Pesic (Secerbegovic, 46), Mirocevic (Cukrov, 68), Repcic.

FINLAND: Isoaho, Lahtinen, Helin, Virtanen, Heikkinen (Vilen, 63), Turunen, Dahllund (Kuuluvainen, 63), Pullainen, Himanka, Tissari, Alila.

21st July 1980

Venue: The Republican Stadium, Kiev.

IRAQ 3 (Ahmed 45, Saeed 49, Hassan, 75)
COSTA RICA 0

Half-time: 1-0

Referee: Nyirenda Chayu (Zambia)

IRAQ: Jassim Abdul Fatah, Hassoun Hassan Farhan, Kadhum Ibrahim Ali, Hafidh Adil Khdhayir, Mutar Adnan Derchal, Khdhayir Alaa Ahmed, Jasim Falah Hassan, Mohammed Hussain Saeed, Salman Nazar Ashraf (Nasir Ali Kadhum, 46), Basheer Hadi Ahmed (Mohammed Saad Jassim, 83), Hamza Jamal Ali.

COSTA RICA: Morales, Masis, Garcia, Toppings, Obando, Velasquez, Arroyo, White, Alvarez (Quesada, 54), Hernandez, Fernandez (Marshall, 59).

23rd July 1980

Venue: The Dinamo Stadium, Minsk.

YUGOSLAVIA 3 (Zlatko Vujovic 6, 46, Primorac 24)
COSTA RICA 2 (White 35, Arroyo 90)

Half-time: 2-1

Referee: Bassey Eyo-Honesty (Nigeria)

YUGOSLAVIA: Cukrov, Hrstic, Klincarski, Krsticevic, Secerbegovic, Matijevic, Mirocevic (Repcic, 46), Pesic (Sestic, 46), Ivkovic, Primorac, Zlatko Vujovic.

COSTA RICA: Morales, Masis, Garcia, Toppings, Jimenez (Alpizar, 14), Hernandez, Velazquez, White, Alvarez (Avila, 60), Obando, Arroyo.

23rd July 1980

Venue: The Republican Stadium, Kiev.

FINLAND 0
IRAQ 0

Half-time: 0-0

Referee: Ramon Calderon Castro (Cuba)

FINLAND: Isoaho, Lahtinen, Helin, Virtanen, Vilen, Turunen, Dahllund, Pullainen, Himanka, Tissari (Soini, 24), Alila (Jalo, 74).

IRAQ: Jassim Abdul Fatah, Hassoun Hassan Farhan, Hamza Jamal Ali, Basheer Hadi Ahmed, Salman Nazar Ashraf (Nasir Ali Kadhum, 62), Hafidh Adil Khdhayir, Khdhayir Alaa Ahmed, Jasim Falah Hassan, Mohammed Hussain Saeed, Mutar Adnan Derchal, Kadhum Ibrahim Ali.

25th July 1980

Venue: *The Dinamo Stadium, Minsk.*

YUGOSLAVIA 1 (Zoran Vujovic 63)
IRAQ 1 (Hassan 61)

Half-time: 0-0

Referee: Andre Daina (Switzerland)

YUGOSLAVIA: Pantelic, Cukrov, Jovin (Hrstic, 75), Matijevic, Primorac, Klincaski, Zlatko Vujovic (Zoran Vujovic, 41), Sestic, Repcic, Mirocevic, Secerbegovic.

IRAQ: Jassim Abdul Fatah, Hassoun Hassan Farhan, Kadhum Ibrahim Ali, Mutar Adnan Derchal, Hafidh Adil Khdhayir, Basheer Hadi Ahmed, Khdhayir Alaa Ahmed, Hamza Jamal Ali (Muhyi Wathiq Aswad, 85), Elias Thamir Assoufi (Salman Nazar Ashraf, 62), Jasim Falah Hassan, Nasir Ali Kadhum.

Quarter-Finals

27th July 1980

Venue: *The Dynamo Stadium, Moscow.*

U.S.S.R. 2 (Tcherenkov 30, Gavrilov 51)
KUWAIT 1 (Sultan 59)

Half-time: 1-0

Referee: Lamberto Rubio Vazquez (Mexico)

U.S.S.R.: Dasaev, Sulakvelidze, Tchivadze, Khidiatullin, Romantsev, Shavio, Andreev, Bessanov, Gavrilov (Gazzaev, 80), Tcherenkov, Tchelebadze (Oganesyan, 46).

KUWAIT: Altarabulsi, Na'eem Mubarek, Mahboub Mubarek, Algabendi, Almubarek (Alhashash, 61), Bohamed, Alshemmari (Alsuwayed, 67), Alhouti, Aldakhil, Marzouq, Sultan.

25th July 1980

Venue: *The Republican Stadium, Kiev.*

FINLAND 3 (Tissari 18, Alila 58, Soini 88)
COSTA RICA 0

Half-time: 1-0

Referee: Ali Albannai Abdulwahab (Kuwait)

FINLAND: Isoaho, Lahtinen, Helin, Virtanen, Turunen, Dahllund, Pulliainen, Himanka (Soini, 61), Tissari (Rissanen, 78), Alila, Vilen.

COSTA RICA: Morales, Masis (Marshall, 69), Garcia, Toppings, Hernandez, Velasquez, White, Alvarez (Quesada, 46), Obando, Alpizar, Arroyo.

27th July 1980

Venue: *The Kirov Stadium, Leningrad.*

CZECHOSLOVAKIA 3 (Vizek 29, 59, Pokluda 90)
CUBA 0

Half-time: 1-0

Referee: Enrique Labo Revoredo (Peru)

CZECHOSLOVAKIA: Seman, Macela, Mazura, Radimec, Vizek, Berger, Pokluda, Licka, Rott, Sreiner, Kunzo.

CUBA: Madera, Sanchez, Dreke, Roldan, Povea, Lara, Nunez, Pereira (Hernandez, 64), Delgado, Masso, Loredo.

	P	W	D	L	F	A	Pts
YUGOSLAVIA	3	2	1	0	6	3	5
IRAQ	3	1	2	0	4	1	4
FINLAND	3	1	1	1	2	2	3
COSTA RICA	3	0	0	3	3	9	0

27th July 1980

Venue: *The Republican Stadium, Kiev.*

EAST GERMANY 4 (Schnuphase 4, Netz 11, Steinbach 17, Terletzki 22)
IRAQ 0

Half-time: 4-0 Attendance: 100,000

Referee: Romualdo Arppi Filho (Brazil)

EAST GERMANY: Rudwaleit, Trieloff, Muller, Hause, Baum, Terletzki (Liebers, 72), Schnuphase, Steinbach, Bahringer, Kuhn (Trautmann, 46).

IRAQ: Jassim Abdul Fatah (Abdulsada Kadom Shibib, 23), Hassoun Hassan Farhan, Mutar Adnan Derchal, Mohammed Hussain Saeed, Basheer Hadi Ahmed, Nasir Ali Kadhum, Khdhayir Alaa Ahmed, Hafidh Adil Khdhayir, Jasim Falah Hassan, Hamza Jamal Ali (Salman Nazar Ashraf, 74), Kadhum Ibrahim Ali.

27th July 1980

Venue: The Dinamo Stadium, Minsk.

YUGOSLAVIA 3   (Mirocevic 5, Sestic 19, Zoran Vujovic 70)

ALGERIA 0

Half-time: 2-0

Referee: Klaus Scheurell (East Germany)

YUGOSLAVIA: Pantelic, Cukrov, Hrstic, Klincarski, Matijevic, Mirocevic (Gudelj, 81), Primorac, Repcic, Sestic (Krsticevic, 77), Zlatko Vujovic, Zoran Vujovic.

ALGERIA: Amara, Guendouz, Mahiouz, Merzekane, Kheddis, Madjer, Fergani, Bensaoula, Belloumi, Assad (Menadi, 73), Larbes.

Semi-Finals

29th July 1980

Venue: The Lenin Stadium, Moscow.

EAST GERMANY 1   (Netz 16)

U.S.S.R. 0

Half-time: 1-0   Attendance: 95,000

Referee: Ulf Eriksson (Sweden)

EAST GERMANY: Rudwaleit, Ullrich, Hause, Baum (Uhlig, 83), Schnuphase (Liebers, 90), Terletzki, Steinbach, Kuhn, Trieloff, Muller, Netz.

U.S.S.R.: Dasaev, Sulakvelidze, Chivadze, Khidiatullin, Romantsev, Shavlo, Andreev, Bessanov, Gavrilov, Cherenkov, Gazzaev.

29th July 1980

Venue: The Dynamo Stadium, Moscow.

CZECHOSLOVAKIA 2   (Licka 4, Sreiner 18)

YUGOSLAVIA 0

Half-time: 2-0

Referee: Franz Wohrer (Austria)

CZECHOSLOVAKIA: Seman, Mazura, Vaclavicek, Radimec, Kunzo, Rott, Berger, Vizek, Pokluda (Nemec, 72), Licka (Svoboda, 84), Sreiner.

YUGOSLAVIA: Pantelic, Zoran Vujovic, Hrstic, Matijevic, Primorac, Klincarski, Zlatko Vujovic, Sestic, Cukrov (Krsticevic), Mirocevic, Repcic.

Bronze Medal Game

1st August 1980

Venue: The Dynamo Stadium, Moscow.

U.S.S.R. 2   (Oganesyan 67, Andreev 82)

YUGOSLAVIA 0

Half-time: 0-0

Referee: Robert Valentine (Scotland)

U.S.S.R.: Dasaev, Sulakvelidze, Chivadze, Khidiatullin, Romantsev, Shavlo, Andreev, Bessanov, Gavrilov, Cherenkov (Baltacha, 72), Gazzaev (Oganesyan, 46).

YUGOSLAVIA: Ivkovic, Zoran Vujovic, Klincarski, Gudelj, Primorac, Krsticevic (Repcic, 78), Zlatko Vujovic, Sestic, Pesic, Cukrov, Secerbegovic.

Final

2nd August 1980

Venue: The Loujniki Stadium, Moscow.

CZECHOSLOVAKIA 1   (Svoboda 77)

EAST GERMANY 0

Half-time: 0-0   Attendance: 70,000

Referee: Eldar Azim-Zade (U.S.S.R.)

CZECHOSLOVAKIA: Seman, Macela, Mazura, Radimec, Rigel, Vizek (Svoboda, 73), Berger, Pokluda (Nemec, 63), Licka, Rott, Stambacher.

EAST GERMANY: Rudwaleit, Trieloff, Muller, Hause (Liebers, 81), Ullrich, Schnuphase, Terletzki, Baum, Netz, Kuhn (Peter, 58), Steinbach.

21st Olympiad – 1984 – Los Angeles

Peace returned to the athletic scene in time for the 1984 Olympics and the result was one of the better competitions, perhaps because for the first time professionals were officially permitted to take part. However, there were restrictions as to which professionals. Players who had taken part in the previous World Cup and were from Europe or South America were barred, while those from the rest of the world were not. The result was that the host nation United States along with Canada, who had qualified for the first time, could field virtually their strongest teams, as could nations like Cameroon and Iraq, while countries like France, Italy, Yugoslavia and West Germany could field teams just below World Cup strength.

The competition was played at two sites on the east coast and two on the west, while the final stages of the competition were only staged on the west coast. Italy, Chile, France, Egypt, Brazil, Canada, Yugoslavia and West Germany qualified for the Quarter-finals. For Canada it was a first and the Canadians might have advanced even to the Semi-finals but for a puzzling refereeing decision which denied them a second goal when they led Brazil 1-0. Eventually Brazil scored the equalising goal and won the game in the penalty kick shoot out.

The Canadian squad, coached by former England international goalkeeper Tony Waiters, included the following players: Tino Lettieri (Minnesota Strikers), Sven Habermann (Toronto Blizzard), Bob Lenarduzzi (Vancouver Whitecaps), Bruce Wilson (Toronto Blizzard), Terry Moore (Tulsa Roughnecks), Ian Bridge (Vancouver Whitecaps), Mike Sweeney (Golden Bay Earthquakes), Craig Martin, Pasquale DeLuca (Toronto Blizzard), Randy Ragan (Toronto Blizzard), David Norman (Vancouver Whitecaps), Paul James (Toronto Blizzard), Gerry Gray (New York Cosmos), John Catliff (Harvard University), Ken Garraway (Victoria Athletics), Dale Mitchell (Tacoma Stars), igor Vrablic (Golden Bay Earthquakes). Many of these players went on to play for Canada in the 1986 World Cup Finals.

Brazil over Italy and France over Yugoslavia won the Semi-finals thus putting Brazil and France into an Olympic Final for the first time. The French, at that time were on a high, having been denied a place in the 1982 World Cup Final only by a penalty shoot out, and this was virtually their second team, full of talented players. On the other hand Brazil were not really a true national team at all, but a club side, Internacional of Porto Alegre bolstered by one or two players. Thus it was remarakble that the Brazilians had even reached the Final, and when it was over France had won the gold medal 2-0.

Looking back on these Finals it is interesting to note some of the players taking part. For Italy, Pietro Vierchowod and Franco Baresi along with Danielle Massaro and Aldo Serena; for West Germany, Andreas Brehme; for Cameroon, Roger Milla and for Norway, Eric Thorsvedt.

Despite the fact that the Olympics were being held in a country where football was not amongst the most popular sports, football drew larger crowds than any other sport. Huge crowds watched the football with a total attendance of 1,421,627, for an average of 45,300. A record attendance for a football game in the U.S. of 101,970 watched the Final

Group A

29th July 1984

Venue: The Harvard Stadium in Cambridge, Massachusetts.

CHILE 0
NORWAY 0

Half-time: 0-0   Attendance: 25,000

Referee: David Socha (U.S.A.)

CHILE: Fourniel, Mosquera, Ahumada, Contreras, Martinez, Baeza (Marchant, 76), Figueroa, Hisis, Vera (Ramos, 60), Santis, Olmos.

NORWAY: Thorsvedt, Fjaelberg, Kojedal, Eggen, Gran, Herlovsen, Ahlsen, Sundby, Johansen, Krogsaeter, Seland (Vaadal, 83).

29th July 1984

Venue: The Navy-Marine Corps Stadium in Annapolis, Maryland.

FRANCE 2   (Garande 43, Xuereb 61)
QATAR 2   (Khalid Al Mohamadi 55, 60)

Half-time: 1-0   Attendance: 29,240

Referee: Romualdo Arppi Filho (Brazil)

FRANCE: Rust, Thouvenal, Senac, Zanon, Ayache, Lacombe, Lemoult, Bijotat, Toure (Rohr), Xuereb, Brisson (Cubaynes).

QATAR: Lari, Alali, Alsowaidi, Malalla, Almass, Alkhater, Issa Al Mohamadi, Khalid Al Mohamadi, Alsadah (Salem, 89), Ahmed, Bakheet.

31st July 1984

Venue: The Harvard Stadium in Cambridge, Massachusetts.

FRANCE 2   (Brisson 11, 56)
NORWAY 1   (Ahlsen 34)

Half-time: 1-1   Attendance: 27,832

Referee: Volker Roth (West Germany)

FRANCE: Rust, Jeannol, Thouvenal, Senac, Ayache, Lacombe, Lemoult, Bijotat, Toure (Rohr, 75), Xuereb, Brisson (Cubaynes, 84).

NORWAY: Thorsvedt, Fjaelberg, Eggen, Kojedal, Mordt, Herlovsen, Ahlsen, Sundby, Kollshaugen (Johansen, 67), Seland, Krogsaeter (Berg, 82).

31st July 1984

Venue: The Navy-Marine Corps Stadium in Annapolis, Maryland.

CHILE 1   (Baeza 52)
QATAR 0

Half-time: 0-0   Attendance: 14,508

Referee: Luis Siles Calderon (Chile)

CHILE: Fourniel, Mosquera, Ahumada, Martinez, Contreras, Hisis, Marchant, Olmos, Ramos, Baeza (Nunez, 66), Figueroa (Santis, 45).

QATAR: Lari, Alali, Alsowaidi, Malalla, Almass, Alkhater, Issa Al Mohamadi, Khalid Al Mohamadi (Salem, 74), Alsadah, Ahmad, Bakheet.

2nd August 1984

Venue: The Navy-Marine Corps Stadium in Annapolis, Maryland.

CHILE 1   (Santis 4)
FRANCE 1   (Lemoult 49)

Half-time: 1-0   Attendance: 28,114

Referee: Jan Keizer (Netherlands)

CHILE: Fournier, Mosquera, Ahumada, Martinez, Contreras, Hisis, Marchant (Vera, 55), Olmos, Ramos (Figueroa, 55), Baeza, Santis.

FRANCE: Rust, Jeannol, Thouvenal, Senac, Ayache, Lacombe, Bijotat (Rohr, 77), Lemoult, Toure, Xuereb, Brisson.

2nd August 1984

Venue: The Harvard Stadium in Cambridge, Massachusetts.

NORWAY 2   (Vaadal 22, 52)
QATAR 0

Half-time: 1-0   Attendance: 17,529

Referee: Bester Kalombo (Malawi)

NORWAY: Thorsvedt, Fjaelberg (Gran, 45), Eggen, Kojedal, Mordt, Herlovsen, Ahlsen, Sundby, Johansen, Seland (Krogsaeter, 34), Vaadal.

QATAR: Lari, Alali, Alsowaidi, Malalla, Waleed, Almass, Alkhater, Issa Al Mohamadi, Alammari, Bakheet, Alsadah (Ahmed, 63).

	P	W	D	L	F	A	Pts
FRANCE	3	1	2	0	5	4	4
CHILE	3	1	2	0	2	1	4
NORWAY	3	1	1	1	3	2	3
QATAR	3	0	1	2	2	5	1

Group B

30th July 1984

Venue: The Harvard Stadium in Cambridge, Massachusetts.

CANADA 1 (Gray 70)
IRAQ 1 (Saeed Mohammed 83)

Half-time: 0-0   Attendance: 16,730

Referee: Jesus Diaz (Colombia)

CANADA: Lettieri, Lenarduzzi, Bridge, Moore, Wilson, James (Norman, 67), Gray, Ragan, Sweeney, Vrablic (Garroway, 80), Mitchell.

IRAQ: Hammoudi, Karim Allawi, Dirjal, Mutashar, Khalil Allawi, Munir (Saddam, 74), Benwan, Awne, Shehab (Fadhil, 59), Mohmoud, Saeed Mohammed.

30th July 1984

Venue: The Navy-Marine Corps Stadium in Annapolis, Maryland.

YUGOSLAVIA 2 (Nikolic 40, Cvetkovic 71)
CAMEROON 1 (Milla 33)

Half-time: 1-1   Attendance: 15,010

Referee: Jan Keizer (Netherlands)

YUGOSLAVIA: Ivkovic, Miljus, Elsner, Radanovic, Baljic, Gracan, Smajic, Bazdarevic, Djurovski (Deveric, 75), Katanec (Stojkovic, 36), Nikolic.

CAMEROON: Bell, Toube, Doumbe, Aoudou, Mbassi, Abega, Sinkot, Ebongue, Mfeede, Ekeke, Milla.

1st August 1984

Venue: The Harvard Stadium in Cambridge, Massachusetts.

CAMEROON 1 (Bahoken 7)
IRAQ 0

Half-time: 1-0   Attendance: 18,236

Referee: David Socha (U.S.A.)

CAMEROON: Bell, Toube, Doumbe, Aoudou, Mbassi, Abega, Kunde, Dang, Bahoken, Milla, Mfeede (Ebongue, 45).

IRAQ: Hammoudi, Dirja, Fadhil, Mutashar, Khalil Allawi (Shehab, 76), Muner, Awne, Karim Allawi, Benwan, Mahmoud, Saeed Mohammed (Saddam, 58).

1st August 1984

Venue: The Navy-Marine Corps Stadium in Annapolis, Maryland.

YUGOSLAVIA 1 (Nikolic 77)
CANADA 0

Half-time: 0-0   Attendance: 19,243

Referee: M. Hossam El Din (Egypt)

YUGOSLAVIA: Ivkovic, Miljus, Radanovic, Baljic, Gracan, Smajic (Stojkovic, 45), Capljic, Djurovski (Mrkela, 70), Bazdarevic, Cvetkovic, Nikolic.

CANADA: Lettieri, Lenarduzzi, Moore, Bridge, Wilson, James (Norman, 70), Ragan, Gray, Sweeney, Vrablic (Catliff, 61), Mitchell.

3rd August 1984

Venue: The Navy-Marine Corps Stadium in Annapolis, Maryland.

YUGOSLAVIA 4 (Deveric 55, 76, 87, Nikolic 86)
IRAQ 2 (Saeed Mohammed 17, Shehab 44)

Half-time: 0-2   Attendance: 24,430

Referee: Toshikazu Sano (Japan)

YUGOSLAVIA: Pudar, Capljic, Elsner, Radanovic, Baljic, Gracan, Smajic (Bazdarevic, 45), Stojkovic (Nikolic, 45), Katanec, Deveric, Mrkela.

IRAQ: Hammoudi, Mutar, Hamed, Shehab, Minshed (Awne, 78), Mohammed, Mahmoud, K.M. Allawi, Nasser, Awne, Hassan (Yacoub, 45).

3rd August 1984

Venue: The Harvard Stadium in Cambridge, Massachusetts.

CANADA 3 (Mitchell 43, 82, Vrablic 73)
CAMEROON 1 (Mfeede 76)

Half-time: 1-0   Attendance: 27,621

Referee: Enzo Barbaresco (Italy)

CANADA: Lettieri, Lenarduzzi, Moore, Bridge, Wilson, James, Ragan, Gray, Sweeney, Mitchell, Vrablic.

CAMEROON: Bell, Toube, Doumbe, Bilamo, Mbassi, Abega, Kunde, Aoudou, Dang (Ekeke, 47), Milla, Bahoken (Mfeede, 47).

30th July 1984

Venue: The Rose Bowl in Pasadena, California.

BRAZIL 3 (Oliveira 14, Paiva 51, Verri 60)
SAUDI ARABIA 1 (Mohammed Majed 68)

Half-time: 1-0   Attendance: 40,779

Referee: Brian McGinlay (Scotland)

BRAZIL: Rinaldi, Silva, Brunn, Galvao, Ademir, Ferreira, Verri, Oliveira, Paiva, Gil (Milton Cruz, 89), Vidal.

SAUDI ARABIA: Al Husain, Aldawasare (Bakhshwein, 85), Albishi, Bishy, Abdulshak, Alnasisah (Masod, 60), Majed, Mosaibeth, Aldosari, Abduljawad, Al Dossary.

	P	W	D	L	F	A	Pts
YUGOSLAVIA	3	3	0	0	7	3	6
CANADA	3	1	1	1	4	3	3
CAMEROON	3	1	0	2	3	5	2
IRAQ	3	0	1	2	3	6	1

1st August 1984

Venue: Stanford Stadium in Palo Alto, California.

BRAZIL 1 (Oliveira 86)
WEST GERMANY 0

Half-time: 0-0   Attendance: 75,239

Referee: Cha Kyong-Bok (South Korea)

BRAZIL: Rinaldi, R. Silva, Brum (D. Silva, 39), Galvao, Ademir, Ferreira, Verri, Oliveira, Paiva, Gil, Vidal.

WEST GERMANY: Franke, Bockenfeld (Dickgiesser, 83), Bast, Buchwald, Wehmeyer, Bommer, Groh, Rahn, Brehme, Schatzschneider (Schreier, 73), Mill.

Group C

30th July 1984

Venue: Stanford Stadium in Palo Alto, California.

WEST GERMANY 2 (Rahn 44, Brehme 52)
MOROCCO 0

Half-time: 1-0   Attendance: 23,228

Referee: Tony Evangelista (Canada)

WEST GERMANY: Franke, Bockenfeld, Bast, Buchwald, Wehmeyer, Bommer, Groh, Rahn, Brehme, Schatzschneider (Schreier, 87), Mill (Lux, 84).

MOROCCO: Badou, Dahan, Lamris, Elbiyaz, Bouyahiaoui, Dolmy, Elhadaoui (Elghrissi, 60), Mouttaqui, Hanini (Elbied, 69), Timoumi, Merry.

1st August 1984

Venue: The Rose Bowl in Pasadena, California.

MOROCCO 1 (Mustapha Merry 72)
SAUDI ARABIA 0

Half-time: 0-0   Attendance: 36,909

Referee: Bester Kalombo (Malawi)

MOROCCO: Badou, Dahan, Lamris, Bouyahiaoui, Dolmy, Mouttaqui (Elhadaoui, 70), Hanini (Elbied, 45), Timoumi, Merry, Ouadani, Elghrissi.

SAUDI ARABIA: Al Husain, Aldawasare, Albishi, Bishy, Abdulshak, Masod, Majed, Mosaibeth, Aldosari, Abduljawad, Al Dossary (Alnasisah, 78).

3rd August 1984

Venue: *The Stanford Stadium in Palo Alto, California.*

WEST GERMANY 6 (Bommer 23, 71, Schreier 8, 67, Mill 32, Rahn 24)

SAUDI ARABIA 0

Half-time: 4-0   Attendance: 26,242

Referee: Ion Igna (Romania)

WEST GERMANY: Franke, Bockenfeld, Bast, Buchwald, Wehmeyer, Bommer, Groh (Schoen, 45), Rahn (Lux, 64), Brehme, Mill, Schreier.

SAUDI ARABIA: Al Husain, Aldawasare, Albishi, Bishy, Abdulshakor, Bayazid, Majed, Mosaibeth, M. Aldosari (Al Dossary, 60), Abduljawad (S. Aldosari, 32), Bakhshwein.

3rd August 1984

Venue: *The Rose Bowl in Pasadena, California.*

BRAZIL 2 (Silva 61, Kita 70)

MOROCCO 0

Half-time: 0-0   Attendance: 49,355

Referee: Victoriano Sanchez Arminio (Spain)

BRAZIL: Rinaldi, Silva, Galvao, Ademir, Verri, Oliveira, Paiva, Winck, Silva, Gil, Vidal (Neto, 60).

MOROCCO: Badou, Dahan, Lamris, Elbiyaz, Bouyahiaoui, Dolmy, Timoumi, Elbied, Merry, Ouadani (Janina, 80), Elghrissi.

	P	W	D	L	F	A	Pts
BRAZIL	3	3	0	0	6	1	6
W. GERMANY	3	2	0	1	8	1	4
MOROCCO	3	1	0	2	1	4	2
SAUDI ARABIA	3	0	0	3	1	10	0

Group D

29th July 1984

Venue: *Stanford Stadium in Palo Alto, California.*

UNITED STATES 3 (Davis 23, 86, Willrich 35)

COSTA RICA 0

Half-time: 2-0   Attendance: 78,265

Referee: Joel Quiniou (France)

U.S.A.: Brcic, Savage, Kapp, Crow, Thompson, Borja (Hooker, 60), DiBernardo, Davis, Perez (Fox, 55), Willrich, Moyers.

COSTA RICA: Rojas, Toppings, Simpson, Hines, Obando, Echevarria, Santana, Rivers, Solano (Coronado, 45), Guardia (Flores, 67), Diaz.

29th July 1984

Venue: *The Rose Bowl in Pasadena, California.*

ITALY 1 (Serena 63)

EGYPT 0

Half-time: 0-0   Attendance: 37,430

Referee: Caston Castro Makuc (Chile)

ITALY: Tancredi, Ferri, Tricella, Vierchowod, Nela, Bagni, Baresi, Battistini (Massaro, 59), Serena, Fanna, Iorio (Vignola, 59).

EGYPT: El Maamour, Hamed, Yassine, Magdy Abdelghani, Sedky, Youssef Ibrahim, Abouzeid, Shawki (Ismail, 83), Nabil, Hassan, Suleiman (El Khatib, 78).

31st July 1984

Venue: *Stanford Stadium in Palo Alto, California.*

EGYPT 4 (El Khatib 32, 62, Abdelghani 35, Gadallah 71)

COSTA RICA 1 (Coronado 87)

Half-time: 2-0   Attendance: 20,645

Referee: Antonio Marquez (Mexico)

EGYPT: El Maamour, Gadallah, Youssif, Gharib, Abdelghani, El Khatib, Suleiman, Abouzeid, Hamed, Salem, Helmy.

COSTA RICA: Gonzales, Toppings, Simpson, Alpizar, Obrando, Echevarria, Santana (Rivers, 45), Coronado, Solano, Guardia, Diaz (Cayasso, 45).

31st July 1984

Venue: The Rose Bowl in Pasadena, California.

ITALY 1   (Fanna 54)
UNITED STATES 0

Half-time: 0-0   Attendance: 63,624

Referee: El Selmy (Kuwait)

ITALY: Tancredi, Ferri, Vierchowod, Tricella, Galli, Bagni, Baresi, Vignola, Fanna (Sabato, 80), Massaro, Serena (Iorio, 76).

U.S.A.: Brcic, Savage, Crow, Kapp, Thompson, DiBernardo, Davis, Borja (Hooker, 61), Perez, Moyers, Willrich (Fox, 67).

	P	W	D	L	F	A	Pts
ITALY	3	2	0	1	2	1	4
EGYPT	3	1	1	1	5	3	3
U.S.A.	3	1	1	1	4	2	3
COSTA RICA	3	1	0	2	2	7	2

Quarter-Finals

2nd August 1984

Venue: The Rose Bowl in Pasadena, California.

COSTA RICA 1   (Rivers 34)
ITALY 0

Half-time: 1-0   Attendance: 41,291

Referee: Gebreyesus Tesfaye (Ethiopia)

COSTA RICA: Rojas, Toppings (Santana, 63), Alpizar, Hines, Obando, Echevarria, Rivers, Coronado (Flores, 45), Guardia, Galagarza, Simpson.

ITALY: Zenga, Ferri, Tricella, Vierchowod, Galli, Massaro, Baresi (Vignola, 45), Battistini, Sabato, Briaschi, Iorio (Serena, 67).

5th August 1984

Venue: Stanford Stadium in Palo Alto, California.

ITALY 1   (Vignola 97)
CHILE 0

Half-time: 0-0   Attendance: 67,039

Referee: Brian McGinlay (Scotland)

ITALY: Tancredi, Ferri (Battistini, 45), Galli, Tricella, Vierchowod, Bagni, Sabato, Vignola, Fanna, Masaro, Serena (Iorio, 82).

CHILE: Fourniel, Mosquera, Ahumada, Martinez, Contreras, Hisis, Nunez, Olmos (Santis, 45), Ramos, Baeza, Figueroa (Marchant, 58).

2nd August 1984

Venue: Stanford Stadium in Palo Alto, California.

UNITED STATES 1   (o.g. 8)
EGYPT 1   (Suleiman 27)

Half-time: 1-1   Attendance: 54,973

Referee: Jorge Romero (Argentina)

U.S.A.: Brcic, Thompson, Crow, Durgan (Perez, 35), Kapp, DiBernardo (Hooker, 82), Fox, Davis, Savage, Moyers, Boja.

EGYPT: El Maamour, B. Mahmoud, El Zeer, Youssef, Yassine, Gharib, Sayed, Abouzeid, Abdou (Saleh, 53), El Khatib, Suleiman (M. Mahmoud, 89).

5th August 1984

Venue: The Rose Bowl in Pasadena, California.

FRANCE 2   (Xuereb 29, 52)
EGYPT 0

Half-time: 1-0   Attendance: 66,228

Referee: Cha Kyong-Bok (South Korea)

FRANCE: Rust, Jeannol, Thouvenal, Senac, Ayache, Lacombe, Bijotat, Lemoult, Toure (Rohr, 12), Brisson, Xuereb (Garande, 76).

EGYPT: Morsy,, Yassine, Hamed, Abdelghani, Youssif, Gharib, Abouzeid, El Khatib (Helmy, 65), El Zeer, Salem, Suleiman (M. Ismail, 71).

6th August 1984

Venue: Stanford Stadium in Palo Alto, California.
(Result is after extra time – Brazil won on penalties)

BRAZIL 1   (Oliveira 72)
CANADA 1   (Mitchell 58)

Half-time: 0-0   Attendance: 36,150

Referee: Luis Siles Calderon (Costa Rica)

BRAZIL: Rinaldi, Ronaldo, Pinga, Galvao, Ademir, Andre, Tonho (Santos, 58), Silva, Oliveira, Chicao (Kita, 68), Silvinho.

CANADA: Lettieri, Lenarduzzi, Bridge, Moore, Wilson, James, Gray, Ragan, Sweeney, Mitchell, Vrablic (Garraway, 111).

6th August 1984

Venue: The Rose Bowl in Pasadena, California.

YUGOSLAVIA 5   (Cvetkovic 21, 58, 70, Radanovic 27, Gracan 47)
WEST GERMANY 2   (Bommer 1, Rahn 29)

Half-time: 2-2   Attendance: 58,439

Referee: Jorge Romero (Argentina)

YUGOSLAVIA: Ivkovic, Miljus, Elsner, Radanovic, Baljic, Gracan, Katanec, Bazdarevic (Mrkela, 89), Cvetkovic, Nikolic, Deveric (Stojkovic, 78).

WEST GERMANY: Franke, Bockenfeld, Bast, Buchwald, Wehmeyer, Bommer, Groh, Rahn, Brehme, Mill, Schreier (Schatzschneider, 68).

Semi-Finals

8th August 1984

Venue: Stanford Stadium in Palo Alto, California.

BRAZIL 2   (Oliveira 53, Ronaldo 95)
ITALY 1   (Fanna 62)

Half-time: 0-0   Attendance: 83,642

Referee: David Socha (U.S.A.)

BRAZIL: Rinaldi, Ronaldo, Pinga, Galvao, Ademir, Andre, Tonho (Milton Cruz, 99), Dunga, Kita (Chicao, 78), Oliveira, Silvinho.

ITALY: Tancredi, Galli, Vierchowod, Baresi, Nela, Bagni, Tricella, Serena, Fanna, Sabato (Battistini, 77), Massaro (Iorio, 60).

8th August 1984

Venue: The Rose Bowl in Pasadena, California
(Result is after extra time)

FRANCE 4   (Bijotat 6, Jeannol 15, Lacombe 96, Xuereb 119)
YUGOSLAVIA 2   (Cvetkovic 63, Deveric 73)

Half-time: 2-0   Attendance: 97,451

Referee: Antonio Marquez (Mexico)

FRANCE: Rust, Thouvenal (Bibard, 22), Senac (Zenon, 45), Jeannol, Ayache, Lemoult, Bijotat, Rohr, Lacombe, Xuereb, Brisson.

YUGOSLAVIA: Ivkovic, Miljus, Elsner, Radanovic, Baljic, Gracan. Katanec, Bazdarevic, Cvetkovic, Deveric, Nikolic.

Bronze Medal Game

10th August 1984

Venue: The Rose Bowl in Pasadena, California.

YUGOSLAVIA 2   (Baljic 59, Deveric 81)
ITALY 1   (Vignola 27)

Half-time: 0-1   Attendance: 100,374

Referee: Brian McGinlay (Scotland)

YUGOSLAVIA: Pudar, Capljic, Katanec, Elsner, Baljic, Miljus, Radanovic, Gracan, Deveric, Bazdarevic, Stojkovic.

ITALY: Tancredi, Galli, Vierchowod, Baresi, Nela, Tricella, Massaro, Bagni, Iorio (Briaschi, 43), Vignola, Serena (Battistini, 77).

Final

11th August 1984

Venue: The Rose Bowl in Pasadena, California.

FRANCE 2   (Brisson 50, Xuereb 62)
BRAZIL 0

Half-time: 0-0   Attendance: 101,970

Referee: Jan Keizer (Holland)

FRANCE: Rust, Jeannol, Bibard, Zanon, Ayache, Lacombe, Bijotat, Rohr, Lemoult, Brisson (Garande, 79), Xuereb (Cubaynes, 87).

BRAZIL: Rinaldi, Ronaldo, Pinga, Galvao, Ademir, Andre Luiz, Tonho (Milton Cruz, 58), Dunga, Kita (Chicao 58), Oliveira, Silvinho.

22nd Olympiad – 1988 – Seoul

In 1988 Brazil reached the Final for the second time only to lose to the Soviet Union, winners for the second time, while the Bronze Medal Game pitted West Germany against Italy. Once again the same regulations prevailed thus allowing the United States and other nations outside of Europe and South America to field their full national teams.

The performance of the U.S. national team in the 1988 Olympic games led to the team qualifying for the World Cup Finals for the first time in 50 years. The players on that team were David Vanole (Los Angeles Heat), Jeff Duback (Boston Bolts), Steve Trittschuh (St. Louis Steamers), John Doyle (University of San Francisco), Paul Krumpe (Chicago Sting), Desmond Armstrong (Cleveland Force), Paul Caligiuri (SV Meppen, Germany), Kevin Crow (San Diego Sockers), John Harkes (University of Virginia), Rick Davis (Tacoma Stars), Bruce Murray (Washington Stars), John Stollmeyer (Cleveland Force), Tab Ramos (New Jersey Eagles), Brian Bliss (Cleveland Force), Jim Gabarra (Los Angeles Lazers), Peter Vermes (New Jersey Eagles), Hugo Perez (San Diego Sockers), Brent Goulet (Bournemouth F.C.), Frank Klopas (Chicago Sting). The team was coached by Lothar Osiander.

Groups A and C were played in Pusan and Teagu and groups B and D in Taejon, Kwangju and Seoul. Pusan staged a quarter Final and a semi-Final, Taegu and Kwangju a quarter Final, and Seoul a quarter Final, semi-Final and Final

Once again the result was that a number of very talented players appeared in the Olympics. For West Germany, Jurgen Klinsmann and Thomas Hassler, for Sweden, Mats Dahlin and Andreas Limpar, for Italy, Andreas Carnevale, for Brazil, Taffarel, Romario and Bebeto and for the Soviet Union, Alexei Mikhailichenko.

Attendances in South Korea were not as large as those in the Soviet Union in 1980, or the United States in 1984. However, 728,712 watched football, for an average of 22,772.

Group A

17th September 1988

Venue: Pusan

WEST GERMANY 3   (Wuttke 31, Mill 60, 89)
CHINA 0

Half-time: 1-0   Attendance: 24,000

Referee: Juan Cardellino (Uruguay)

WEST GERMANY: Kamps, Horster, Schulz, Funkel, Grahammer, Gortz, Fach (Schreier, 39), Hassler, Wuttke (Kleppinger, 32), Klinsmann, Mill.

CHINA: Zhang Kuikang, Gao Sheng, Zhu Bo, Jia Xiuquan, Mai Chao, Xie Yuxinn (Li Hui, 39), Guo JiJun, Liu Haiguang, Tang Yaodong, Ma Lin (Wang Baoshan, 43), Duan Ju.

17th September 1988

Venue: Taegu

SWEDEN 2   (Thern 44, Hellstrom 45)
TUNISIA 2   (Tarek Dhiab 16, Nabil Maloul 43)

Half-time: 2-2   Attendance: 15,000

Referee: Edgardo Codesal (Mexico)

SWEDEN: S. Andersson, Vaattovaara, Lonn, Arnberg, R. Nilsson, Thern, M. Andersson, Rehn, J. Nilsson, Eskilsson (Dahlin, 65), Hellstrom (Limpar, 85).

TUNISIA: Chouchane: Ouahchi, Mahjoubi, Ben Yahia, Misouri, Sm**IRAN**i, Maaloul, Baouab, Dhiab, Rouissi, Limam.

19th September 1988

Venue: Pusan

WEST GERMANY 4 (Grahammer 4, Fach 50, Mill 55, Wuttke 75)
TUNISIA 1 (Nabil Maaloul 26)

Half-time: 1-1   Attendance: 14,000
Referee: Kenneth Hope (Scotland)
WEST GERMANY: Kamps, Horster, Funkel, Grahammer, Schulz, Fach, Hassler, Wuttke (Schreier, 76), Gortz (Kleppinger, 79), Klinsmann, Mill.
TUNISIA: Chouchane, Ouahchi, Mahjoubi, SmIRANi (Abid, 30), Ben Yahia, Mizouri, Baouab, Maaloul, Rannene, Dhiab, Rouissi.

21st September 1988

Venue: Taegu

SWEDEN 2 (Engqvist 64, Lonn 85)
WEST GERMANY 1 (Walter 60)

Half-time: 0-0   Attendance: 17,000
Referee: Kurt Rothlisberger (Switzerland)
SWEDEN: S. Andersson, R. Nilsson, Lonn, Arnberg, Ljung, Limpar, Engqvist, M. Andersson, J. Nilsson, Dahlin (Rehn, 77), Hellstrom.
WEST GERMANY: Kamps, Horster, Grahammer, Kleppinger, Schulz, Gortz, Hassler, Fach, Wuttke (Schreier, 66), Mill (Walter, 45), Klinsmann.

19th September 1988

Venue: Taegu

SWEDEN 2 (Lonn 19, Hellstrom 42)
CHINA 0

Half-time: 2-0   Attendance: 17,000
Referee: Badara Sene (Senegal)
SWEDEN: S. Andersson, R. Nilsson, Lonn, Arnberg, Ljung, Limpar, M. Andersson, Engqvist, J. Nilsson (Palmer, 84), Dahlin (Lindman, 75), Hellstrom.
CHINA: Zhang Kuikang, Zhu Bo, Guo Jijin, Jia Xiuquan, Mai Chao, Duan Ju, Tang Yaodong, Xie Yuxinn, Gao Sheng, Liu Haiguang (Wang Boashan, 82), Ma Lin.

	P	W	D	L	F	A	Pts
SWEDEN	3	2	1	0	6	3	5
W. GERMANY	3	2	0	1	8	3	4
TUNISIA	3	0	2	1	3	6	2
CHINA	3	0	1	2	0	5	1

Group B

17th September 1988

Venue: Taejon

ZAMBIA 2 (Nyirenda 44, Kalusha Bwalya 66)
IRAQ 2 (Ahmed Radhi 36, Karim Alawi 71)

Half-time: 1-1   Attendance: 29,600
Referee: Jesus Diaz (Colombia)
ZAMBIA: Chabala (R. Mwansa, 60), Chitalu, Melu, Chomba, Mumba, J. Bwalya, Makinka, K. Bwalya, Musonde, Nyirenda, Chansa.
IRAQ: Mohammed Ahmed, Alahi Karim, Ahmed Hassan Kamal, Motar Adnan Dirjal, Jasim Ghaeim, Abo-Awn Natik, Hanna Basil (Sharef Ismael, 46), Noarman Saad Kies, Okal Hibeeb Jafar, Mohammed Hussain Said, Amish Ahmed Radhi.

21st September 1988

Venue: Pusan

TUNISIA 0
CHINA 0

Half-time: 0-0   Attendance: 17,000
Referee: Lennox Sirjuesingh (Trinidad & Tobago)
TUNISIA: Fessi, Bousnina, Ben Neji, Ben Yahia, Chahat, Mahjoubi, Maaloul, Baouab, Mheddhebi (Abid, 58), Dhiab, Rannene (Yakoubi, 67).
CHINA: Zhang Kuikang, Zhu Bo, Jia Xiuquan, Guo Jijun, Zhang Xiaooen, Tang Yaodong, Gao Sheng, Xie Yuxinn, Li Hui, Liu Haiguang (Wang Baoshan, 82), Duan Ju.

17th September 1988

Venue: Kwangju

ITALY 5 (Carnevale 3, Evani 11, Virdis 34, Ferrara 38, Desideri 75)

GUATEMALA 2 (Casteneda Mendez 7, Onelio Paniagua 79)

Half-time: 4-1   Attendance: 12,000

Referee: Shizuo Takada (Japan)

ITALY: Tacconi, Cravero, Tassotti, Ferrara, De Agostini, Colombo, Iachini (Desideri, 69), Evani (Galia, 60), Carnevale, Mauro, Virdis.

GUATEMALA: Jerez Hidalgo, Wellman, Davila Lopez, Mazariegos Bitron (Ortiz Obergon, 78), Monzon Perez, Batres Morales, Castaneda Mendez, Funes Hernandez, Rodas Hurtarte, Paniagua, Perez Solorzano.

19th September 1988

Venue: Taejon

IRAQ 3 (Ahmed Radhi 57, Mudhafar Taufek 67, o.g. 77)

GUATEMALA 0

Half-time: 0-0   Attendance: 23,500

Referee: Jean-Fidele Diramba (Gabon)

IRAQ: Mohammed Ahmed, Motar Adnan Dirjal, Taufek Mudhafar, Ahmed Hassan Kamal, Jasim Ghaeim, Okal Hibeeb Jafar, Hanna Basil (Shahib Laith, 45), Sharef Ismael, Noaman Saad Kies, Mohammed Hussain Said (Sadkhan Younis, 78) Amish Ahmed Radhi.

GUATEMALA: Piccinini, Wellman, Davila Lopez, Mazariegos Bitron, Monzon Perez, Batres Morales (Sandoval, 81), Castaneda Mendez, Funes Hernandez, Rodas Hurtarte (Delva Noriega, 69), Paniagua, Perez Solorzano.

19th September 1988

Venue: Kwangju

ZAMBIA 4 (Kalusha Bwalya 40, 55, 90, Johnson Bwalya 63)

ITALY 0

Half-time: 1-0   Attendance: 9,800

Referee: Keith Hackett (England)

ZAMBIA: Chabala, Chabinga, Melu, Chomba, Mumba, J. Bwalya, Musonda, Makinka, K. Bwalya, Nyirenda (Chikabala, 71), Chansa.

ITALY: Tacconi, Cravero (Crippa, 61), Tassotti, Iachini, Ferrara, Colombo (Pellegrini, 61), Mauro, Galia, De Agostini, Carnevale, Virdis.

21st September 1988

Venue: Kwangju

ZAMBIA 4 (Makinka 53, 85, Kalusha Bwalya 79, 82)

GUATEMALA 0

Half-time: 0-0   Attendance: 9,000

Referee: Mandi Jassim (Bahrain)

ZAMBIA: Chabala, Chabinga, Melu, Mulenga, Mumba, Chambeshi, Musonda, Makinka, K. Bwalya, Nyirenda (P. Mwanza, 79), Chansa.

GUATEMALA: Jerez Hidalgo, Monzon Perez (Batres Morales, 45), Davila Lopez, Mazariegos Bitron, Ortiz Obergon, Rodas Hurtarte, Lopez Meneses, Sandoval (Gardiner Walton, 60), Perez Solorzano, Delva Noriega, Castaneda Mendez.

21st September 1988

Venue: Seoul/Dongdaemon

ITALY 2 (Rizzitelli 59, Mauro 63)
IRAQ 0

Half-time: 2-0   Attendance: 13,000

Referee: Hernan Silva Arce (Chile)

ITALY: Tacconi, Tassotti, Brambati, Ferrara, De Agostini, Crippa, Mauro (Colombo, 81), Iachini, Evani, Virdis, Rizzitelli (Carnevale, 80).

IRAQ: Mohammed Ahmed, Motar Adnan Dirjal, Taufek Mudhafer, Ahmed Hassan Kamal, Jasim Ghaeim, Okal Hibeeb Jafar, Amish Ahmed Radhi, Sharef Ismael, Noaman Saa Kies (Mahmoud Samir Shakir, 45), Mohammed Hussain Said (Alahi Karim, 70), Shahib Laith.

	P	W	D	L	F	A	Pts
ZAMBIA	3	2	1	0	10	2	5
ITALY	3	2	0	1	7	6	4
IRAQ	3	1	1	1	5	4	3
GUATEMALA	3	0	0	3	2	12	0

Group C

18th September 1988

Venue: Pusan

SOUTH KOREA 0
U.S.S.R. 0

Half-time: 0-0   Attendance: 30,000

Referee: Tullio Lanese (Italy)

SOUTH KOREA: Cho Byung-Deuk, Cho Min-Kook, Park Kyung-Hoon, Chung Yong-Hwan, Ku Sang-Bun, Choi Kang-Hee, Yeo Bum-Kyu (Choi Yun-Kyum, 62), Kim Joo-Sung, Byun Byung-Joo, Choi Soon-Ho, Chung Hae-Won (Choi Sang-Kook. 24).

U.S.S.R.: Kharine, Gorloukovitch, Lossev, Ketachvili, Tcherednik, Ponomarev, Mikhailichenko, Dobrovolski, Narbekovas, Borodiuk (Lioutyi, 45), Savitchev (Tatartchouk, 58).

18th September 1988

Venue: Taegu

UNITED STATES 1 (Windischmann, 78)
ARGENTINA 1 (Alfaro Moreno 83)

Half-time: 0-0   Attendance: 18,500

Referee: Jamal Al-Sharif (Syria)

U.S.A.: Vanole, Caligiuri, Krumpe, Crow, Murray, Armstrong, Davis, Ramos (Harkes, 74), Bliss, Vermes, Goulet (Windischmann, 68).

ARGENTINA: Islas, Fabbri, Aguero, Perez, Mayor (Lucca, 54), Lorenzo, Diaz, Siviski, Alfaro, Comas (Aires, 81), Ruidiaz.

20th September 1988

Venue: Pusan

SOUTH KOREA 0
UNITED STATES 0

Half-time: 0-0   Attendance: 22,000

Referee: Baba Laouissi (Morocco)

SOUTH KOREA: Cho Byung-Deuk, Cho Min-Kook, Park Kyung-Hoon, Chung Yong-Hwan, Ku Sang-Bun, Kim Joo-Sung, Choi Kang-Hee (Lee Tae-Ho, 25) (Kim Yong Se, 74), Choi Yun-Kyum, Choi Sang-Kook, Choi Soon-Ho, Byun Byung-Soo.

U.S.A.: Vanole, Caligiuri, Krumpe, Crow, Bliss, Davis, Ramos (Doyle, 45), Harkes (Stollmeyer, 76), Armstrong, Goulet, Klopas.

20th September 1988

Venue: Taegu

U.S.S.R. 2 (Dobrovolski 7, Mikhailichenko 22)
ARGENTINA 1 (Alfaro Moreno 77)

Half-time: 2-0   Attendance: 25,000

Referee: Gerard Biguet (France)

U.S.S.R.: Kharine, Gorloukovitch, Lossev, Ketachvili, Tcherednik, Kouznetsov, Mikhailichenko, Dobrovolski, Narbekovas (Savitchev, 61), Lioutyi, Tatarchouk (Iarovenko, 79).

ARGENTINA: Islas, Lucca, Lorenzo, Aguero, Fabbri, Perez, Cabrera (Aires, 68), Diaz, Siviski, Comas, Alfaro.

22nd September 1988

Venue: Pusan

ARGENTINA 2 (Alfaro Moreno 3, Fabbri 73)
SOUTH KOREA 1 (Noh Soo-Jin)

Half-time: 1-1   Attendance: 30,000
Referee: Christopher Bambridge (Australia)

ARGENTINA: Islas, Monzon, Lorenzo (Cabrera, 74), Lucca, Perez (Russo, 60), Siviski, Diaz, Fabrri, Comas, Alfaro, Aires.

SOUTH KOREA: Cho Byung-Deuk, Chung Yong-Hwan, Park Kyung-Hoon, Cho Min-Kook, Ku Sang-Bun, Byun Byung-Joo, Noh Soo-Jin (Yeo Bum-Kyu, 70), Choi Kang-Hee (Kim Yong-Se, 81), Choi Soon-Ho, Kim Joo-Sung, Choi Sang-Kook.

22nd September 1988

Venue: Taegu

U.S.S.R. 4 (Mikhailichenko 7, Narbekovas 19, Dobrovolski 45)
UNITED STATES 2 (Goulet 65, Doyle 85)

Half-time: 3-0   Attendance: 20,000
Referee: Arnaldo Coelo (Brazil)

U.S.S.R.: Kharine, Gorloukovitch, Lossev, Ketachvili, Iarovenko, Kouznetsov, Mikhailichenko (Borodiuk, 59), Dobrovolski (Ianonis, 54), Narbekovas, Lioutyi, Savitchev.

U.S.A.: Vanole, Caligiuri, Krumpe (Armstrong, 65), Crow, Bliss, Stollmeyer (Goulet, 45), Davis, Doyle, Klopas, Vermes, Murray.

	P	W	D	L	F	A	Pts
U.S.S.R.	3	2	1	0	6	3	5
ARGENTINA	3	1	1	1	4	4	3
SOUTH KOREA	3	0	2	1	1	2	2
U.S.A.	3	0	2	1	3	5	2

Group D

18th September 1988

Venue: Kwangju

AUSTRALIA 1 (Farina 48)
YUGOSLAVIA 0

Half-time: 0-0   Attendance: 12,000
Referee: Juan Carlos Loustau (Argentina)

AUSTRALIA: Olver, Yankos, Davidson, Dunn, Jennings, Peterson, Crino, Wade, Mitchell, Arnold, Farina.

YUGOSLAVIA: Levkovic (Stojanovic, 30), Sabandzovic, Stanojkovic, Barbaric, Spasic, Stojkovic, Katanec, Brnovic, Djukic, Tuce, Milinkovic (Mihic, 69).

18th September 1988

Venue: Taejon

BRAZIL 4 (Edmar 59, Romario 74, 84, Bebeto 86)
NIGERIA 0

Half-time: 0-0   Attendance: 29,512
Referee: Vincent Mauro (U.S.A.)

BRAZIL: Taffarel, Andre Cruz, Luis Carlos, Aloisio, Jorginho, Geovani, Ademir, Edmar (Neto, 63), Milton, Romario, Careca (Bebeto, 73).

NIGERIA: Ngodigha, Nwanu, Ezeogu (Obobaifo, 67), Andrew, Adeshina, Sadi, Eguavon, Okpala, Okwaraji, Yekini, Jorfa (Siasia, 60).

20th September 1988

Venue: Taejon

YUGOSLAVIA 3 (Stojkovic 35 67, Sabanadzovic 49)
NIGERIA 1 (Yekini)

Half-time: 1-0   Attendance: 24,000
Referee: Choi Gil-Soo (South Korea)

YUGOSLAVIA: Stojanovic, Barbaric, Stanojkovic, Jozic, Spasic, Stojkovic, Katanec, Savevski, Sabanadzovic (Brnovic, 69), Mihic, Suker (Milosevic, 69).

NIGERIA: Obi, Nwanu, Adeshina, Andrew, Omokaro (Obiku, 45), Okwaraji (Odegbami, 79), Eguavon, Okpala, Sadi, Siasia, Yekini.

10th September 1988

Venue: Seoul/Dongdaemon

BRAZIL 3 (Romario 20, 57, 61)
AUSTRALIA 0

Half-time: 1-0   Attendance: 15,000
Referee: Karl-Heinz Tritschler (West Germany)
BRAZIL: Taffarel, Aloisio, Batista, Ademir, Andre Cruz, Milton (Joao Paulo, 81), Luis Carlos, Geovani, Edmar, Careca (Bebeto, 75), Romario.
AUSTRALIA: Olver, Yankos, Davidson, Dunn (Van Egmond, 60), Jennings, Paterson, Crino, Wade, Mitchell, Arnold, Farina (Slater, 75).

	P	W	D	L	F	A	Pts
BRAZIL	3	3	0	0	9	1	6
AUSTRALIA	3	2	0	1	2	3	4
YUGOSLAVIA	3	1	0	2	4	4	2
NIGERIA	3	0	0	3	1	8	0

Quarter-Finals

22nd September 1988

Venue: Taejon

BRAZIL 2 (Andre Cruz 25, Bebeto 56)
YUGOSLAVIA 1 (Sabanadzovic 69)

Half-time: 1-0   Attendance: 31,200
Referee: Alexei Spirin (U.S.S.R.)
BRAZIL: Taffarel, Aloisio, Luis Carlos, Batista, Andre Cruz, Ademir, Careca (Andrade, 45), Edmar (Bebeto, 45), Geovani, Milton, Romario.
YUGOSLAVIA: Stojanovic, Jozic, Barbaric, Spasic, Brnovic (Milosevic, 45), Stojkovic, Stanojkovic, Katanec, Sabanadzovic, Mihic (Suker, 60), Tuce.

25th September 1988

Venue: Taegu   (Result is after extra time)

SWEDEN 1 (Hellstrom 84)
ITALY 2 (Virdis 50, Crippa 98)

Half-time: 0-0   Attendance: 3,000
Referee: Gerard Biguet (France)
SWEDEN: S. Andersson, R. Nilsson, Ljung, Lonn, Arnberg, Thern, Limpar (Eskilsson, 23), Engqvist, Hellstrom, M. Andersson, J. Nilsson (Dahlin, 73).
ITALY: Tacconi, Brambali, De Agostini, Tassotti, Ferrara, Iachini, Mauro, Crippa, Virdis, Evani (Colombo, 73), Rizzitelli (Carnevale, 80).

22nd September 1988

Venue: Seoul/Dongdaemon

AUSTRALIA 1 (Kosmina 76)
NIGERIA 0

Half-time: 0-0   Attendance: 12,800
Referee: Michal Listkiewicz (Poland)
AUSTRALIA: Olver, Yankos, Van Egmond, Dunn (Koczka, 69), Jennings, Davidson, Crino, Wade, Mitchell, Arnold, Kosmina (Ollerenshaw, 84).
NIGERIA: Obi, Eguavon, Adeshina, Andrew, Sadi, Okwaraji, Okpala, Siasia, Jorfa (Odegbami, 52), Obiku (Ezeogu, 80), Yekini.

25th September 1988

Venue: Kwangju

WEST GERMANY 4 (Funkel 18, Klinsmann 34, 43, 89)
ZAMBIA 0

Half-time: 3-0   Attendance: 8,200
Referee: Jesus Diaz (Colombia)
WEST GERMANY: Kamps, Schulz, Funkel, Horster, Gortz, Fach, Grahammer, Hassler (Janssen, 77), Wuttke, Klinsmann, Riedle (Kleppinger, 29).
ZAMBIA: Chabala, Chabinga, Melu, Chomba, Mumba, Makinka, J. Bwalya (Mwanza, 54), Musonda, K. Bwalya, Chansa, Nyirenda (Msiska, 54).

25th September 1988

Venue: Pusan

U.S.S.R. 3   (Dobrovolski 50, 54, Mikhailichenko 62)
AUSTRALIA 0

Half-time: 0-0   Attendance: 5,000

Referee: Juan Cardellino (Uruguay)

U.S.S.R.: Kharine, Ketashvili, Cherednik (Fokine, 72), Gorlukovich, Losev, Kuznetsov, Dobrovolski, Mikhailichenko, Tatarchuk (Sklyiarov, 68), Liuti, Narbekovas.

AUSTRALIA: Olver, Van Egmond, Jennings, Yankos, Dunn, Wade, Davidson, Crino, Farina, Mitchell, Graham.

25th September 1988

Venue: Seoul/Dongdaemon

BRAZIL 1   (Geovani 76)
ARGENTINA 0

Half-time: 0-0   Attendance: 21,857

Referee: Kurt Rothlisberger (Switzerland)

BRAZIL: Taffarel, Luiz Carlos, Andre Cruz, Aloisio, Jorginho, Andrade, Milton (Careca, 65), Geovani, Ademir, Bebeto, Romario.

ARGENTINA: Islas, Lorenzo, Lucca, Aguero, Fabbri (Mayor, 65), Hernan Diaz, Perez (Russo, 80), Siviski, Airez, Moreno, Comas.

Semi-Finals

27th September 1988

Venue: Pusan   (Result is after extra time)

U.S.S.R. 3   (Dobrovolski 78, Narbekovas 92, Mikhailichenko 106)
ITALY 2   (Virdis 50, Carnevale 118)

Half-time: 0-0   Attendance: 10,000

Referee: Jamal Al Sharif (Syria)

U.S.S.R.: Kharine, Ketashvili, Cherednik (Yarovenko, 46), Gorlukovich, Losev, Kuznetsov, Dobrovolski, Mikhailichenko, Tatarchuk (Savichev 70), Liufi, Narbekovas.

ITALY: Tacconi, Brambati, Carobbi, Tassotti, Ferrara, Iachini, Mauro, Crippa, Virdis, Evani (Desideri 70), Rizzitelli (Carnevale 88).

27th September 1988

Venue: Seoul/Olympic
(Results is after extra time – Brazil won on penalties)

BRAZIL 1   (Romario 79)
WEST GERMANY 1   (Fach 50)

Half-time: 0-0   Attendance: 55,000

Referee: Keith Hackett (England)

BRAZIL: Taffarel, Luiz Carlos, Andre Cruz, Aloisio, Jorginho, Andrade, Careca, Geovani, Ademir (Milton, 72), Bebeto (Joao Paulo, 62), Romario.

WEST GERMANY: Kamps, Horster, Funkel, Grahammer, Schulz, Hassler, Fach, Wuttke, Gortz (Kleppinger, 96), Mill (Janssen 106), Klinsmann.

Bronze Medal Game

30th September 1988

Venue: The Olympic Stadium, Seoul.

WEST GERMANY 3   (Klinsmann 5, Kleppinger 18, Schreier 68)
ITALY 0

Half-time: 2-0   Attendance: 8,000

Referee: Juan Carlos Loustau (Argentina)

WEST GERMANY: Kamps, Schulz, Funkel, Horster, Sievers (Bommer, 85), Kleppinger, Grahammer, Hassler, Wuttke (Schreier, 61), Klinsmann, Mill.

ITALY: Tacconi, Galia, Carobbi, Tassotti, Brambati, Crippa, Mauro, Colombo, Carnevale, De Agostini, Virdis (Rizzitelli, 58).

Final

1st October 1988

Venue: The Olympic Stadium, Seoul.
(Result is after extra time)

U.S.S.R. 2   (Dobrovolski 60, Savichev 103)
BRAZIL 1   (Romario 29)

Half-time: 0-1   Attendance: 73,000

Referee: Gerard Biguet (France)

U.S.S.R.: Kharine, Ketashvili, Yarovenko, Gorlukovich, Losev, Kuznetsov, Dobbrovolski, Mikhailichenko, Tatarchuk, Liuti (Skliyarov, 115), Narbekovas (Savichev).

BRAZIL: Taffarel, Luiz Carlos, Andre Cruz, Aloisio, Jorginho, Andrade, Milton, Neto (Edmar, 73), Careca, Bebeto (Joao Paulo, 75), Romario.

23rd Olympiad – 1992 – Barcelona

The regulations changed once again before the start of qualifying for Spain in 1992. This time FIFA decreed that the Olympics would be restricted to players Under 23 years of age, creating to a certain degree a world Under-23 championship. However, each country was allowed to field three overage players. The change did not please the International Olympic Committee and the resulting poor attendances led FIFA to charge that the IOC had deliberately downplayed the competition. Only 466,300 watched football for an average of 14,572 per game.

Nevertheless, as Spain advanced to the Final the crowds increased and there were 95,000 in the Camp Nou Stadium in Barcelona to see Spain win the gold medal by defeating Poland 3-2. In effect many of the future stars of world football were on view: Mats Brolin of Sweden, Fausto Asprilla of Colombia, Dino Baggio of Italy and Luis Enrique of Spain. But perhaps most incredible of all was that Ghana won the bronze medal over Australia – another indication of the growing strength of African football.

Group A

24th July 1992

Venue: The Camp Nou Stadium, Barcelona.

ITALY 2   (Melli 14, Albertini 21)
UNITED STATES 1   (Moore 65)

Half-time: 1-0   Attendance: 18,000

Referee: Manuel Diaz Vega (Spain)

ITALY: Antonioli, Verga, Baggio, Bonomi, Favalli (Rossini, 70), Corini, Albertini (Sordo, 85), Matrecano, Marcolin, Melli, Buso.

U.S.A.: Friedel, Rast, Huwiler (Onalfo, 62), Dayak (Moore, 25), Lapper, Reyna, Burns, Imler, Washington, Jones, Allnutt.

24th July 1992

Venue: The La Romereda Stadium, Zaragoza.

POLAND 2   (Juskowiak 7, 80)
KUWAIT 0

Half-time: 1-0   Attendance: 2,000

Referee: Juan Francisco Escobar (Paraguay)

POLAND: Klak, Lapinski, Waldoch, Kozminski, Adamczuk, Staniek, Gesior (Jalocha, 46), Brzeczek, Swierczewski, Juskowiak (Waligora, 83), Kowalczyk.

KUWAIT: Al-Majidi, Abdullah, Al-Lanqawi, Al-Dokhi, Al-Dhafairi (Marzoug, 62), Al-Hamad, Saihan, Al-Khodhari (Al-Eisa, 77), Mohammed, Al-Hadiyah, Al-Huwaidi.

27th July 1992

Venue: The Sarria Stadium, Barcelona.

ITALY 0
POLAND 3 (Juskowiak 4, Staniek 48, Mielcarski 90)

Half-time: 0-1 Attendance: 15,000

Referee: Philip Don (England)

ITALY: Antonioli, Verga, Luzardi, Bonomi, Sordo (Mussi, 57), Corini, Albertini, Marcolin, Favalli (Rossini, 56), Buso, Melli.

POLAND: Klak, Lapinski, Waldoch, Jalocha, Kozminski (Bajar, 82), Adamczuk, Staniek, Brzeczek, Swierczewski, Juskowiak (Mielcarski, 78), Kowalczyk.

27th July 1992

Venue: The La Romereda Stadium, Zaragoza.

UNITED STATES 3 (Brose 56, Lagos 79, Snow 85)
KUWAIT 1 (Al-Hadiyah 16)

Half-time: 0-1 Attendance: 4,500

Referee: An-Yan Lim Kee Chong (Mauritius)

U.S.A.: Friedel, Onalfo, Rast, Lapper, Jones (Allnutt, 70), Moore, Burns, Brose (Lagos, 63), Huwiler, Snow, Reyna.

KUWAIT: Al-Majidi, Abdullah, Al-Lanqawi, Al-Dokhi, Haji, Al-Ahmad, Mohammad (Marzoug, 78), Al-Khodhari, Saihan, Al-Hadiyah, Al-Huwaidi (Ben Hajji, 65).

29th July 1992

Venue: The Sarria Stadium, Barcelona.

ITALY 1 (Melli 9)
KUWAIT 0

Half-time: 1-0 Attendance: 8,000

Referee: Arturo Brizio Carter (Mexico)

ITALY: Antonioli, Verga, Baggio, Matrecano, Bonomi, Favalli, Sordo (Muzzi, 57), Rocco (Rossini, 75), Marcolin, Buso, Melli.

KUWAIT: Al-Majidi, Al-Khaledi, Abdullah, Al-Dokhi, Haji, Thamer Al-Enizi, Al-Anzi (Salamah Al-Enizi, 81), Al-Lanqawi, Al-Hamda, Al-Huwaidi (Ben Hajji, 85), Al-Hadiyah.

29th July 1992

Venue: The La Romereda Stadium, Zaragoza.

UNITED STATES 2 (Imler 20, Snow 52)
POLAND 2 (Kozminski 31, Juskowiak 40)

Half-time: 1-2 Attendance: 3,000

Referee: An-Yan Lim Kee Chong (Mauritius)

U.S.A.: Friedel, Onalfo, Huwiler, Lalas (Moore 45), Allnutt, Lapper, Burns, Reyna, Imler, Lagos (Jones, 72), Snow.

POLAND: Klak, Lapinski, Waldoch, Kozminski, Adamczuk (Kobylanski, 83), Staniek, Bajar (Gesior, 45), Brzeczek, Jalocha, Juskowiak, Kowalczyk.

	P	W	D	L	F	A	Pts
POLAND	3	2	1	0	7	2	4
ITALY	3	2	0	1	3	4	4
U.S.A.	3	1	1	1	6	5	3
KUWAIT	3	0	0	3	1	6	0

Group B

24th July 1992

Venue: The Luis Casanova Stadium, Valencia.

SPAIN 4 (Guardiola 10, Quico 37, Berges 41, Luis Enrique 69)
COLOMBIA 0

Half-time: 3-0 Attendance: 18,000

Referee: Markus Merk (Germany)

SPAIN: Toni, Ferrer, Lopez, Solozabal, Lasa, Luis Enrique, Guardiola (Soler, 83), Abelardo, Berges, Quico, Alfonso (Miguel, 62).

COLOMBIA: Calero, Santa, Bermudez, Cassiani, Osorio, Gaviria, Lozano, Perez (Pacheco, 46), Aristizabal (Canas, 46), Valenciano, Asprilla.

24th July 1992

Venue: The Nova Creu Alta Stadium, Sabadell.

EGYPT 0
QATAR 1 (Nooralla 75)

Half-time: 0-0   Attendance: 2,000

Referee: Philip Don (England)

EGYPT: N. Ibrahim, ElSheshiny, Abdelhamid, ElManzalawy, ElNouemany, Rayyan, Sakr, Khashba, Abdelrazik (El Ghandour, 67), Mostafa Ibrahim, Mohamed Ibrahim (El Masry, 73).

QATAR: Saleh, Al-Mohannadi, Al-Atteya, Suwaid, Al-Kuwari, Maayof, Nooralla, Al-Obaidly (Al-Kuwari, 65), Al-Mulla, Johar (Al-Waheebi, 80), Souf.

29th July 1992

Venue: The Luis Casanova Stadium, Valencia.

SPAIN 2 (Alfonso 40, Quico 80)
QATAR 0

Half-time: 1-0   Attendance: 19,300

Referee: Arturo A. Angeles (U.S.A.)

SPAIN: Toni, Ferrer, Abelardo, Solozabal, Lasa, Soler, Guardiola (Villabona, 63), Berges, Luis Enrique, Alfonso (Pinilla, 69), Quico.

QATAR: Saleh, Al-Mohannadi, Al-Atteya, Suwaid, Al-Kuwari, Maayof, Johar (AlAbdulla 46), Al-Obaidy (Mahmoud, 62), Al-Mulla, Nooralla, Souf.

27th July 1992

Venue: The Luis Casanova Stadium, Valencia.

SPAIN 2 (Solozabal 56, Soler 72)
EGYPT 0

Half-time: 0-0   Attendance: 15,000

Referee: Marcio Rezende de Freitas (Brazil)

SPAIN: Toni, Miguel, Ferrer, Solozabal, Lasa, Luis Enrique, Soler, Guardiola, Berges (Amavisca, 85), Alfonso, Quico (Villabona, 83).

EGYPT: N. Ibrahim, ElSheshiny, ElManzalawy, Sakr, Khafaga, Khashba, Abdelhamid, Adbelrazak, ElNouemany, Mostafa Ibrahim (Mohamed Ibrahim, 65), ElMasry (Rayyan, 59).

29th July 1992

Venue: The Nova Creu Alta Stadium, Sabadell.

COLOMBIA 3 (Gaviria 8, Pacheco 14)
EGYPT 4 (Abdelrazik 27, El Masry 48, Khashba 90, 91)

Half-time: 2-1   Attendance: 4,500

Referee: Ali Mohammed Bujsaim (U.A.E.)

COLOMBIA: Mondragon, Bermudez, Santa, Marulanda, Moreno, Restrepo, Lozano (Uribe, 46), Aristizabal, Gaviria, Asprilla (Calanche, 70), Pacheco.

EGYPT: N. Ibrahim, Abuelw (Sakr, 30), Khafaga, Khaled, ElManzalawy, ElGhandour, Abdelrazik, Khashba, ElNouemany, ElMasry, Sadek (Ibrahim Mostafa, 54).

27th July 1992

Venue: The Nova Creu Alta Stadium, Sabadell.

COLOMBIA 1 (Aristizabal 62)
QATAR 1 (Soufi 89)

Half-time: 1-1   Attendance: 4,000

Referee: Arturo Brizio Carter (Mexico)

COLOMBIA: Calero, Bermudez, Santa, Marulanda, Moreno, Lozano (Canas, Uribe, 46), Gaviria, Restrepo, Pacheco, Asprilla, Aristizabal.

QATAR: Saleh, Al-Mohannadi, Maayof, Suwaid, Al-Kuwari, Al-Atteya, Johar (Al Kuwari, 78), Al-Obaidly, Al-Mulla (Jaloof, 78), Nooralla, Souf.

	P	W	D	L	F	A	Pts
SPAIN	3	3	0	0	8	0	6
QATAR	3	1	1	1	2	3	3
EGYPT	3	1	0	2	4	6	2
COLOMBIA	3	0	1	2	4	9	1

Group C

26th July 1992

Venue: *The Sarria Stadium, Barcelona.*

SWEDEN 0
PARAGUAY 0

Half-time: 0-0 *Attendance:* 15,000

Referee: Lube Spassov (Bulgaria)

SWEDEN: Ekholm, Johansson, Andersson, Bjorklund, Apelstav, Alexandersson (Jansson, 78), Mild, Landberg, Fursth, Brolin, Rodlund (Simpson, 70).

PARAGUAY: Ruiz Diaz, Duarte Villamayor, Gamarra Pavon, Ayala Gavilan, Jara Martinez, Arce Rolon, Neffa Rodriguez (Alvarenga, 54), Sanabria Acuna, Sosa Franco, Ferreira Romero, Campos Velazquez.

26th July 1992

Venue: *The Luis Casanova Stadium, Valencia.*

MOROCCO 1 (Bahja 64)
SOUTH KOREA 1 (Jung Kwang-Seok, 73)

Half-time: 0-0 *Attendance:* 2,000

Referee: Arturo A. Angeles (U.S.A.)

MOROCCO: Achab, Bouhlal, Abrami, Moudakkar (Azim, 85), Naybet, Samadi, Azzouzi, ElHadrioui, Rokbi, Raghib, ElBadraoui (Bahja, 57).

SOUTH KOREA: Sin Bum-Chul, Jung Kwang-Seok, Lee Lim-Saeng, Lee Seung-Hyup, Jung Jae-Kwon, Na Seung-Howa, Noh Jung-Yoon, Cho Jung-Hyun (Sin Tae-Yong, 51), Kim Gwi-Hwa, Seo Jung-Won (Han Jung-Kook, 67), Gwak Kyung-Keun.

28th July 1992

Venue: *The Nova Creu Alta Stadium, Sabadell.*

SWEDEN 4 (Brolin 13, 68, Mild 19, Rodlund 20)
MOROCCO 0

Half-time: 2-0 *Attendance:* 5,000

Referee: Jose Torres Cadena (Colombia)

SWEDEN: Ekholm, Andersson, Johansson, Lilius, Bjorklund, Alexandersson (Gudmundsson 73), Landberg, Mild, Fursth, Brolin, Rodlund (Axeldal, 75).

MOROCCO: Achab, Naybet, Azzouzi, Moudakkar, Bouhlal (Chippo, 85), Abrami, Azim, Dmiai, Ahnouta (Rokbi, 45), ElBadraoui, Bahja.

28th July 1992

Venue: *The Luis Casanova Stadium, Valencia.*

PARAGUAY 0
SOUTH KOREA 0

Half-time: 0-0 *Attendance:* 2,000

Referee: Mohamed Sendid (Algeria)

PARAGUAY: Ruiz Diaz, Gamarra, Sanabria, Ayala, Duarte, Arce, Bourdier, Sosa, Jara, Ferreira (Yegros, 71), Campos (Benitez, 46).

SOUTH KOREA: Sin Bum-Chul, Jung Kwang-Seok, Lee Seung-Hyup, Lee Lim-Saeng, Jung Jae-Kwon, Na Seung-Howa, Noh Jung-Yoon (Han Jung-Kook, 74), Kim Gwi-Hwa, Cho Jung-Hyun (Sin Tae-Yong, 36), Seo Jung-Won, Gwak Kyung-Keun.

30th July 1992

Venue: *The Sarria Stadium, Barcelona.*

SWEDEN 1 (Rodlund 50)
SOUTH KOREA 1 (Seo Jung-Won 28)

Half-time: 0-1 *Attendance:* 12,000

Referee: Manuel Diaz Vega (Spain)

SWEDEN: Ekholm, Andersson, Johansson, Lilius, Bjorklund, Alexandersson, Mild, Landberg (Jansson, 83), Fursth (Gudmundsson, 72), Brolin, Rodlund.

SOUTH KOREA: Sin Bum-Chul, Kang Chul, Lee Lim-Saeng, Lee Seung-Hyup (Noh Jung-Yoon, 57), Na Seung-Howa, Han Jung-Kook, Jung Kwang-Seok, Kim Gwi-Hwa (Gwak Kyung-Keun, 80), Sin Tae-Yong, Jung Jae-Kwon, Seo Jung-Won.

30th July 1992

Venue: *The Luis Casanova Stadium, Valencia.*

PARAGUAY 3 (Arce 43, Caballero 57, Gamarra 70)
MOROCCO 1 (Naybet 87)

Half-time: 1-0 *Attendance:* 2,000

Referee: Markus Merk (Germany)

PARAGUAY: Ruiz Diaz, Sanabria, Gamarra, Ayala, Jara (Marecos, 74), Duarte, Arce, Sosa, Campos, Ferreira (Neffa, 46), Caballero.

MOROCCO: Achab, Bouhlal, Abrami, Moudakkar, Naybet, ElHadrioui, Raghib, Azim, Dmiai, Samadi, Rokbi (Bahja 65).

	P	W	D	L	F	A	Pts
SWEDEN	3	1	2	0	5	1	4
PARAGUAY	3	1	2	0	3	1	4
SOUTH KOREA	3	0	3	0	2	2	3
MOROCCO	3	0	1	2	2	8	1

28th July 1992

Venue: The La Romereda Stadium, Zaragoza.

DENMARK 0
GHANA 0

Half-time: 0-0   Attendance: 5,000

Referee: Juan Francisco Escobar (Paraguay)

DENMARK: Jorgensen, Thomsen, Laursen, Kjeldberg, Helveg, Ekelund (Moller, 62), Hojer Nielsen, Tofting, Larsen (Frank, 23), Molnar, Frandsen.

GHANA: Mensah, Acheampong, Amankwah, Asare, Adjei, Kumah, Lamptey (Preko, 53), Gargo, Quaye, Ayew, Konadu.

Group D

26th July 1992

Venue: The La Romereda Stadium, Zaragoza.

DENMARK 1 (Thomsen 85)
MEXICO 1 (Rotlan pen. 39)

Half-time: 0-1   Attendance: 8,000

Referee: Fabio Baldas (Italy)

DENMARK; Jorgensen, Thomsen, Helveg, Laursen, Frank, Ekelund (Hojer Nielsen, 58), Frandsen, Kjeldberg, Tofting, Mollar (Andersen, 64), Molnar.

MEXICO: Guadarrame, Macias, Cadena, Vidrio, Hernandez (Lopez, 87), Morales, Casteneda, Delgado, Rangel, Rotan, Vazquez (Pineda, 75).

28th July 1992

Venue: The Sarria Stadium, Barcelona.

MEXICO 1 (Castaneda 64)
AUSTRALIA 1 (Arambasic 23)

Half-time: 0-1   Attendance: 10,000

Referee: Kiichiro Tachi (Japan)

MEXICO: Guadaramma, Macias, Vidrio, Hernandez, Cadena, Morales (Arteaga, 50), Delgado, Rangel, Castaneda, Rotlan (Pineda, 75), Alvarez.

AUSTRALIA: Bosnich, Zelic, Mori, Longo, Murphy, Vidmar, Blagojevic, Slifkas, Refenes, Arambasic (Seal, 78), Corica (Veart, 46).

26th July 1992

Venue: The Nova Creu Alta Stadium, Sabadell.

GHANA 3 (Gargo 15, Ayew 80, 90)
AUSTRALIA 1 (Vidmar 91)

Half-time: 1-0   Attendance: 4,000

Referee: Ali Mohammed Bujsaim (U.A.E.)

GHANA: Mensah, Acheampong, Amankwah, Asare, Adjei, Lamptey, Kumah (Preko, 53), Gargo (Kuffour, 60), Aryee, Ayew, Konadu.

AUSTRALIA: Filan, Zelic, Blagojevic, Longo, Murphy, Mori, Slifkas, Okon (Corica, 58), Vidmar, Arambasic (Seal, 46), Refenes.

30th July 1992

Venue: The La Romereda Stadium, Zaragoza.

DENMARK 0
AUSTRALIA 3 (Markovski 32, Mori 60, Vidmar 75)

Half-time: 0-1   Attendance: 3,000

Referee: Fabio Baldas (Italy)

DENMARK: Jorgensen, Thomsen (J.C. Madsen, 60), Helveg, Hojer Nielsen, Laursen, Kjeldberg, Frandsen, Tofting, Larsen, Moller (J.C.M. Madsen, 71) Molnar.

AUSTRALIA: Bosnich, Zelic, Longo, Murphy, Vidmar, Blagojevic (Veart, 44), Okon, Slifkas, Markovski, Mori, Seal.

30th July 1992

Venue: *The Nova Creu Alta Stadium, Sabadell.*

MEXICO 1   (Rotlan 29)
GHANA 1   (Ayew 83)

Half-time: 1-0   Attendance: 6,000

Referee: Jose Torres Cadena (Colombia)

MEXICO: Guadarrama, Macias, Cadena, Vidrio, Hernandez, Lopez (Romero, 59), Castaneda, Delgado, Alvarez, Arteaga, Rotlan (Pineda, 50).

GHANA: Mensah, Acheampong, Amankwah, Asare, Adjei, Kumah, Gargo, Lamptey, Quaye (Preko, 46), Konadu (Amandu, 60), Ayew.

1st August 1992

Venue: *The Luis Casanova Stadium, Valencia.*

SPAIN 1   (Quico 38)
ITALY 0

Half-time: 1-0   Attendance: 28,000

Referee: Marcio Rezende de Freitas (Brazil)

SPAIN: Toni, Solozabal, Lopez, Abelardo, Lasa, Amavisca, Soler, Guardiola, Berges, Alfonso, Quico (Vidal, 85).

ITALY: Antonioli, Verga, Luzardi, Matrecano, Favalli, Baggio, Rocco (Rossini, 77), Albertini, Marcolin, Melli (Muzzi, 77), Buso.

	P	W	D	L	F	A	Pts
GHANA	3	1	2	0	4	2	4
AUSTRALIA	3	1	1	1	5	4	3
MEXICO	3	0	3	0	3	3	3
DENMARK	3	0	2	1	1	4	2

2nd August 1992

Venue: *The Camp Nou Stadium, Barcelona.*

SWEDEN 1   (Andersson 62)
AUSTRALIA 2   (Markovski 30, Murphy 55)

Half-time: 0-1   Attendance: 30,000

Referee: Arturo Brizio Carter (Mexico)

SWEDEN: Ekholm, Andersson, Johansson, Lilius, Bjorklund, Landberg, Jansson (Axeldal, 59), Mild, Fursth, Rodlund, Brolin (Gudmundsson, 30).

AUSTRALIA: Bosnich, Okon, Longo, Murphy, Vidmar, Mori, Zelic, Blagojevic, Markovski, Veart (Refenes, 74), Arambasic (Seal, 63).

Quarter-Finals

1st August 1992

Venue: *The Camp Nou Stadium, Barcelona*

POLAND 2   (Kowalczyk 42, Jalocha 74)
QATAR 0

Half-time: 1-0   Attendance: 25,000

Referee: Mohamed Sendid (Algeria)

POLAND: Klak, Lapinski, Waldoch, Jalocha, Kozminski, Adamczuk (Gesior, 80), Staniek, Brzeczek, Swierczewski, Juskowiak (Kobylanski, 86), Kowalczyk.

QATAR: Saleh, Al-Mohammadi, Mahmoud, Al-Obaidly (Ibrahim, 75), Maayof, AlAbdulla, Al-Kuwari, Al-Atteya, Johar, Al-Waheebi (Jaloof, 46), Souf.

2nd August 1992

Venue: *The La Romereda Stadium, Zaragoza.*
(Result is after extra time)

GHANA 4   (Ayew 17, 55 121, Rahman 114)
PARAGUAY 2   (o.g. 78, Campos 81)

Half-time: 1-0   Attendance: 5,000

Referee: Ali Mohammed Bujsaim (U.A.E.)

GHANA: Mensah, Acheampong, Amankwah, Kuffour, Asare, Lamptey, Aryee (Rahman, 46), Nyarko (Kalilu, 73), Kumah, Preko, Ayew.

PARAGUAY: Ruiz Diaz, Gamarra, Sanabria, Ayala, Duarte, Alvarenga (Neffa, 61), Sosa, Arce, Jara, Ferreira, Caballero (Campos, 46).

Semi-Finals

5th August 1992

Venue: The Camp Nou Stadium, Barcelona.

POLAND 6 (Kowalczyk 28, 90, Juskowiak 43, 55, 80, o.g. 70)

AUSTRALIA 1   (Veart 36)

Half-time: 2-1   Attendance: 45,000

Referee: Marcio Rezende de Freitas (Brazil)

POLAND: Klak, Lapinski, Waldoch, Kozminski, Jalocha (Bjor, 81), Adamczuk, Brzeczek (Gesior, 83), Staniek, Swierczewski, Juskowiak, Kowalczyk.

AUSTRALIA: Bosnich, Okon, Longo, Murphy, Mori (Arambasic 79), Blagojevic, Zelic, Slifkas, Markovski (Seal 68), Vidmar, Veart.

5th August 1992

Venue: The Luis Casanova Stadium, Valencia.

SPAIN 2   (Abelardo 26, Berges 54)

GHANA 0

Half-time: 1-0   Attendance: 36,000

Referee: Arturo Brizio Carter (Mexico)

SPAIN; Toni, Solozabal, Lopez, Abelardo, Lasa, Luis Enrique, Ferrer, Guardiola, Berges, Amavisca (Vidal, 86), Quico (Pinilla, 78).

GHANA: Mensah, Kalilu, Kuffour, Gargo, Amankwah, Lamptey, Kumah, Asare, Aryee (Rahman, 64), Ayew, Preko.

Bronze Medal Game

7th August 1992

Venue: The Camp Nou Stadium, Barcelona.

AUSTRALIA 0

GHANA 1   (Asare 20)

Half-time: 0-1   Attendance: 15,000

Referee: Manuel Diaz Vega (Spain)

AUSTRALIA; Filan, Zelic, Longo, Murphy (Popovic, 25), Mori, Maloney (Markovski, 72), Blagojevic, Okon, Vidmar, Hasler, Refenes.

GHANA: Dossey (Addo, 63), Acheamponmg, Amankwah, Asare, Adjei, Gargo, Kumah, Lamptey (Quaye, 46), Aryee, Preko, Ayew.

Final

8th August 1992

Venue: The Camp Nou Stadium, Barcelona.

POLAND 2   (Kowalczyk 46, Staniek 75)

SPAIN 3   (Abelardo 65, Quico 70, 90)

Half-time: 1-0   Attendance: 95,000

Referee: Jose Torres Cadena (Colombia)

POLAND: Klak, Lapinski, Waldoch, Kozminski, Jalocha (Swierczewski, 55), Staniek, Brzeczek, Kobylanski, Gesior, Kowalczyk, Juskowiak.

SPAIN: Toni, Lopez, Solozabal, Abelardo, Lasa (Amavisca, 51), Ferrer, Guardiola, Luis Enrique, Berges, Alfonso, Quico.

24th Olympiad – 1996 – Atlanta

Men's Competition

Nigeria became the first African nation to win a major soccer title when they defeated Argentina 3-2 to win the gold medal in Athens, Georgia on 3rd August. Atlanta '96 was something of a misnomer as far as soccer was concerned because none of the soccer was played in the Olympic City itself. Instead the games were spread around the American south with Birmingham, Alabama, Orlando and Miami in Florida, Washington D.C. and Athens, Georgia playing host. Attendances, as they were in the Los Angeles games of 1984, were very high and the games were lively, skilful and entertaining with a much higher number of goals being scored than in other international tournaments during this time frame.

Brazil were the pre-tournament favourites, but they received a setback when defeated by Japan in the Group Competition. However, they did go on to reach the semi-final and when they were leading 3-1 against Nigeria, a team they had beaten earlier, it appeared as if the prediction was going to come true. But the Nigerians had other ideas and staged a great comeback to win 4-3 and advance to the Final against Argentina. The Final, the Semi-finals and the Bronze Medal Game were all played in Sanford Stadium at the University of Georgia in Athens, Georgia. Overall 1,364,142 fans watched the games for an average of 40,122 a game – hugely in excess of the total in Barcelona '92 where the average was just 14,572.

Group A

20th July 1996

Venue: *Legion Field in Birmingham, Alabama.*

UNITED STATES 1 (Reyna 1)
ARGENTINA 3 (G. Lopez 27, Crespo 56, Simeone 90)

Half-time: 1-1   Attendance: 83,810

Referee: Lucien Bouchardeau (Niger)

U.S.A.: Keller, Peay (Vargas, 85), Lalas, Pope, Hejduk, Maisonneuve, Silvera (McKeon, 72), Reyna, Baba, Kirovski, Wood (Joseph, 46).

ARGENTINA: Bossio, Zanetti, Ayala (Paz, 83), Sensini, Chamot, Simeone, Almeyda, G. Lopez, Ortega (C. Lopez, 70), Delgado (Gallardo, 65), Crespo.

20th July 1996

Venue: *R.F.K. Stadium in Washington D.C.*

PORTUGAL 2 (Afonso Martins 13, 68)
TUNISIA 0

Half-time: 1-0   Attendance: 34,746

Referee: Antonio Pereira Da Silva (Brazil)

PORTUGAL: Costinha, Rui Bento, Peixe, Andrade, Nuno Capucho (Dominguez, 57), Paulo Alves (Nuno Gomes, 70), Afonso Martins, Rui Jorge, Vidigal, Litos, Dani (Kennedy, 78).

TUNISIA: ElQuaer, Badra (Gabsi, 82), Mkacher (Baccouche, 46), Chouchane, Beya, Ghodbane, Sellimi, Bouazizi, Jaidi, Chrouda, Ben Simane (Ben Younes, 35).

22nd July 1996

Venue: Legion Field in Birmingham, Alabama.

UNITED STATES 2 (Kirovski 38, Maisonneuve 90)
TUNISIA 0

Half-time: 1-0   Attendance: 45,687

Referee: Hugh Dallas (Scotland)

U.S.A.: Keller, Hejduk, Lalas, Pope, Peay, Joseph, Silvera, Reyna, Maisonneuve, Baba, Kirovski (Wood, 90).

TUNISIA: ElQuaer, Baccouche (Bokri, 57), Badra, Chouchane, Beya, Gabai, Ghodbane (Ben Younes, 63), Sellimi, Jaballah, Jaidi, Ben Chrouda.

24th July 1996

Venue: Legion Field in Birmingham, Alabama.

ARGENTINA 1 (Ortega 5)
TUNISIA 1 (Mkacher 74)

Half-time: 1-0   Attendance: 16,826

Referee: Pirom Un-Prasert (Thailand)

ARGENTINA: Cavallero, Ayala, Chamot, Zanetti, Simeone (Bassedas), Crespo (Delgado), Ortega, Paz, G. Lopez, Almeyda, C. Lopez (Gallardo).

TUNISIA: El Ouaer, Baccouche, Badra, Mkacher, Jaidi, Kanzari, Beya, Bouazizi, Ben Younes (Gabsi), Ghodbane, Sellimi.

22nd July 1996

Venue: R.F.K. Stadium in Washington D.C.

ARGENTINA 1 (Ortega 45)
PORTUGAL 1 (Nuno Gomes 70)

Half-time: 1-0   Attendance: 25,811

Referee: Omar Saleh Saad Al Muhanna (Saudi Arabia)

ARGENTINA: Bossio, Zanetti, Ayala, Sensini, Chamot, Simeone, Almeyda, Ortega, Morales (G. Lopez, 77), C. Lopez, Crespo.

PORTUGAL: Costinha (Nuno, 40), Calado, Rui Bento, Peixe (Paulo Alves, 12), Nuno Capucho, Afonso Martins, Rui Jorge, Vidigal, Litos, Dani (Porfirio, 46), Nuno Gomes.

	P	W	D	L	F	A	Pts
ARGENTINA	3	1	2	0	5	3	5
PORTUGAL	3	1	2	0	4	2	5
U.S.A.	3	1	1	1	4	4	4
TUNISIA	3	0	1	2	1	5	1

Group B

24th July 1996

Venue: R.F.K. Stadium in Washington D.C.

UNITED STATES 1 (Maisonneuve 75)
PORTUGAL 1 (Paulo Alves 33)

Half-time: 0-1   Attendance: 58,012

Referee: Edward Lennie (Australia)

U.S.A.: Keller, Pope, Peay (Pollard, 67), Lalas, Hejduk, Joseph, Reyna, Silvera (Wood, 53), Maisonneuve (McKeon, 83), Baba, Kirovski.

PORTUGAL: Nuno Herlander, Rui Bento, Andrade, Rui Jorge, Litos, Vidigal, Calado, Kenedy, Dominguez (Dani, 61, Beto, 84), Paulo Alves, Porfirio (Capucho, 55).

20th July 1996

Venue: The Citrus Bowl in Orlando, Florida

SPAIN 1 (Oscar 80)
SAUDI ARABIA 0

Half-time: 0-0   Attendance: 28,174

Referee: Pierluigi Collina (Italy)

SPAIN: Mora, Mendieta, Aranzabal, Santi, Corino, Jose Ignacio, De la Pena (Karanka, 72), Idiakez (Roberto, 63), Morientes (Oscar, 63) Lardin, Raul.

SAUDI ARABIA: Al-Sadig, Al-Khilaiwi, Zebermawi, Al-Jahani, Anwar Amin, Suliman (Sifein, 82), Al-Harbi, Al-Dossary, Fatatah.

20th July 1996

Venue: The Orange Bowl in Miami, Florida.

FRANCE 2 (Pires 11, Maurice 74)
AUSTRALIA 0

Half-time: 1-0   Attendance: 14,322

Referee: Roberto Ruben Ruscio (Argentina)

FRANCE: Letizi, Djetou, Bonnissel, Moreau, Candela, Makelele, Dhorasoo, Dacourt (Sibierski, 46), Legwinski, Maurice (Vairelles, 80), Pires (Wiltord, 89).

AUSTRALIA: Juric, Moric, Babic, Muscat, Casserly, Horvat (Aloisi, 79), Corica, Foxe, Tiatto, Viduka (Spiteri, 69), Vidmar.

24th July 1996

Venue: The Citrus Bowl in Orlando, Florida.

SPAIN 3 (Raul 40, 90, Santi 86)
AUSTRALIA 2 (Vidmar 3, 11)

Half-time: 1-2   Attendance: 12,050

Referee: Hugh Dallas (Scotland)

SPAIN: Mora, Mendieta (Lardin, 32), Aranzabal, Javi Navarro, Santi, Karanka, Oscar, Jose Ignacio (De la Pena, 60), Paul, Morientes (Idiakez, 70) Dani.

AUSTRALIA: Juric, Babic, Muscat, Horvat, Casserly, Moric (Aloisi, 56), Tsenkenis, Corica, Viduka, Vidmar (Lozanovski, 72), Spiteri (Tiatto, 36).

22nd July 1996

Venue: The Orange Bowl in Miami, Florida.

AUSTRALIA 2 (Tsekenis 11, Viduka 63)
SAUDI ARABIA 1 (Al-Kilaiwi 37)

Half-time: 1-1   Attendance: 5,997

Referee: Esfandiar Baharmast (U.S.A.)

AUSTRALIA: Juric, Babic, Moric, Muscat, Casserly, Corica, Tsekenis, Aloisi, Vidmar, Viduka, Spiteri.

SAUDI ARABIA: Al-Sadig, Al-Khilaiwi, Zebermawi, Al-Jahani, Anwar Amin, Suliman (Al-Marzoug, 26, Rahman, 70), Al-Harbi, Al-Rashaid, Al-Garni (Al-Dosari, 26), Falatah, Al-Dosary.

24th July 1996

Venue: The Orange Bowl in Miami, Florida.

FRANCE 2 (Maurice 20, Sibierski 49)
SAUDI ARABIA 1 (Anwar Amin 26)

Half-time: 1-0   Attendance: 4,615

Referee: Benito Archundia Tellez (Mexico)

FRANCE: Letizi, Djetou (Moreau, 85), Laville, Candela, Dieng, Dacourt, Bonnissel, Dhorasso, Sibierski (Wiltord, 62), Maurice, Pires (Legwinski, 73).

SAUDI ARABIA: Al Sadig, Al Jahni (Al Shahrani, 75), Al Kilaiwi, Zebermawi, Suliman, Anwar Amin, Al Harbi, Al Rashaid, Al Dossari, Falatah (Al Karai, 46), Al Dossary.

22nd July 1996

Venue: The Citrus Bowl in Orlando, Florida.

FRANCE 1 (Legwinski 38)
SPAIN 1 (Oscar 85)

Half-time: 1-0   Attendance: 16,773

Referee: Pirom Un-Prasert (Thailand)

FRANCE: Letizi, Djetou, Moreau, Toyes, Candela, Dieng, Makelele (Sibierski, 90), Dhorasoo, Legwinski, Vairelles, Wiltord (Pires, 79).

SPAIN: Mora, Javi Navarro, Santi, Corino (Lardin), Oscar, Roberto (Aranzabal, 65), Jose Ignacio, Karanka, Sietes (De la Pena, 65), Raul, Dani.

	P	W	D	L	F	A	Pts
FRANCE	3	2	1	0	5	2	7
SPAIN	3	2	1	0	5	3	7
AUSTRALIA	3	1	0	2	4	6	3
SAUDI ARABIA	3	0	0	3	2	5	0

Group C

21st July 1996

Venue: R.F.K. Stadium in Washington D.C.

SOUTH KOREA 1   (Yoon Jong Hwan 42)
GHANA 0

Half-time: 1-0   Attendance: 45,946
Referee: Edward Lennie (Australia)
SOUTH KOREA: See Dong Myong, Choi Sung Yong, Lee Sang Hun, Lee Ki Hyung, Yoon Jong Hwan (Chung Sang Nam, 78), Kim Hyun Su, Kim Sang Hoon, Lee Lim Saeng, Choi Yoon Yeol, Ha Seok Ju, Hwang Sun Hong (Choi Yong Su, 79).
GHANA: S. Addo, Welbeck (Amoako, 80), J. Addo, Duodu, Osei S. Kuffor, Ahinful, Kennedy (Aboagye, 56), Hagan, Sabah, Akunnor, Duah.

21st July 1996

Venue: Legion Field in Birmingham, Alabama.

MEXICO 1   (Palencia 82)
ITALY 0

Half-time: 0-0   Attendance: 44,211
Referee: Hugh Dallas (Scotland)
MEXICO: Campos, Suarez, Villa, Davino, Lara, J. Garcia, Sol, Pardo, Alfaro (Blanco, 69), Abundis (Panencia, 66), I. Garcia.
ITALY: Pagliuca, Nesta, Cannavaro, Galante, Fresi, Crippa, Brambilla (Morfeo, 64), Tommasi, Pecchia, Branca, Lucarelli (Delvecchio, 77).

23rd July 1996

Venue: Legion Field in Birmingham, Alabama.

MEXICO 0
SOUTH KOREA 0

Half-time: 0-0   Attendance: 26,111
Referee: Lucian Bouchardeau (Niger)
MEXICO: Campos, Suarez, Davino, Pardo, Villa, Lara, R. Garcia, Sol, Blanco (Alfaro, 62), L. Garcia, Palencia (Abundis, 69).
SOUTH KOREA: Seo Dong Myung, Choi Sung Yong, Lee Sang Hun, Kim Hyun Su, Lee Lim Saeng (Lee Kyung Soo, 16), Lee Ki Hyung, Yoon Jong Hwan, Choi Yoon Yeol, Choi Yong Su, Ha Seok Ju, Hwang Sun Hong (Lee Won Shik 35, Sam Nam Chung, 89).

23rd July 1996

Venue: R.F.K. Stadium in Washington D.C.

GHANA 3   (Sabah 15, 74, Ahinful 63)
ITALY 2   (Branca 8, 44)

Half-time: 1-2   Attendance: 27,849
Referee: Jose Garcia Aranda (Spain)
GHANA: S. Addo, J. Addo, Osei M. Kuffour, Sabah, Duodu, Hagan, Ahinful, Akunnor (Yahaya, 31), Duah, Aboagye, Amoako.
ITALY: Pagliuca, Sartor (Pistone, 78), Nesta, Cannavaro, Galante, Fresi, Crippa, Tommasi, Bernardini (Pecchia, 69), Branca, Lucarelli (Delvecchio, 46).

25th July 1996

Venue: R.F.K. Stadium in Washington D.C.

MEXICO 1   (Abundis 65)
GHANA 1   (Hagan 44)

Half-time: 0-1   Attendance: 30,237
Referee: Antonio Pereira da Silva (Brazil)
MEXICO: Campos, Suarez, Davino, Pardo, Villa, Lara, R. Garcia (Blanco, 62), Sol (Arellano, 52), L. Garcia, Alfaro, Abundis (Palencia, 68).
GHANA: S. Addo, J. Addo, Osei M. Kuffour, Sabah, Duodu (Baidoo, 46), Yahaya, Hagan (Welbeck, 74), Ahinful, Duah, Aboagye, Amoako.

25th July 1996

Venue: Legion Field in Birmingham, Alabama.

ITALY 2   (Branca 24, 82)
SOUTH KOREA 1   (Lee Ki Hyung 62)

Half-time: 1-0   Attendance: 28,319
Referee: Robert Ruben Ruscio (Argentina)
ITALY: Pagliuca, Nesta, Cannavaro, Fresi, Pistone, Tommasi, Ametrano, Crippa, Brambilla (Pecchia, 75), Branca, Delvecchio (Morfeo, 53).
SOUTH KOREA: Seo Dong Myung, Choi Sung Yong, Lee Sang Hun, Kim Hyun Su, Lee Lim Saeng, Choi Yoon Yeol, Lee Kyung Soo (Chung Sang Nam, 79), Lee Ki Hyung, Yoon Jong Hwan, Choi Yong Su, Ha Seok Ju.

	P	W	D	L	F	A	Pts
MEXICO	3	1	2	0	2	1	5
GHANA	3	1	1	1	4	4	4
SOUTH KOREA	3	1	1	1	2	2	4
ITALY	3	1	0	2	4	5	3

23rd July 1996

Venue: The Orange Bowl in Miami, Florida.

BRAZIL 3 (Ronaldinho 35, Juninho 61, Bebeto 84)
HUNGARY 1 (Madar 58)

Half-time: 1-0   Attendance: 34,871

Referee: Gamal Mahmoud El-Ghandour (Egypt)

BRAZIL: Dida, Ze Maria, Aldair, Ronaldo Guira, Roberto Carlos, Flavio Conceicao, Juninho, Ze Elias, Bebeto, Rivaldo (Amaral, 75), Ronaldinho (Savio, 75).

HUNGARY: Safar, Bukszegi, Sebok, Herzceg, Peto, Lendvai, Molnar, Dragoner (Madar, 46), Lisztes (Szanto, 65), Szatmari, Dombi.

Group D

21st July 1996

Venue: The Citrus Bowl in Orlando, Florida.

NIGERIA 1 (Kanu 77)
HUNGARY 0

Half-time: 0-0   Attendance: 25,303

Referee: Pirom Un-Prasert (Thailand)

NIGERIA: Dosu, C. Babayaro, West, Kanu (Ikpeba, 80), Ukechukwu, Amunike (Lawal, 75), Babangida, Okocha, Amokachi, Oliseh, Obaraku.

HUNGARY: Safar, Sebok, Peto, Lendvai, Molnar, Dragoner, Szatmari, Lisztes, Dombi, Sandor (Preisinger, 83), Egressy (Herzceg, 75).

23rd July 1996

Venue: The Citrus Bowl in Orlando, Florida.

NIGERIA 2 (Babangida 82, Okocha pen. 89)
JAPAN 0

Half-time: 0-0   Attendance: 22,734

Referee: Pierluigi Collina (Italy)

NIGERIA: Dosu, C. Babayaro, West, Ukechukwu, Amunike (Lawal, 72), Okocha, Oliseh, Obaraku, Kanu (Ikpeba, 86), Babangida, Amokachi.

JAPAN: Kawaguchi, Shirai, Suzuki, Tanaka (Akiba, 72), Matsuda, Hattori (Hironaga, 86), Maezono, Ito, Nakata, Michiki, Jo.

21st July 1996

Venue: The Orange Bowl in Miami, Florida.

JAPAN 1 (Ito 72)
BRAZIL 0

Half-time: 0-0   Attendance: 46,713

Referee: Benito Archundia Tellez (Mexico)

JAPAN: Kawaguchi, Suzuki, Tanaka, Hattori, Maezono, Ito, Jo (Matsubara, 86), Endo (Shirai, 75), Matsuda, Nakata (Uemura, 82), Michiki.

BRAZIL: Dida, Ze Maria, Aldair, Ronaldo Guira, Flavio Conceicao, Roberto Carlos, Bebeto, Amaral (Ze Elias, 46), Juninho, Rivaldo, Savio (Ronaldo, 64).

25th July 1996

Venue: The Orange Bowl in Miami, Florida.

BRAZIL 1 (Ronaldinho 30)
NIGERIA 0

Half-time: 1-0   Attendance: 55,650

Referee: Esfandiar Baharmast (U.S.A.)

BRAZIL: Dida, Ze Maria, Aldair, Ronaldo Guira, Roberto Carlos, Flavio Conceicao, Juninho, Ze Elias, Bebeto, Rivaldo (Amaral, 71), Ronaldinho (Savio, 83).

NIGERIA: Dosu, West, Ukechukwu, Oliseh, Obaraku, Amunike (Ikpeba, 63), Okocha, Obafemi (Lawal, 47), Kanu, Babangida (Babatunde, 81), Amokachi.

25th July 1996

Venue: The Citrus Bowl in Orlando, Florida.

JAPAN 3   (Maezono 39, 90, Uemura 90)
HUNGARY 2   (Sandor 2, Madar 48)

Half-time: 0-1   Attendance: 20,834

Referee: Lucian Bouchardeau (Niger)

JAPAN: Kawaguchi, Suzuki, Tanaka, Matsuda, Hattori, Maezono, Ito, Michiki, Jo, Morioka (Hironaga, 36), Matsubara (Uemura, 89).

HUNGARY: Safar, Bukszegi, Peto, Lendvai, Molnar, Madar, Lisztes (Szanto, 76), Dombi, Sandor, Egressy, Preisinger (Zavadsky, 74).

	P	W	D	L	F	A	Pts
BRAZIL	3	2	0	1	4	2	6
NIGERIA	3	2	0	1	3	1	6
JAPAN	3	2	0	1	4	4	6
HUNGARY	3	0	0	3	3	7	0

Quarter-Finals

27th July 1996

Venue: The Orange Bowl in Miami, Florida.

PORTUGAL 2   (Nuno Capucho 7, Calado pen. 105)
FRANCE 1   (Maurice pen. 49)

Half-time: 1-0   Attendance: 22,339

Referee: Pierluigi Collina (Italy)

PORTUGAL: Nuno Herlander, Rui Bento, Peixe, Andrade, Nuno Capucho (Dani, 51), Rui Jorge (Afonso Martins, 62), Vidigal, Calado, Litos (Beto, 13), Kenedy, Paulo Alves.

FRANCE: Letizi, Djetou, Bonnissel, Moreau, Dieng, Makefele, Dhorasoo, Maurice, Dacourt (Vairelles, 61), Legwinski, Pires, Wiltord.

27th July 1996

Venue: Legion Field in Birmingham, Alabama.

ARGENTINA 4   (Crespo 47, pen 88, o.g. 52, C. Lopez 66)
SPAIN 0

Half-time: 0-0   Attendance: 43,507

Referee: Gamal Mahmoud El-Ghandour (Egypt)

ARGENTINA: Cavallero, Ayala, Zanetti, Sensini, Pineda, Bassedas (Simeone, 78), Almeyda, Crespo, Ortega (Gallardo, 75), Morales (G. Lopez, 80), C. Lopez.

SPAIN: Mora, Aranzabal, Navarro, Corino, Karanka, Oscar, Roberto (Lardin, 56), Jose Ignacio, Idiakez (De La Pena, 56), Raul, Dani.

29th July 1996

Venue: Legion Field in Birmingham, Alabama.

MEXICO 0
NIGERIA 2   (Okocha 20, C. Babayaro 85)

Half-time: 0-1   Attendance: 44,788

Referee: Omar Saleh Saad Al-Muhanna (Saudi Arabia)

MEXICO: Campos, Suarez, Davino, Perdo, Villa, Lara, R. Garcia (Blanco, 46), Sol (Arellano, 24). L. Garcia, Alfaro (Alvarado, 66), Abundis.

NIGERIA: Dosu, C. Babayaro, West, Ukechukwu, Oliseh, Obaraku, Amunike (Lawal, 86), Okocha, Kanu (Fatusi, 67), Babangida (Ikpeba, 56), Amokachi.

28th July 1996

Venue: The Orange Bowl in Miami, Florida.

BRAZIL 4   (o.g. 17, Ronaldinho 56, 62, Bebeto 72)
GHANA 2   (Akunnor 23, Aboagye 53)

Half-time: 1-1   Attendance: 45,257

Referee: Pirom Un-Prasert (Thailand)

BRAZIL: Dida, Ze Maria, Aldair, Ronaldo Guira, Roberto Carlos (Andre Luiz, 86), Flavio Conceicao, Juninho, Ze Elias, Amaral (Rivaldo, 65) Bebeto, Ronaldinho.

GHANA: S. Addo, J. Addo, Osei M. Kuffour, Sabah, Duodo, Yahaya, Ahinful, Akunnor, Duah (Osei Kuffour, 88), Aboagye, Amoako (Hagan, 35).

Semi-Finals

30th July 1996

Venue: Sanford Stadium in Athens, Georgia.

ARGENTINA 2 (Crespo 55, 62)
PORTUGAL 0

Half-time: 0-0   Attendance: 78,212
Referee: Esfandiar Baharmast (U.S.A.)
ARGENTINA: Cavallero, Zanetti, Ayala, Sensini, Chamot, Almeyda, Morales (G. Lopez, 67), Bassedas (Simeone, 70), Ortega, C. Lopez, Crespo (Gallardo, 79)
PORTUGAL: Nuno Herlander, Andrade (Paulo Alves, 65), Peixe, Rui Bento, Rui Jorge, Vidigal, Calado, Afonso Martins (Porfirio, 58), Beto (Nuno Afonso, 8), Dominguez, Nuno Gomes.

31st July 1996

Venue: Sanford Stadium in Athens, Georgia.

NIGERIA 4 (o.g. 20, Ikpeba 77, Kanu 90, 94)
BRAZIL 3 (Flavio Conceicao 2, 37, Bebeto 27)

Half-time: 1-3   Attendance: 78,587
Referee: Jose Garcia-Aranda (Spain)
NIGERIA: Dosu, C. Babayaro, Ukechukwu, West, Obaraku (Oruma, 83), Babangida (Fatusi, 68), Lawal, Okocha, Amunike (Ikpeba, 46), Kanu, Amokachi.
BRAZIL: Dida, Ze Maria, Aldair, Ronaldo Guira, Roberto Carlos, Flavio Conceicao, Amaral, Juninho (Rivaldo, 67), Ze Elias, Bebeto, Ronaldinho (Savio, 85).

Bronze Medal Game

2nd August 1996

Venue: Sanford Stadium in Athens, Georgia.

BRAZIL 5 (Ronaldinho 5, Flavio Conceicao 10, Bebeto pen 47, 54, 75)
PORTUGAL 0

Half-time: 2-0   Attendance: 68,173
Referee: Gamal Mahmoud El-Ghandour (Egypt)
BRAZIL: Dida, Ze Maria, Aldair (Narciso, 81), Ronaldo Guira, Roberto Carlos, Flavio Conceicao, Amaral (Marcelinho Paulista, 85), Juninho, Ze Elias, Bebeto, Ronaldinho (Luizao, 79).
PORTUGAL: Paulo Costinha, Rui Bento, Peixe (Rui Jorge, 57), Nuno Capucho (Afonso Martins, 46), Nuno Afonso, Videgal, Calado, Kenedy, Donmingues, Dani, Paulo Alves (Nuno Gomes, 46).

Final

3rd August 1996

Venue: Sanford Stadium in Athens, Georgia

NIGERIA 3 (C. Babayaro 28, Amokachi 74, Amunike 89)
ARGENTINA 2 (C. Lopez 2, Crespo pen 50)

Half-time: 1-1   Attendance: 86,117
Referee: Pierluigi Collina (Italy)
NIGERIA: Dosu, C. Babayaro, West, Ukechukwu, Obaraku (Oruma, 61), Oliseh, Ikpeba (Amunike, 72), Okocha (Lawal, 59), Babangida, Kanu, Amokachi.
ARGENTINA: Cavallero, Zanetti, Ayala, Sensini, Chamot, Almeyda, C. Lopez, Bassedas, Ortega, Crespo, Morales (Simeone, 58).

Women's Competition

Women's soccer became an Olympic sport for the first time in 1996 with overwhelming success. Almost totally ignored and overshadowed by the men's game for many years, women's soccer started to make an impact when the first World Championship was held in China in 1991, but it really came of age during the Atlanta games attracting huge crowds. The Final itself drew 76,481 – the largest crowd ever to watch a women's sporting event of any kind anywhere. The gold medal was won by the United States, who had also won the first World Championship by beating Norway in the Final, and had always been in the forefront of the rise in popularity of women's soccer. The Americans beat China in an exciting and well played Olympic Final after overcoming arch-rivals Norway in the semi-final. One year before this, the Norwegians had beaten the Americans in the semi-final of the second World Championship and gone on to capture the title. Now it was time for the Americans to turn the tables once again.

Group E

21st July 1996

Venue: *The Citrus Bowl in Orlando, Florida.*

UNITED STATES 3   (Venturini 36, Hamm 40, Milbrett 49)
DENMARK 0

Half-time: 2-0   Attendance: 25,003
Referee: Claudia Vasconcelos Guedes (Brazil)
U.S.A.: Scurry, Overbeck, Chastain, Fawcett, MacMillan, Foudy, Venturini, Lilly, Hamm (Gabarra, 76), Milbrett (Roberts, 67), Akers (Parlow, 62).
DENMARK: Larsen, B. Madsen, Flaeng, Holm, C. Pedersen, Christensen, Kolding (Laursen, 68), Krogh (Bonde, 80), L. Madsen (Jensen, 46), Terp, Nielsen.

21st July 1996

Venue: *The Orange Bowl in Miami, Florida.*

CHINA 2   (Shi Guihong 30, Zhao Lihong 31)
SWEDEN 0

Half-time: 2-0   Attendance: 46,713
Referee: Gamal Mahmoud El-Ghandour (Egypt)
CHINA: Gao Hong, Wang Liping (Liu Ying, 64), Fan Yunjie, Xie Hulin, Zhao Lihong, Shui Qingxia (Yu Hongqti, 59), Sun Wen, Liu Ailing, Sun Qingmei, Wen Lirong, Shi Guihong (Wei Haiying, 59).
SWEDEN: Nilsson, Sandell, Jakobsson (Svensson, 46), Nessvold, Bengtsson, Pohjanen, Sundhage, Swedberg, Kalte (Ljungberg, 71), Videkull, Kun (Andersson, 64).

23rd July 1996

Venue: *The Citrus Bowl in Orlando, Florida.*

UNITED STATES 2   (Venturini 15, MacMillan 61)
SWEDEN 1   (o.g. 64)

Half-time: 1-0   Attendance: 22,734
Referee: Bente Skogvang (Norway)
U.S.A.: Scurry, Overbeck, Chastain, Fawcett, MacMillan (Wilson, 90), Foudy, Venturini, Lilly, Hamm (Gabarra, 85), Milbrett (Roberts, 58), Akers.
SWEDEN: Nilsson, Sandell (Jakobsson, 68), Nessvold, Bengtsson, Sundhage, Swedberg, Andersson, Kalte (Kun, 85), Videkull, Svensson, Carlsson (Ljungberg, 57).

23rd July 1996

Venue: *The Orange Bowl in Miami, Florida.*

CHINA 5   (Shu Guihong 10, Liu Ailing 14, Sun Qingmei 29, 59, Fan Yunjie 36)
DENMARK 1   (L. Madsen 55)

Half-time: 3-0   Attendance: 22,734
Referee: Benito Archunda Tellez (Mexico)
CHINA: Gao Hong, Fan Yunjie, Wang Lipang, Xie Hulin, Zhao Lihong, Shui Qingxia, Liu Ailing (Yu Honggi, 84), Sun Qingmei (Liu Ying, 61), Wen Lirong, Sun Wen (Chen Yufeng, 43), Shi Guihong.
DENMARK: Larsen, B. Madsen, Flaeng, Holm, Terp, Pedersen (Laursen, 83), Christensen, Kolding, Jensen (Nielsen, 46), Krogh, Bonde (L. Madsen, 41).

25th July 1996

Venue: The Orange Bowl in Miami, Florida.

UNITED STATES 0
CHINA 0

Half-time: 0-0   Attendance: 43,525

Referee: Pierluigi Collina (Italy)

U.S.A.: Scurry, Overbeck, Fawcett, Chastain, Roberts, MacMillan, Foudy, Venturini (Parlow, 62), Akers, Lilly, Milbrett (Gabarra, 29).

CHINA: Gao Hong, Wang Liping, Fan Yunjie, Xie Hulin, Wen Lirong, Zhao Lihong, Sun Wen, Liu Ailing, Sun Qingmei, Shi Guihong (Wei Haiying, 86), Shui Qingxia (Chen Yufeng, 54).

25th July 1996

Venue: The Citrus Bowl in Orlando, Florida.

SWEDEN 3   (Swedberg 62, 68, Videkull 76)
DENMARK 1   (Jensen 90)

Half-time: 0-0   Attendance: 17,224

Referee: Claudia Vasconcelos Guedes (Brazil)

SWEDEN: Nilsson (Karlsson, 31), Sandell (Jakobsson, 27), Nessvold, Bengtsson, Svensson, Pohjanen, Sundhage, Swedberg, Andersson, Kalte (Kun, 84), Videkull.

DENMARK: Larsen, Laursen (Jensen, 45), B. Madsen, Flaeng, Holm, Terp, C. Pedersen (M. Pedersen, 69), Christensen, Nielsen, Krogh, L. Madsen.

Group F

21st July 1996

Venue: R.F.K. Stadium in Washington D.C.

BRAZIL 2   (Pretinha 57, 89)
NORWAY 2   (Medalen 32, Aarones 69)

Half-time: 0-1   Attendance: 45,946

Referee: Jose Garcia-Aranda (Spain)

BRAZIL: Meg, Nene (Marisa 90), Fanta, Marcia Taffarel, Elane, Pretinha (Michael Jackson, 90), Formiga, Sissi, Roseli, Tania Maria, Sonia (Katia, 84).

NORWAY: Nordby, Carlsen, Espeseth, N. Nymark Andersen, Myklebust, Riise, A. Nymark Andersen, Stoere (Sandaune, 32), Medalen, Haugen (Svensson, 76), Aarones.

21st July 1996

Venue: Legion Field in Birmingham, Alabama.

GERMANY 3   (Wiegmann 5, o.g. 29, Mohr 62)
JAPAN 2   (Kioka 18, Noda 33)

Half-time: 2-2   Attendance: 44,211

Referee: Sonia Denoncourt (Canada)

GERMANY: Goller, Nardenbach, Austermuehl, Fitschen, Voss, Wiegmann, Mohr, Neid, Brocker (Prinz, 54), Minnert, Wunderlich (Stegemann, 65).

JAPAN: Ozawa, Tomei, Yamaki, Haneta, Obe, Nishina, Sawa, Takakura, Kioka, Noda, Uchiyama (Handa, 73).

23rd July 1996

Venue: Legion Field in Birmingham, Alabama.

BRAZIL 2   (Katia 68, Pretinha 77)
JAPAN 0

Half-time: 0-0   Attendance: 26,111

Referee: Ingrid Jonsson (Sweden)

BRAZIL: Didi, Sonia (Katia, 36), Nene, Fanta, Marcia Taffarel, Elane, Formiga, Sissi, Pretinha, Roseli, Tania Maria.

JAPAN: Ozawa, Tomei, Yamaki, Haneta, Obe, Nishina, Sawa, Takakua (Otake, 72), Kioka, Noda, Uchiyama.

	P	W	D	L	F	A	Pts
CHINA	3	2	1	0	7	1	7
U.S.A.	3	2	1	0	5	1	7
SWEDEN	3	1	0	2	4	5	3
DENMARK	3	0	0	3	2	11	0

23rd July 1996

Venue: R.F.K. Stadium in Washington D.C.

NORWAY 3 (Aarones 6, Medalen 35, Riise 66)
GERMANY 2 (Wiegmann 33, o.g. 62)

Half-time: 2-1   Attendance: 27,849

Referee: Edward Lennie (Australia)

NORWAY: Nordby, Carlsen, Espeseth, N. Nymark Andersen, Myklebust, Svensson (Haugen, 77), Riise, A. Nymark Andersen, Aarones, Pettersen (Tangeraas, 66), Medalen.

GERMANY: Goller, Nardenbach, Austermuehl, Fitschen, Minnert, Voss, Wiegmann, Neid (Lingor, 77), Wunderlich (Stegemann, 55), Mohr, Brocker (Prinz, 53).

	P	W	D	L	F	A	Pts
NORWAY	3	2	1	0	9	4	7
BRAZIL	3	1	2	0	5	3	5
GERMANY	3	1	1	1	6	6	4
JAPAN	3	0	0	3	2	9	0

Semi-Finals

25th July 1996

Venue: Legion Field in Birmingham, Alabama.

BRAZIL 1 (Sissi 53)
GERMANY 1 (Wunderlich 4)

Half-time: 0-1   Attendance: 28,319

Referee: Sonia Denoncourt (Canada)

BRAZIL: Meg, Nene, Katia (Sonia, 86), Fanta, Marcia Taffarel, Elane, Formiga, Sissi, Pretinha, Roseli, Tania Maria.

GERMANY: Goller, Nardenbach (Stegemann, 46), Austermuehl, Fitschen, Minnert, Wunderlich, Voss, Wiegmann, Neid (Pohlmann, 68), Mohr, Brocker (Prinz, 42).

25th July 1996

Venue: R.F.K. Stadium in Washington D.C.

NORWAY 4 (Pettersen 25, 86, Medalen 60, Tangeraas 74)
JAPAN 0

Half-time: 1-0   Attendance: 30,237

Referee: Omar Saleh Saad Al-Muhanna (Saudi Arabia)

NORWAY: Nordby, Carlsen, Espeseth (Haugen, 77), N. Nymark Andersen, Myklebust, Svensson, Riise (Sandaune, 70), A. Nymark Andersen, Aarones, Pettersen, Medalen (Tangeraas, 61).

JAPAN: Onodera, Tomei, Yamaki, Haneta, Obe (Kadohara, 78), Nishina, Sawa, Takakura, Kioka, Noda, Uchiyama (Izumi, 81).

28th July 1996

Venue: Sanford Stadium in Athens, Georgia.

CHINA 3 (Sun Qingmei 5, Wei Haiying 83, 90)
BRAZIL 2 (Roseli 67, Pretina 72)

Half-time: 1-0   Attendance: 54,241

Referee: Ingrid Jonsson (Sweden)

CHINA: Gao Hong, Fan Yunjie, Wen Lirong, Wang Liping, Xie Hulin, Zhao Lihong, Shui Qingxia (Yu Honggi, 70), Liu Ailing, Sun Qingmei, Sun Wen, Shi Guihong (Wei Haiying, 55)

BRAZIL: Meg, Nene, Katia (Suzi, 46), Fanta, Marcia Taffarel, Elane, Formiga, Sissi, Pretinha, Roseli, Tania Maria.

28th July 1996

Venue: Sanford Stadium in Athens, Georgia.

UNITED STATES 2 (Akers pen 77, MacMillan 100)
NORWAY 1 (Medalen 18)

Half-time: 0-1   Attendance: 64,196

Referee: Sonia Denoncourt (Canada)

U.S.A.: Scurry, Overbeck, Fawcett, Chastain, Roberts, Foudy, Venturini, Lilly, Hamm, Akers, Milbrett (MacMillan, 96)

NORWAY: Nordby, Carlsen, Espeseth, N. Nymark Andersen, Myklebust, Riise, A. Nymark Andersen, Pettersen, Medalen, Svensson (Tangeraas, 75), Aarones.

Bronze Medal Game

1st August 1996

Venue: Sanford Stadium in Athens, Georgia.

NORWAY 2 (Aarones 21, 24)
BRAZIL 0

Half-time: 2-0   Attendance: 62,015

Referee: Ingrid Jonsson (Sweden)

NORWAY: Nordby, Espeseth, N. Nymark Andersen (Svensson, 46), Myklebust, Riise, A. Nymark Andersen, Pettersen (Haugen, 89), Medalen, Sandaune, Tangeraas, Aarones (Frustol, 90).

BRAZIL: Meg, Suzi, Fabta, Marcia Taffarel (Katia, 46), Elane, Pretinha, Fomiga, Sissi (Nene, 86), Roseli, Marisa, Sonia (Michael Jackson, 71).

Women's Competition Final

1st August 1996

Venue: Sanford Stadium in Athens, Georgia

UNITED STATES 2 (MacMillan 18, Milbrett 68)
CHINA 1 (Sun Wen 32)

Half-time: 1-1   Attendance: 76,481

Referee: Bente Skogvang (Norway)

U.S.A.: Scurry, Overbeck, Chastain, Fawcett, MacMillan, Foudy, Lilly, Venturini, Akers, Hamm (Gabarra, 90), Milbrett (Roberts, 71).

CHINA: Gao Hong, Wang Lipang (Yu Hongqti, 87), Fan Yunjie, Xie Huilin, Zhao Lihong, Shui Qingxia, Sun Wen, Liu Ailing, Sun Qingmei, Liu Ying, Shi Guihong (Wei Haiying, 70).

25th Olympiad – 2000 – Sydney

Cameroon became the second African nation to win a men's Olympic gold medal when they defeated Spain at the Olympic Stadium in Sydney on penalty kicks.

In the second Olympic competition for women Norway upset the United States with a golden goal scored by Dagny Mellgren after 112 minutes. Football was played in Melbourne, Adelaide, Canberra and Brisbane in addition to Sydney.

The Final between Cameroon and Spain ended 2-2 after extra time and in the penalty shoot-out Cameroon converted five of its kicks as against three for Spain. An excellent crowd of 98,212 watched this Final.

Perhaps the surprise team of the men's competition was the United States who advanced to the Semi-finals for the first time only to lose to Spain, and then lose the Bronze Medal Game to Chile. However, it underscored the growing quality of the game in the United States. Once again a number of talented players made their mark on the Olympics. Ivan Zamorano (Chile), Milan Baros (Czech Republic), Lauren (Cameroon), Landon Donovan (United States), Mark Viduka (Australia) and Ronaldinho and Edu (Brazil).

Unlike the men's competition, restricted largely to players under 23 years of age, the women's competition featured the best players in the game, and the final, the top two teams. The rivalry between the U.S.A. and Norway goes back to the first Women's World Cup in China in 1991.

Once again over a million people watched this Olympic football tournament.

Men's Competition

Group A

13th September 2000

Venue: Adelaide

NIGERIA 3 (Igbinadolar 57, Agali 79, Ayegbeni 90)
HONDURAS 3 (D. Suazo 36 pen, 77, Leon 61)

Half-time: 0-1 Attendance: 13,000
Referee: Lubos Michel (Slovakia)

NIGERIA: Etafia, Okunowo (C. Kanu 83), Babayaro, Iyenemi (Okoronkwo), Okpara, Oliseh, Lawal, Igbinadolar (Agali 65), Ayegbeni, Ikedia, Aghahowa.

HONDURAS: Valladares, Guerrero, Montoya, Izaguirre, Rosales, Turcios, M. Suazo, Chirinos, D. Suazo (Ramirez 90), Leon (Pavon 90), Martinez (Scott 70).

13th September 2000

Venue: Melbourne

AUSTRALIA 0
ITALY 1 (Pirlo 82)

Half-time: 0-0 Attendance: 93,200
Referee: Peter Prendergast (Jamaica)

AUSTRALIA: Milosevic, Foxe, Laybutt, Colosimo, Lazaridis, Skoko (Neill 80), Emerton, Wehrman (Bresciano 67), Grella (Rizzo 87), Curcija, Viduka.

ITALY: Abbiati, Grandoni, Zanchi, Cirillo, Gattuso, Comandini, Baronio (Zanetti 59), Zambrotta, Ambrosini, Ventola (Margiotta), Pirlo.

16th September 2000

Venue: Adelaide

ITALY 3 (Comandini 12, 22, Ambrosini 18)
HONDURAS 1 (own goal 29)

Half-time: 3-1   Attendance: 18,301

Referee: Jun Lu (China)

ITALY: Abbiati, Grandoni, Zanchi, Cirillo, Gattuso, Comandini (Margiotta), Baronio (Vannucchi 82), Zambrotta, Ambrosini, Zanetti, Ventola.

HONDURAS: Valladares, Guerrero, Montoya, Izaguirre (Ramirez 61), Rosales, J.C. Suazo, M. Suazo, Turcios, Chirinos (Paes de Oliveira 58), Leon, Martinez (Pavon 70).

16th September 2000

Venue: Sydney

AUSTRALIA 2 (Foxe 41, Wehrman 44)
NIGERIA 3 (Ikedia 16, Aghaowa 22, Agali 64)

Half-time: 2-2   Attendance: 38,080

Referee: Carlos Eugenio Simon (Brazil)

AUSTRALIA: Milosevic, Foxe, Laybutt, Colosimo (Rizzo 74), Lazaridis, Skoko, Emerton, Wehrman (Neill 61), Grella, Curcija (Zane 79), Viduka.

NIGERIA: Etafia, Babayaro, Okpara, Okoronkwo, C. Kanu, Oliseh, Lawal, Aghahowa, Ikedia (Johnson 85), Agali (Kaku 81), Ayegbeni.

19th September 2000

Venue: Adelaide

ITALY 1 (own goal 65)
NIGERIA 1 (Lawal pen 40)

Half-time: 0-1   Attendance: 18,340

Referee: Felipe D. Jesus Ramos Rizo (Mexico)

ITALY: Abbiati, Mezzano, Ferrari, Cirillo, Rivalta, Comandini, Baronio (Ambrosini 80), Zanetti (Zambrotta 80), Vannucchi, Margiotta, Pirlo.

NIGERIA: Etafia, Okunowo, Okpara, Okoronkwo, C. Kanu, Oliseh, Lawal, Aghahowa, Ikedia, Iginadolor (Kaku 69), Agali.

19th September 2000

Venue: Sydney

AUSTRALIA 1 (Curcija 51)
HONDURAS 2 (D. Suazo 3, 60)

Half-time: 0-1   Attendance: 37,788

Referee: Mourad Daami (Tunisia)

AUSTRALIA: Milosevic, Laybutt, Colosimo (Bresciano 46), Foxe, Lazaridis, Skoko, Neill, Wehrman (Zane 79), Grella (Culina 30), Curcija, Viduka.

HONDURAS: Valladares, Guerrero, Montoya, Lopez (Izaguirre 46), Paes de Oliveira (Pavon 77), Turcios, Chirinos, Rosales, M. Suazo, Leon (J.C. Suazo 90), D. Suazo.

	P	W	D	L	F	A	Pts
ITALY	3	2	1	0	5	2	7
NIGERIA	3	1	2	0	7	6	5
HONDURAS	3	1	1	1	6	7	4
AUSTRALIA	3	0	0	3	3	6	0

Group B

14th September 2000

Venue: Adelaide

SOUTH KOREA 0
SPAIN 3 (Velamazan 10, Jose Mari 26, Xavi 37)

Half-time: 0-3   Attendance: 14,000

Referee: Felipe D. Jesus Ramos Rizo (Mexico)

SOUTH KOREA: Kim Yong Dae, Park Jae Hong, Park Dong Hyuk, Kim Do Kyun,

Kang Chul (Sim Jae Won 32), Park Ji Sung, Lee Young Pyo. Lee Chun Soo (Park Ji Sung 78) Ko Jong Su, Kim Sang Sik (Lee Dong Gook 60) Kim Do Hoon.

SPAIN: Aranzubia, Lacruz, Capdevila, Marchena, Amaya, Albelda (Ismael 80), Xavi, Gabri, Velamazan (Ferron 69), Jose Mari (Luque 76), Tamudo.

14th September 2000

Venue: Melbourne

MOROCCO 1 (Ouchia 79)
CHILE 4 (Zamorano 36 pen, 45, 55, Navia 72 pen)

Half-time: 0-2   Attendance: 22,500

Referee: Saad Kameel Mane (Kuwait)

MOROCCO: El Jarmouni, Romani, Chbouki, El Brazi, Kharbouch, Oulmers (Uchla 59), Safri, Aboub, El Khattari (Zairi 86), El Moubarki, Benkouar (El Assas 44)

CHILE: N. Tapia, Alvarez, Contreras, Reyes, Olarra, Maldonado, Pizarro, Nunez (Arrue 70), Ormazabal (Ibarra 76), Zamorano (Gonzalez 74), Navia.

17th September 2000

Venue: Adelaide

SOUTH KOREA 1 (Lee Chun Soo 52)
MOROCCO 0

Half-time: 0-0   Attendance: 12,753

Referee: Herbert Fandel (Germany)

SOUTH KOREA: Kim Yong Dae, Sim Jae Won, Park Jae Hong, Park Ji Sung, Lee Young Pyo, Kang Chul, Lee Chun Soo, Park Jin Sub (Kim Do Kyun 62), Kim Sang Sik, Lee Dong Gook (Ko Jong Su), KIm Do Hoon (Choi Tai Uk 80).

MOROCCO: El Jarmouni, Romani, El Brazi, Karbouch, Nater, El Assas, Safri, Benkouar (Oulmers 66), Aboub, El Moubarki (Uchla 85), El Khattan.

17th September 2000

Venue: Melbourne

SPAIN 1 (Lacruz 54)
CHILE 3 (Olarra 24, Navia 41, 90)

Half-time: 0-2   Attendance: 58,061

Referee: Felix Tangawarima (Zimbabwe)

SPAIN: Aranzubia, Lacruz, Capdevila (Puyol 82), Amaya, Marchena, Albelda, Xavi, Gabri, Velamazan (Ferron 69), Angulo (Alberto Luque 69), Tamudo.

CHILE: N. Tapia, Alvarez, Contreras, Reyes, Olarra, Maldonado, Pizarro, Nunez (Tello 85), Ormazabal (Henriquez 82), Zamorano, Navia.

20th September 2000

Venue: Adelaide

SOUTH KOREA 1 (Lee Dong Gook 28)
CHILE 0

Half-time: 1-0   Attendance: 16,068

Referee: Lubos Michel (Slovakia)

SOUTH KOREA: Kim Yong Dae, Sim Jae Won, Park Jae Hong, Park Ji Sung, Lee Young Pyo, Kang Chul, Song Chong Gug, Lee Chun Soo, Kim Sang Sik, Choi Chul Woo (Kim Do Hoon 61, Ko Jong Su 67), LeeDong Gook (Park Dong Hyuk 82).

CHILE: N. Tapia, Alvarez, Maldonado (Henrique 58), Contreras, Reyes, Pizarro, Nunez (Tello), Olarra, Ormazabal (Arrue), Gonzalez, Navia.

20th September 2000

Venue: Melbourne

SPAIN 2 (Mari 33, Gabri 90)
MOROCCO 0

Half-time: 1-0   Attendance: 24,623

Referee: Jun Lu (China)

SPAIN: Aranzubia, Capdevila, Unai, Puyol, Amaya, Albelda, Xavi (Ismael 90), Velamazan (Ferron 75), Angulo, Jose Mari (Gabri 65), Tamudo.

MOROCCO: El Jarmouni, Romani (Zairi 43), Ouchla, El Brazi, El Assas, Kacemi, Safri, Aboub (Outmers 79), El Barodi (Nater 46), El Moubarki, El Khattari.

	P	W	D	L	F	A	Pts
CHILE	3	2	0	1	7	3	6
SPAIN	3	2	0	1	6	3	6
SOUTH KOREA	3	2	0	1	2	3	6
MOROCCO	3	0	0	3	1	7	0

Group C

13th September 2000

Venue: Brisbane

CAMEROON 3 (Alnoudji 38, Mboma 77, own goal 87)

KUWAIT 2 (Al Mutairi 64, Abdulrahman 89)

Half-time: 1-0   Attendance: 26,700

Referee: Bruce Grimshaw (New Zealand)

CAMEROON: Bekono, Wome, Mimpo, Abanda, Alnoudji, Njitap, Etame, Nguimbat, Branco (Epalle 79), Eto'o, Mboma (Suffo 80).

KUWAIT: Kankone, Salman, Abdulrahman, Saihan (Al Humaidan 87), Al Tayyar, Al Azeni, Zayed, Al Kandari, Al Othman, Abdulaziz, Saeid (Al Mutairi 47).

13th September 2000

Venue: Canberra

UNITED STATES 2 (Albright 22, Wolff 45)

CZECH REPUBLIC 2 (Jankulovski 29, Lukas Dosek 53 pen)

Half-time: 2-1   Attendance: 24,800

Referee: Carlos Eugenio Simon (Brazil)

U.S.A.: Friedel, McCarty, Agoos, Hejduk, Califf, O'Brien, Olsen, Vagenas, Albright (Corrales 86), Wolff, Casey.

CZECH REPUBLIC: Drobny, Lukas Dosek, Petrous, Kovac, Lengyel, Tyce, Sionko (Kucera 86), Ujfalusi (Simak 60), Jankulovski, Baros (Libor Dosek 69), Heinz.

16th September 2000

Venue: Brisbane

CZECH REPUBLIC 2 (Heinz 2, Lengyel 90)

KUWAIT 3 (Al Mutairi 56, Saeid 64, 73)

Half-time: 1-0   Attendance: 22,182

Referee: Mourad Daami (Tunisia)

CZECH REPUBLIC: Drobny, Petrous, Kovac (Simak 68), Lengyel, Tyce, Sionko, Ujfalusi, Jankulovski, Kucera (Dosek 80), Baros, Heinz.

KUWAIT: Kankone, Salman, Abdulrahman, Saihari, Al Tayyar, Al Mutairi (Al Anezi 89), Al Azemi, Al Kandari, Al Othman (Zayed 80), Abdulaziz, Saeid.

16th September 2000

Venue: Canberra

UNITED STATES 1 (Vagenas pen 64)

CAMEROON 1 (Mboma pen 16)

Half-time: 0-1   Attendance: 22,397

Referee: Mario Sanchez Yanten (Chile)

U.S.A.: Friedel, Hajduk, Califf, McCarty, Agoos, O'Brien, Vagenas, Albright, Olsen, Wolff, Casey.

CAMEROON: Bekono, Wome, Mimpo, Abanda, Alnoudji, Njitap, Lauren, Nguimbat, Epalle (Ngome Kome 65), Eto'o, Mboma (Mbami 77).

19th September 2000

Venue: Brisbane

CZECH REPUBLIC 1 (Lukas Dosek 74)

CAMEROON 1 (Lauren 24)

Half-time: 0-1   Attendance: 23,442

Referee: Simon Micallef (Australia)

CZECH REPUBLIC: Chvalovsky, Lucas Dosek (Vozabal 85), Petrous, Kovac (Jankulovski 53), Lengyel, Libor Dosek (67), Tyce, Sionko, Ujfalusi, Kucera, Baros, Simak.

CAMEROON: Bekono, Wome, Mimpo, Abanda, Alnoudji, Njitap, Lauren, Nguimbat, Branco, Eto'o, Mboma (Meyong Ze 64).

19th September 2000

Venue: Melbourne

UNITED STATES 3 (Califf 40, Albright 63, Donovan 88)

KUWAIT 1 (Najem 83)

Half-time: 1-0   Attendance: 19,684

Referee: Herbert Fandel (Germany)

U.S.A.: Friedel, Hejduk, Califf, McCarty, Agoos, O'Brien, Vagenas, Albright, Olsen (DiGiamarino 62), Wolff, Casey (Donovan).

KUWAIT: Kankone, Salman, Abdulrahman, Al Anezi, Al Tayyar (Al Omran 66), Al Mutairi, Al Azeni, Al Kandari, Al Othman, Abdulaziz (Najem 68), Saeid.

	P	W	D	L	F	A	Pts
U.S.A.	3	1	2	0	5	4	6
CAMEROON	3	1	2	0	5	4	5
KUWAIT	3	1	0	2	6	8	3
CZECH REP.	3	0	2	1	5	6	2

Group D

14th September 2000

Venue: Brisbane

BRAZIL 3 (Edu 30, Fabio Aurelio 69, Alex 90)
SLOVAKIA 1 (Porazik 26)

Half-time: 1-1   Attendance: 24,600
Referee: Simon Micallef (Australia)

BRAZIL: Helton, Baiano, Fabio, Bilica, Alvaro, Fabio Aurelio, Ronaldinho (Lucas 80), Marcos Paulo, Fabiano, Edu (Roger 90), Alex, Geovanni (Mozart 88).

SLOVAKIA: Contofalsky, Cisovsky, Hlinka, Lerant, Krsko, Kisel, Pancik (Barcik 81), Czinege, Slahor (Vyskoc 77), Petras, Porazik (Drobnak 76).

14th September 2000

Venue: Canberra

SOUTH AFRICA 1 (Nomvethe 32)
JAPAN 2 (Takahara 45, 80)

Half-time: 1-1   Attendance: 17,500
Referee: Stephane Bre (France)

SOUTH AFRICA: Baron, F. McCarthy, Kannenmeyer, Matombo (Fredericks 56), Booth, Fortune, Nteo, Mokoena, Nomvethe (Nhleko 88), Buckley (Pule 88), B. McCarthy.

JAPAN: Narazaki, Nakazawa, Morioka, Inamoto, K. Nakata, Myojin, Nakamura, Sakai, Yanagisawa (Motoyama 80), H. Nakata, Takahara.

17th September 2000

Venue: Brisbane

BRAZIL 1 (Edu 12)
SOUTH AFRICA 3 (Fortune 11, Nomvethe 74, Lekoelea 88)

Half-time: 1-1   Attendance: 36,326
Referee: Bruce Grimshaw (New Zealand)

BRAZIL: Helton, Baiano (Roger 80), Fabio Bilica, Alvaro, Marcos Paulo (Lucas 75), Fabio Aurelio, Fabiano, Edu, Alex, Ronaldinho, Geovanni (Mozart 61).

SOUTH AFRICA: Baron, F. McCarthy, Kannemeyer, Booth, Fortune, Nhleko (Nomvethe 36, Matsaw 85), Pule (Lekoelea 55), Nteo, Mokoena, Buckley, B. McCarthy.

17th September 2000

Venue: Canberra

SLOVAKIA 1 (Porazik 83)
JAPAN 2 (H. Nakata 67, Inamoto 74)

Half-time: 0-0   Attendance: 22,000
Referee: Falla Ndoye (Senegal)

SLOVAKIA: Lipcak, Hlinka, Lerant, Krsko, Kisel, Czinege, Slahor (Pancik 77), Petras, Mintal (Drobnak 77), Kral, Porazik.

JAPAN: Narazaki, Nakazawa, Morioka, Inamoto, K. Nakata, Myojin, Nakamura (Motoyama 79), Miura, Yanagisawa (Sakai 54), H. Nakata, Takahara (Hirase 90).

20th September 2000

Venue: Brisbane

BRAZIL 1 (Alex 5)
JAPAN 0

Half-time: 1-0   Attendance: 36,608
Referee: Stephane Bre (France)

BRAZIL: Helton, Baiano, Fabio Bilica, Alvaro, Marcos Paulo, Fabio Aurelio, Fabiano, Edu, Alex, Ronaldinho (Lucas 65), Geovanni (Roger 80).

JAPAN: Narazaki, Nakazawa, Miyamoto, K. Nakata (Matsuda 71), Inamoto, Myojin, Nakamura, Miura, Sakai, Yanagisawa (Hirase 80), Takahara (Motoyama 90).

20th September 2000

Venue: Canberra

SLOVAKIA 2 (Czinege 47, Slahor 72)
SOUTH AFRICA 1 (B. McCarthy 75)

Half-time: 0-0 Attendance: 14,562

Referee: Mario Sanchez Yanten (Chile)

SLOVAKIA: Lipcak, Drobnak (Cisovsky 69), Hlinka, Lerant, Krsko, Pancik, Czinege, Slahor (Supka), Petras, Kral, Porazik (Vyskoc 90)

SOUTH AFRICA: Baron, F. McCarthy, Kannemeyer, Matombo (Leoelea 67), Booth, Fredericks, Nhleko (Nomvethe 58), Nteo, Mokoena, Buckley, B. McCarthy.

	P	W	D	L	F	A	Pts
BRAZIL	3	2	0	1	5	4	6
JAPAN	3	2	0	1	4	3	6
SOUTH AFRICA	3	1	0	2	5	5	3
SLOVAKIA	3	1	0	2	4	6	3

Quarter-Finals

23rd September 2000

Venue: Adelaide

JAPAN 2 (Yanagisawa 30, Takahara 72)
UNITED STATES 2 (Wolff 68, Vagenas 90 pen)

Half-time: 1-0 Attendance: 18,345

Referee: Felix Tangawarima (Zimbabwe)

JAPAN: Narazaki, Nakazawa, Morioka, Matsuda, Myojin, Inamoto, Sakai, Nakamura, Nakata, Takahara, Yanagisawa (Miura 65)

U.S.A.: Friedel, Hejduk, McCarty, Califf, Agoos, O"Brien (Whitfield 107), Olsen (Donovan 46), Albright (Victorine 91), Vagenas, Casey, Wolff.

The United States won 5-4 on penalties.

23rd September 2000

Venue: Brisbane (Result is after extra time)

BRAZIL 1 (Ronaldinho 90)
CAMEROON 2 (Mboma 17, Nguimbat 113)

Half-time: 0-1 Attendance: 37,332

Referee: Herbert Fangel (Germany)

BRAZIL: Helton, Baiano, Fabio Bilica (Lucio 46), Alvaro, Athirson (Roger 46), Fabio Aurelio, Marcos Paulo, Fabiano, Alex, Lucas (Geovanni 59), Ronaldinho.

CAMEROON: Kameni, Wome, Mimpo, Abanda, Alnoudji, Njitap, Lauren, Nguimbat, Branco (Mbami 71), Eto'o (Meyong Ze 81), Mboma (Suffo 63)

23rd September 2000

Venue: Sydney

ITALY 0
SPAIN 1 (Gabri 86)

Half-time: 0-0 Attendance: 38,134

Referee: Carlos Eugenio Simon (Brazil)

ITALY: Abbiati, Grandoni, Zanchi, Cirillo, Gattuso, Comandini (Margiotta 88), Zanetti, Vanucchi, Ambrosini, Ventola, Pirlo.

SPAIN: Aranzubia, Lacruz, Amaya, Marchena (Unai 46), Albelda, Xavi, Puyol, Velamazan, Tamudo (Gabri 70), Angulo, Jose Mari.

23rd September 2000

Venue: Melbourne

CHILE 4 (Contreras 17, Zamorano 18, Navia 42, Tello 65)
NIGERIA 1 (Agali 76)

Half-time: 3-0 Attendance: 44,425

Referee: Saad Kameel Mane (Kuwait)

CHILE: N. Tapia, Alvarez, Contreras, Reyes, Olarra, Maldonado (Henriquez 80), Pizarro, Tello, Ormazabal, Zamorano, Navia (Arrue 75).

NIGERIA: Etafia, Okunowo, Iyenemi (Onwuzuruike 46, Iginadolar 79), Okpara, Okoronkwo, Kaku (C. Kanu 46), Lawal, Aghahowa, Ikedia, Agali, Ayegbeni.

Semi-Finals

26th September 2000

Venue: Sydney

SPAIN 3 (Tamudo 16, Angulo 25, Joe Mari 87)
UNITED STATES 1 (Vagenas pen 42)

Half-time: 2-1   Attendance: 39,800

Referee: Mourad Daami (Tunisia)

SPAIN: Aranzubia, Lacruz, Amaya, Marchena, Puyol, Albelda, Xavi, Valamazan (Gabri 75), Angulo (Ferron 75), Jose Mari (Unai 88), Tamudo.

U.S.A.: Friedel, Hejduk, Califf, McCarthy, Agoos, Albright (Victorine 39), Vagenas, O"Brien, Corrales (Donovan 39), Casey, Wolff.

26th September 2000

Venue: Melbourne

CHILE 1 (own goal 78)
CAMEROON 2 (Mboma 84, Lauren pen 89)

Half-time: 0-0   Attendance: 64,338

Referee: Stephane Bre (France)

CHILE: N. Tapia, Alvarez, Maldonado, Contreras, Reyes, Pizarro, Tello, Olarra, Ormazabal (Henriquez 84), Zamorano, Navia (Gonzales 70).

CAMEROON: Kameni, Wome, Mimpo, Abanda, Beaud, Alnoudji, Lauren, Mbami (Epalle 65), Branco (Ngome 82), Eto'o (Suffo 92), Mboma.

Third Place play-off

29th September 2000

Venue: Sydney

CHILE 2 (Zamorano pen 69, 84)
UNITED STATES 0

Half-time: 0-0   Attendance: 26,381

Referee: Simon Micallef (Australia)

CHILE: Tapia, Alvarez, Contreras, Reyes, Olarra, Maldonado, Ormazabal (Nunez 36), Tello (Rojas 86), Pizarro, Zamorano, Navia (Gonzalez 63).

U.S.A.: Friedel, Hejduk, Califf (Donovan 82), Dunseth, Agoos, Albright, Vagenas, O'Brien, Olsen (Victorine 61), Casey, Wolff.

Final

30th September 2000

Venue: Sydney   (Result is after extra time)

CAMEROON 2 (own goal 53, Eto'o 58)
SPAIN 2 (Xavi 2, Gabri 45)

Half-time: 0-2   Attendance: 98,212

Referee: Felipe D Jesus Ramos Rizo (Mexico)

CAMEROON: Kameni, Wome, Abanda, Nguimbat (Ngom Kome 46), Branco (Epalle 91), Etame-Mayer, Njitap, Alnoudji (Meyong Ze 111), Mimpo, Mboma, Eto'o

SPAIN: Aranzubia, Puyol, Lacruz, Marchena, Amaya, Albeida, Xavi, Toni Velamazan (Gabri 26), Angulo (Capdevila 74), Jose Mari, Tamudo (Ferron 49).

Cameroon won 5-3 on penalties.

Women's Competition

Group E

13th September 2000

Venue: Melbourne

BRAZIL 2 (Pretinha 22, Katia 71)
SWEDEN 0

Half-time: 1-0   Attendance: 58,432

Referee: Sandra Hunt (**U.S.A.**)

BRAZIL: Andreia, Juliana (Monica 78), Daniela, Tania, Simone, Rosana, Formiga, Cidinha, Sissi, Katia (Roseli 82), Pretinha.

SWEDEN: Jonsson, Westberg, Tornqvist (Fagerstroem 85), Larsson, Bengtsson, Sandell, Nordlund, Andersson, Ljungberg, Mostrom, Svensson (Sjogran 76).

13th September 2000

Venue: Canberra

AUSTRALIA 0
GERMANY 3 (Grings 36, Wiegmann 71, Lingor 70)

Half-time: 0-1   Attendance: 24,800

Referee: Bola Elisabeth Abidoye (Nigeria)

AUSTRALIA: Wheeler, Alagich, Tann-Darby, Salisbury, Wainwright, McShea, Forman, Duus (Garriock 72), Wilson, Murray (Golebiowski 62), Hughes (Ferguson 46).

GERMANY: Rottenberg, Stegemann, Jones, Fitschen, Minnert, Hingst, Lingor, Meinert, Wiegmann, Prinz, Grings.

16th September 2000

Venue: Sydney

AUSTRALIA 1 (Salisbury 57)
SWEDEN 1 (Andersson pen 66)

Half-time: 0-0   Attendance: 33,600

Referee: Sonia Denoncourt (Canada)

AUSTRALIA: Wheeler, Alagich, Tann-Darby, Wainwright, Salisbury, McShea, Forman, Duus (Garriock 77), Wilson (Black 46), Ferguson (Golebiowski 78), Hughes.

SWEDEN: Jonsson, Westberg, Tornqvist, Larsson, Bengtsson, Sandell, Andersson, Ljungberg, Mostrom, Nordlund (Fagerstroem), Svensson (Sjogran 54).

16th September 2000

Venue: Canberra

GERMANY 2 (Prinz 33, 41)
BRAZIL 1 (Raquel 72)

Half-time: 2-0   Attendance: 17,000

Referee: Martha Liliana Toro Pardo (Colombia)

GERMANY: Rottenberg, Stegemann, Jones, Fitschen, Wiegmann, Meinert, Minnert, Hingst, Lingor, Prinz, Grings.

BRAZIL: Andreia, Juliana, Monica, Simone (Roseli 46), Rosana, Daniela, Formiga (Nene 46), Cidinha (Raquel 69), Sissi, Katia, Pretinha.

19th September 2000

Venue: Sydney

AUSTRALIA 1 (Hughes 33)
BRAZIL 2 (Raquel 56, Katia 64)

Half-time: 1-0   Attendance: 29,400

Referee: Vibeke Karlsen (Norway)

AUSTRALIA: Wheeler, Starr, Alagich, Tann-Darby, Salisbury, McShea (Golebiowski 74), Forman, Duus (Wilson 62), Black (Garriock 70), Ferguson, Hughes.

BRAZIL: Andreia, Juliana, Simone, Rosana (Maicon 46), Daniela, Tania, Cidinha, Raquel (Formiga 57), Sissi, Katia, Pretinha (Roseli 74).

19th September 2000

Venue: Melbourne

GERMANY 1 (Hingst 88)
SWEDEN 0

Half-time: 0-0   Attendance: 7,000

Referee: Wendy Toms (England)

GERMANY: Rottenberg, Jones, Fitschen, Wunderlich, Wiegmann, Meinert (Brandebusemeyer 87), Minnert, Hingst, Hoffmann (Mueller 46), Prinz, Grings (Lingor 46).

SWEDEN: Jonsson, Westberg, Tornqvist, Larsson, Sandell, Andersson, Ljungberg, Marklund (Johansson 82), Mostroem, Nordlund (Sjogran 46), Svenberg (Svensson 59).

	P	W	D	L	F	A	Pts
GERMANY	3	3	0	0	6	1	9
BRAZIL	3	2	0	1	5	3	6
SWEDEN	3	0	1	2	1	4	1
AUSTRALIA	3	0	1	2	2	6	1

17th September 2000

Venue: Melbourne

UNITED STATES 1 (Foudy 38)
CHINA 1 (Sun 67)

Half-time: 1-0   Attendance: 32,500

Referee: Nicle Petignat (Switzerland)

U.S.A.: Mullinix, Pearce, Sobrero, Fawcett, Chastain (Parlow 62), Fair, Foudy, Lilly, MacMillan (Serlenga 80), Hamm, Milbrett.

CHINA: Gao, Wang, Fan Yunjie, Ba, Zhao, Jin (Zhang 61), Wen, Liu Ailing, Pu, Sun, Liu Ying.

Group F

14th September 2000

Venue: Melbourne

UNITED STATES 2 (Milbrett 18, Hamm 24)
NORWAY 0

Half-time: 2-0   Attendance: 16,000

Referee: Eun Ju Im (South Korea)

U.S.A.: Mullinix, Pearce, Sobrero, Fawcett, Chastain, MacMillan, Fair, Foudy, Lilly, Milbrett, Hamm (Parlow 70).

NORWAY: Nordby, Sandaune, Kringen, Toennessen, Espeseth, Riise, Knudsen (S. Gulbrandsen 46), Rapp (R. Gulbrandsen 71), Lehn, Mellgren, Pettersen (Jensen 55)

17th September 2000

Venue: Canberra

NORWAY 3 (Mellgren 22, Riise pen 62, Pettersen 90)
NIGERIA 1 (Akide 78)

Half-time: 1-0   Attendance: 9,150

Referee: Tammy Ogston (Australia)

NORWAY: Nordby, Kringen, Toennessen (Bekkevold 4), Espeseth, Riise, Gulbrandsen (Knudsen 59), Lehn, Pettersen, Joergensen (Sandaune 80), Mellgren, Gulbradnsen.

NIGERIA: Chime, Kudaisi, Opara, Ajayi, Mbachu, Nwadike, Okosieme, Omagbemi, Mmada (Akide 54), Avre (Chiejene 57), Nkwocha.

14th September 2000

Venue: Canberra

CHINA 3 (Zhao 12, Sun 53, 83)
NIGERIA 1 (Nkwocha pen 85)

Half-time: 1-0   Attendance: 11,000

Referee: Martha Liliana Toro Pardo (Colombia)

CHINA: Gao, Wang, Fan Yunjie, Ba, Wen, Zhao, Liu Ailing, Pu (Xie 82), Liu Ying, Jin (Zhang 71), Sun.

NIGERIA: Chiejine (Chime 81), Kudaisi, Opara, Ajayi, Nwadike, Usieta, Okosieme, Omagbemi, Akide (Mbachu 58), Avre (Chiejene 81), Nkwocha.

20th September 2000

Venue: Melbourne

UNITED STATES 3 (Chastain 26, Lilly 35, MacMillan 56)
NIGERIA 1 (Akide 48)

Half-time: 1-0   Attendance: 9,000

Referee: Im Eun Ju (South Korea)

U.S.A.: Mullinix, Pearce, Fawcett, Sobrero, Chastain, MacMillan, Fair, Foudy, Lilly (Serlenga 46), Hamm (Parlow 70), Milbrett.

NIGERIA: Chiejine (Chime 64), Kudaisi, Opara, Nkwocha, Ajayi (Avre 20), Akide, Omagbemi (Mmadu 72), Okosieme, Mbachu, Nwadike, Chiejene.

20th September 2000

Venue: Canberra

NORWAY 2 (Pettersen 55, Haugenes 78)
CHINA 1 (Sun pen 75)

Half-time: 0-0   Attendance: 11,532

Referee: Sonia Denoncourt (Canada)

NORWAY: Nordby, Kringen, Espeseth, Jorgensen (Sandaune 84), Bekkevold, Riise, S. Gulbrandsen, Lehn (Knudsen 51), Mellgren (Haugenes 61), R. Gulbrandsen, Pettersen.

CHINA: Gao, Wang, Fan Yunjie, Ba, Wen, Zhao, Liu Ailing, Pu, Liu Ying (Xie 66), Jin (Zhang 46), Sun.

24th September 2000

Venue: Canberra

UNITED STATES 1 (Hamm 60)
BRAZIL 0

Half-time: 0-0   Attendance: 11,200

Referee: Nicole Petignat (Switzerland)

U.S.A.: Mullinix, Pearce, Fawcett, Sobrero, Chastain, MacMillan (Parlow 79), Fair, Foudy, Lilly, Hamm, Milbrett.

BRAZIL: Andreia, Simone, Juliana, Tania, Cidinha, Sissi (Raquel 83), Daniela, Formiga, Maicon, Pretinha, Katia (Roseli 58).

	P	W	D	L	F	A	Pts
U.S.A.	3	2	1	0	6	2	7
NORWAY	3	2	0	1	5	4	6
CHINA	3	1	1	1	5	4	4
NIGERIA	3	0	0	3	3	9	0

Semi-Finals

24th September 2000

Venue: Sydney

NORWAY 1 (own goal 80)
GERMANY 0

Half-time: 0-0   Attendance: 16,710

Referee: Im Eun Ju (South Korea)

NORWAY: Nordby, Sandaune, Kringen, Riise, S. Gulbrandsen, Jorgensen, Bekkevold, R. Gulbrandsen, Boe Jensen (Knudsen 33), Mellgren (Haugenes 55), Pettersen (Lehn 86).

GERMANY: Rottenberg, Stegemann, Jones, Fitschen, Wunderlich, Minnert, Meinert, Hingst, Wiegmann, Prinz, Grings.

Bronze Medal Game

28th September 2000

Venue: Sydney

GERMANY 2 (Lingor 64, Prinz 79)
BRAZIL 0

Half-time: 0-0   Attendance: 11,200

Referee: Im Eun Ju (South Korea)

GERMANY: Rottenberg, Stegemann (Hoffmann 17), Jones, Fitschen, Meinert, Minnert, Wiegmann, Hingst (Gottschich 55), Lingor, Prinz, Grings (Goette 90).

BRAZIL: Andreia, Juliana, Daniela, Tania, Simone (Suzana 75), Formiga (Raquel 68), Cidinha, Sissi, Roseli (Rosana 70), Pretinha, Maicon.

Women's Competition Final

28th September 2000

Venue: Sydney

UNITED STATES 2 (Milbrett 5, 90)

NORWAY 3 (Espeseth 44, R. Gulbrandsen 78, Mellgren 112)

Half-time: 1-1   Attendance: 22,848

Referee: Sonia Denoncourt (Canada)

U.S.A.: Mullinix, Pearce, Fawcett, Sobrero, Chastain, MacMillan (Parlow 69), Fair, Foudy, Lilly, Hamm, Milbrett.

NORWAY: Nordby, Sandaune, Kringen, Espeseth, Riise, S. Gulbrandsen (Lehn 34), Knudsen, Pettersen (Mellgren 82), Jorgensen, Haugenes, R. Gulbrandsen.

Norway won with a Golden Goal during extra time.

26th Olympiad – 2004 – Athens

Argentina won the Olympic Football Championship for the first time in Athens, winning all six games they played without conceding a goal. Carlos Tevez was the star player of the tournament, scoring eight times in total. This was the third time that Argentina reached the Final, losing in 1928 to Uruguay after a replay and losing to Nigeria in 1996 in Athens, Georgia. Paraguay reached the Final for the first time and, while losing to Argentina, took home that countries first ever Olympic medal in any sport.

Crowds were smaller in Greece than at any Olympic Games for a long time probably because the host nation did not fare well, but also because fears of a terrorist attack kept many people away.

Men's Competition

Group A

11th August 2004

Venue: The Kaftanzoglio Stadium in Thessaloniki.

GREECE 2 (Taralidis 78, Papadopoulos 82)
SOUTH KOREA 2 (Kim 43, o.g. 64)

Half-time: 0-1   Attendance: 25,152

Referee: Jorge Larrionda (Uruguay)

GREECE: Amparis, Lagos (Salpingidis, 46), Moras, Vallas, Stoltidis, Agritis (Amanatidis, 46), Nempegleras, Papadopoulos, Fotakis, Sapanis, Vyntra (Taralidis, 74)

SOUTH KOREA: Young Kwang Kim, Won Kwon Kim, Yong Ho Park, Sang Chul Yoo, Do Heon Kim (Nam Il Kim, 84), Chun Soo Lee, Tae Uk Choi (Byung Kuk Cho, 34), Kyu Seon Park (Won Kwon Choi, 59), Dong Jin Kim, Jung Woo Kim, Jae Jin Cho.

11th August 2004

Venue: The Panthessaliko Stadium in Volos.

MALI 0
MEXICO 0

Half-time: 0-0   Attendance: 10,104

Referee: Subkhiddin Salleh Mohd (Malaysia)

MALI: Bathily, Berthe, Tamboura, Kone, Ndiaye (Abouta, 74), Abdou Traore, Dramane Traore (Doucoure, 81), Sissoke, Kebe, Coulibaly, Mamadou Diallo.

MEXICO: Corona, Francisco Rodriguez, Mario Perez, Lopez, Galindo, Zinha (Iniguez, 67), Martinez, Bravo (Garcia, 76), Luis Perez, Marquez (Ponce, 56), Sanchez.

14th August 2004

Venue: *The Karaiskaki Stadium in Athens.*

SOUTH KOREA 1 (Jung Kim 15)
MEXICO 0

Half-time: 1-0   Attendance: 14,026

Referee: Claus Bo Larsen (Denmark)

SOUTH KOREA: Young Kwang Kim, Yong Ho Park, Byung Kuk Cho, Sang Chul Yoo, Do Heon Kim (Won Kwon Choi, 89), Kyung Ho Chung (Sung Kuk Choi, 60) Chun Soo Lee (Tae Uk Choi, 69), Kyu Seon Park, Dong Jin Kim, Jae Jin Cho.

MEXICO: Corona, Francisco Rodriguez, Mario Perez, Lopez, Galindo, Zinha, Martinez (Garcia, 74), Bravo (Pineda, 46), Luis Perez, Marquez, Sanchez (Iniguez 46)

14th August 2004

Venue: *The Kaftanzoglio Stadium in Thessaloniki.*

GREECE 0
MALI 2 (Berthe 2, Ndiaye 45)

Half-time: 0-2   Attendance: 17,123

Referee: Carlos Torres (Paraguay)

GREECE: Amparis, Moras, Vallas, Stoltidis, Nempegleras (Lagos, 46), Salpingidis, Mitrou (Taralidis, 30), Papadopoulos, Fotakis, Sapanis (Galanopoulos, 63), Vyntra.

MALI: Bathily, Berthe, Tamboura, Kone (Abdou Traore, 40), Ndiaye, Diakite, Dramane Traore (Doucoure, 62), Sissoko, Kebe (Sidibe, 72), Coulibaly, Mamadou Diallo.

17th August 2004

Venue: *The Kaftanzoglio Stadium in Thessaloniki.*

SOUTH KOREA 3 (Jae Jin Cho 57, 59, o.g. 64)
MALI 3 (Ndiaye 7, 24, 55)

Half-time: 0-2   Attendance: 3,320

Referee: Eric Poulat (France)

SOUTH KOREA: Young Kwang Kim, Chi Gon Kim, Byung Kuk Cho, Sang Chul Yoo, Do Heon Kim (Sung Kuk Choi, 58), Kyu Seon Park, Dong Jin Kim, Jung Woo Kim, Chun Soo Lee, Tae Uk Choi (Kyung Ho Chung, 38), Jae Jin Cho (Do Namkung, 90).

MALI: Bathily, Tamboura, Boucader Diallo, Traore, Diakite, Coulibaly, Berthe, Sissoko (Doucoure, 37, Sidibe 69), Ndiaye, Traore, Kebe.

17th August 2004

Venue: *The Panthessaliko Stadium in Volos.*

GREECE 2 (Taralidis 82 pen., Stoltidis 93)
MEXICO 3 (Marquez 47, Bravo 70, 86)

Half-time: 0-0   Attendance: 21,597

Referee: Divine Evehe (Cameroon)

GREECE: Giannou, Lagos, Moras, Vallas, Nempegleras, Vyntra (Taralidis, 64), Stoltidis, Fotakis, Sapanis (Agritis, 50), Salpingidis, Papadopoulos.

MEXICO: Corona, Francisco Rodriguez, Mario Perez, Galindo, Martinez (Garcia, 85), Pineda, Lopez, Zinha (Iniguez, 68), Luis Perez, Bravo, Marquez (Ponce, 60).

	P	W	D	L	F	A	Pts
MALI	3	1	2	0	5	3	5
SOUTH KOREA	3	1	2	0	6	5	5
MEXICO	3	1	1	1	3	3	4
GREECE	3	0	1	2	4	7	1

Group B

12th August 2004

Venue: *The Kaftanzoglio Stadium in Thessaloniki.*

PARAGUAY 4 (Gimenz 5, Cardozo 26, 37, Torres 62)
JAPAN 3 (Ono 22, 53, Okubo 81)

Half-time: 3-1   Attendance: 5,318

Referee: Esam Abd El Fatah (Egypt)

PARAGUAY: Diego Barreto, Manzur, Gamarra, Devaca, Esquivel (Bareiro, 70), Gimenez (Martinez, 58), Edgar Barreto, Figueredo, Torres, Cristaldo (Diaz, 77), Cardozo.

JAPAN: Sogahata, Tanaka, Moniwa, Nasu (Matsui, 46), Abe, Konino, Morisaki (Tanaka, 66), Ono, Takamatsu (Hirayama, 74), Tokunaga, Okubo.

12th August 2004

Venue: *The Panthessaliko Stadium in Volos.*

GHANA 2 (Pappoe 36, Appiah 46)
ITALY 2 (Pinzi 49, Gilardino 83)

Half-time: 2-0   Attendance: 7,012

Referee: Horacio Elizondo (Argentina)

GHANA: Owu, Baffour Gyan (Pimpong, 59), Osei, Mensah, Pappoe, Appiah (Asampong Taylor, 79), Asamoah Gyan (Poku, 67), Pantsil, Coleman, Tiero, Chibsah.

ITALY: Pelizzoli, Moretti, Ferrari, Bonera, de Rossi (Donadel, 81), Pinzi (Mesto, 65), Palombo, Gilardino, Pirlo, Sculli (de Nero, 54), Barzagli.

18th August 2004

Venue: *The Karaiskaki Stadium in Athens*

PARAGUAY 1 (Bareiro 14)
ITALY 0

Half-time: 1-0   Attendance: 24,160

Referee: Claus Bo Larsen (Denmark)

PARAGUAY: Diego Barreto, Martinez, Manzur, Gamarra, Torres, Edgar Barreto, Figueredo, Enciso, Gimenez (Esquival, 56), Bareiro (Cristaldo, 56), Cardozo (Gonzalez, 75).

ITALY: Pelizzoli, Moretti, Ferrari, Bonera, Barzagli, de Rossi, Pinzi (Gasbarroni, 62), Palombo, Pirlo (Donadel, 71), Gilardino, Sculli (del Nero, 59).

15th August 2004

Venue: *The Kaftanzoglio Stadium in Thessaloniki.*

PARAGUAY 1 (Gamarra 76)
GHANA 2 (Tiero 81, Appiah 84)

Half-time: 0-0   Attendance: 1,119

Referee: Benito Archundia (Mexico)

PARAGUAY: Diego Barreto, Manzur, Gamarra, Devaca (Gonzalez, 88), Esquival, Torres, Edgar Barreto, Figueredo, Enciso (Diaz, 86), Gimenez (Bareiro, 66), Cardozo.

GHANA: Owu, Osei, Mensah, Pappoe, Coleman, Chibsah, Baffour Gyan (Asampong Taylor, 76), Appiah, Asamoah Gyan, Pimpong (Poku, 54), Tiero.

18th August 2004

Venue: *The Panthessaliko Stadium in Volos.*

JAPAN 1 (Okubo 37)
GHANA 0

Half-time: 1-0   Attendance: 6,813

Referee: Kyros Vassaras (Greece)

JAPAN: Sogahata, Tanaka, Moniwa, Kikuchi, Abe, Konno, Ono, Komano (Morisaki, 23), Ishikawa (Matsui, 62), Takamatsu, Okubo (Tanaka, 82).

GHANA: Owu, Osei, Pappoe, Villars (Lamine, 77), Coleman, Chibsah, Baffour Gyan (Asampong Taylor, 57), Appiah, Asamoah Gyan, Pimpong (Poku, 46), Tiero.

15th August 2004

Venue: *The Panthessaliko Stadium in Volos.*

JAPAN 2 (Abe 20, Takamatsu 91)
ITALY 3 (de Rossi 3, Gilardino 8, 36)

Half-time: 1-3   Attendance: 9,487

Referee: Jorge Larrionda (Uruguay)

JAPAN: Sogahata, Tanaka, Moniwa, Tokunaga (Nasu, 18), Konno, Ono, Matsui (Morisaki, 76), Komano (Tanaka, 46), Takamatsu, Okubo.

ITALY: Pelizzoli, Moretti, Ferrari, Bonera, Barzagli, de Rossi, Pinzi (Mesto, 89), Palombo (Donadel, 62), Pirlo, Gilardino, Sculli (del Nero 54).

	P	W	D	L	F	A	Pts
PARAGUAY	3	2	0	1	6	5	6
ITALY	3	1	1	1	5	5	4
GHANA	3	1	1	1	4	4	4
JAPAN	3	1	0	2	6	7	3

Group C

11th August 2004

Venue: *The Pankritio Stadium in Heraklio, Crete.*

TUNISIA 1 (Zitouni 69)
AUSTRALIA 1 (Aloisi 45)

Half-time: 0-1   Attendance: 15,757
Referee: Kyros Vassaras (Greece)
TUNISIA: Fadhel, Boussaidi, Hagui, Yahia, Ragued, Bhairi (Ayari, 46), Zitouni, Mouelhi (Ltaief, 76), Ben Yahia (Traoui, 57), Clayton, Jedidi.
AUSTRALIA: Galekovic, North, Cansdell-Sherrif, Moore, Madaschi, Elrich (Griffiths, 82), Wilkshire, Aloisi, Cahill, Brosque (Holman 68), Valeri (McKain 84)

11th August 2004

Venue: *The Pampelonnisiako Stadium in Patras.*

ARGENTINA 6 (Delgado 11, Gonzalez 17, Tevez 42, 43, Heinze 74, Rosales 77)
SERBIA & MONTENEGRO 0

Half-time: 4-0   Attendance: 14,657
Referee: Carlos Batres (Guatemala)
ARGENTINA: Lux, Ayala, Coloccini, Mascherano, Heinze, Delgado, Tevez (Medina, 72), Cristian Gonzalez (Rodriguez, 77), Rosales, D'Alessandro (Saviola, 60) Luis Gonzalez.
SERBIA: Milojevic, Lomic, Neziri, Lazarevic, Bisevac, Jokic, Stepanov (Delibasic, 83), Milovanovic, Vukcevic (Petrovic, 70), Krasic, Nikezic (Lovre, 46)

14th August 2004

Venue: *The Pankritio Stadium in Heraklio, Crete.*

SERBIA & MONTENEGRO 1 (Radonjic 72)
AUSTRALIA 5 (Cahill 11, Aloisi 46, 57, Elrich 60, 86)

Half-time: 0-2   Attendance: 8,857
Referee: Subkhiddin Mohd Salleh (Malaysia)
SERBIA: Milojevic, Bisevac, Neziri, Jokic, Basa, Lovre, Delibasic, Vukcevic (Radonjic, 46), Matic (Lomic, 72), Lazarevic (Petrovic, 60), Krasic.
AUSTRALIA: Galekovic, North, Cansdell-Sherriff, Moore, McKain, Madaschi, Elrich, Wilkshire, Aloisi (Holman, 74), Cahill (Danze 64), Brosque (Griffiths, 64).

14th August 2004

Venue: *The Pampelonnisiako Stadium in Patras.*

ARGENTINA 2 (Tevez 39, Saviola 72)
TUNISIA 0

Half-time: 1-0   Attendance: 5,512
Referee: Eric Poulat (France)
ARGENTINA: Lux, Ayala, Coloccini, Mascherano, Heinze, Delgado, Tevez (Burdisso, 86), Cristian Gonzalez, Rosales (Mariano Gonzalez, 63), D'Alessandro (Saviola, 56), Luis Gonzalez.
TUNISIA: Fadhel, Boussaidi, Hagui, Yahia, Trabelsi (Zitouni, 65), Ragued, Mouelhi, Ayari, Ben Yahia, Traoui (Jedidi, 59), Clayton (Ltaief, 70)

17th August 2004

Venue: *The Karaiskaki Stadium in Athens.*

ARGENTINA 1 (D'Alessandro 9)
AUSTRALIA 0

Half-time: 1-0   Attendance: 26,338
Referee: Esam Abd El Fatah (Egypt)
ARGENTINA: Lux, Ayala, Coloccini, Heinze, Mascherano, Cristian Gonzalez (Mariano Gonzalez, 1), D'Alessandro, Luis Gonzalez, Delgado (Burdisso, 30), Tavez (Saviola, 66), Rosales.
AUSTRALIA: Galekovic, North, Cansdell-Sherriff, Moore, Madaschi, Elrich, Wilkshire, Cahill, Valeri (Danze, 73), Aloisi, Brosque (Holman, 72).

17th August 2004

Venue: *The Pampeloponnisiako Stadium in Patras.*

SERBIA & MONTENEGRO 2 (Krasic 70, Vukcevic 87)
TUNISIA 3 (Clayton 41, Jedidi 83 pen, Zitouni 89)

Half-time: 0-1   Attendance: 7,214
Referee: Charles Ariiotime (Tahiti)
SERBIA: Milojevic, Bisevac, Neziri, Stepanov, Jokic, Lovre, Delibasic, Vukcevic, Lomic, Lazarevic, Krasic (Nikezic 89).
TUNISIA: Fadhel, Boussaidi, Hagui, Ragued, Zitouni, Ltaief (Ben Yahia), Ayari, Traoui, Clayton, Merdassi (Yahia, 46), Jedidi.

	P	W	D	L	F	A	Pts
ARGENTINA	3	3	0	0	9	0	9
AUSTRALIA	3	1	1	1	6	3	4
TUNISIA	3	1	1	1	4	5	4
SERBIA & MON.	3	0	0	3	3	14	0

Group D

12th August 2004

Venue: The Pankritio Stadium in Heraklio, Crete.

COSTA RICA 0
MOROCCO 0

Half-time: 0-0   Attendance: 3,212

Referee: Massimo De Santis (Italy)

COSTA RICA: Drummond, Salazar, Umana, Myre, Scott, Lopez, Brenes (Granados, 69), Saborio, Villalobos, Diaz, Hernandez (Wilson, 86).

MOROCCO: Lamyaghri, Zerka, Alioui, El Kaddouri, Talhaoui, Bouden (Kaissi, 69), Taouil, El Moubarki (Ourahou, 91), Souaidy, Erbate, El Assas.

12th August 2004

Venue: The Pampeloponnisiako Stadium in Patras.

IRAQ 4   (Emad 16, Hawar Mulla 29, Younis 56, Salih 93)
PORTUGAL 2   (o.g. 13, Boswinga 45)

Half-time: 2-2   Attendance: 5,689

Referee: Divine Evehe (Cameroon)

IRAQ: Nour Sabri, Bassim Abbas, Haidar Jabar, Nashat Akram (Salih Sadir, 71), Emad Mohammed (Ahmed Manajid, 76), Abdul Wahab Abu Al Hail, Younis Mahmoud, Hawar Mulla Mohammed (Mahdi Karim, 80), Haidar Abdul Razzaq, Qusai Munir, Haidar Abdul Amir.

PORTUGAL: Moreira, Bruno Alves, Ricardo Costa, Fernando Meira (Carlos Martins, 74), Cristiano Ronaldo, Hugo Vianna (Danny, 60), Hugo Almeida, Jorge Ribeiro, Frechaut, Boa Morte, Bosingwa (Raul Meireles, 63).

15th August 2004

Venue: The Karaiskaki Stadium in Athens

COSTA RICA 0
IRAQ 2   (Hawar Mulla Mohammed 67, Mahdi Karim 72)

Half-time: 0-0   Attendance: 12,150

Referee: Charles Ariiotima (Tahiti)

COSTA RICA: Drummond, Salazar, Umana, Myre (Arrieta, 76), Villalobos, Diaz, Lopez, Brenes, Hernandez (Granados, 80), Scott, Saborio (Wilson, 75).

IRAQ: Nour Sabri, Bassim Abbas, Haidar Jabar, Haidar Abdul Razzaq, Haidar Abdul Amir, Nashat Akram (Salih Sadir, 58), Abdul Wahab Abu Al Hail, Hawar Mulla Mohammed, Qusai Munir, Emad Mohammed (Mahdi Karim, 69), Younis Mahmoud (Razzaq Farhan, 79).

15th August 2004

Venue: The Pankritio Stadium in Heraklio, Crete.

MOROCCO 1   (Bouden 85)
PORTUGAL 2   (Ronaldo 40, Costa 73)

Half-time: 0-1   Attendance: 7,581

Referee: Carlos Batres (Guatemala)

MOROCCO: Lamyaghri, Zerka (Sami, 72), El Kaddouri, Souaidy, Erbate, Kaissi, El Assas, Talhaoui, Bouden, Taouil (Aqqal, 78), El Moubarki (Ourahou, 48).

PORTUGAL: Moreira, Bruno Alves, Ricardo Costa, Fernando Meira, Jorge Ribeiro, Frechaut (Mario Sergio, 73), Raul Meireles, Bosingwa, Cristiano Ronaldo, Hugo Almeida (Lourenco, 58), Danny (Carlos Martins, 81).

18th August 2004

Venue: The Pankritio Stadium in Heraklio, Crete.

COSTA RICA 4 (Villalobos 50, o.g. 68, Saborio 71, Brenes 91)

PORTUGAL 2 (Hugo Almeida 29, Jorge Riberio 54)

Half-time: 0-1   Attendance: 11,218

Referee: Carlos Torres (Paraguay)

COSTA RICA: Drummond, Salazar (Scott, 46), Umana, Myre, Villalobos, Diaz, Lopez, Brenes, Hernandez (Granados, 81), Wilson (Saborio, 46), Arrieta.

PORTUGAL: Moreira, Mario Sergio, Ricardo Costa, Fernando Meira, Jorge Ribeiro, Joao Paulo, Raul Meireles, Carlos Martins (Frechaut, 48), Bosingwa (Hugo Viana, 79), Hugo Almeida (Lourenco, 64), Danny.

Quarter-Finals

21st August 2004

Venue: The Karaiskaki Stadium in Athens

MALI 0

ITALY 1 (Bovo 116)

Half-time: 0-0   Attendance: 27,543

Referee: Carlos Torres (Paraguay)

MALI: Bathily, Tamboura, Kone, Diakite, Coulibaly, Berthe (Abdou Traore, 106), Sissoko, Ndiaye, Dramane Traore (Abouta, 82), Kebe (Sidebe, 120), Mamadou Diallo.

ITALY: Pelizzoli, Moretti (Chiellini, 118), Ferrari, Bonera, Bovo, Pinzi (Gasbarroni, 109), Palomobo, Pirlo, Donadel, Gilardino, Sculli (del Nero, 76).

18th August 2004

Venue: The Pampeloponnisiako Stadium in Patras.

MOROCCO 2 (Bouden 69, Aqqal 77)

IRAQ 1 (Salih 63)

Half-time: 0-0   Attendance: 4,019

Referee: Horacio Elizondo (Argentina)

MOROCCO: Lamyaghri, Alioui, El Kaddouri (Zemmama, 46), Souaidy, Sami, Erbate, Kaissi, Ourahou, Bouden, Taouil (Aqqal, 75), El Moubarki (Talhaoui, 58).

IRAQ: Nour Sabri, Saad Attiya, Haidar Abdul Razzaq, Haidar Abdul Amir, Salih Sadir, Abdul Wahab Abu Al Hail, Qusai Munir, Mahdi Karim, Razzaq Farhan, Ahmed Manjid (Emad Mohammed, 58), Ahmed Salah (Hawar Mulla Mohammed, 65).

21st August 2004

Venue: The Pankritio Stadium in Heraklio

IRAQ 1 (Emad 64)

AUSTRALIA 0

Half-time: 0-0   Attendance: 10,023

Referee: Carlos Batres (Guatemala)

IRAQ: Nour Sabri, Bassim Abbas, Haidar Jabar, Haidar Abdul Razzaq, Haidar Abdul Amir, Salih Sadir (Mahdi Karim, 60), Abdul Wahab Abu Al Halil, Hawar Mulla Mohammed, Qusai Munir, Emad Mohammed (Saad Attiya), Younis Mahmoud (Razzaq Farhan, 71).

AUSTRALIA: Galekovic, North, Cansdell-Sherriff, McKain, Madaschi, Wilkshire, Valeri, Danze (Dilevski, 77), Aloisi, Brosque, Holman (Griffiths, 60).

	P	W	D	L	F	A	Pts
IRAQ	3	2	0	1	7	4	6
COSTA RICA	3	1	1	1	4	4	4
MOROCCO	3	1	1	1	3	3	4
PORTUGAL	3	1	0	2	6	9	3

21st August 2004

Venue: *The Pampeloponnisiako Stadium in Patras*

ARGENTINA 4 (Delgado 24, Tevez 43, 82, 83)
COSTA RICA 0

Half-time: 2-0   Attendance: 9,292

Referee: Kyros Vassaras (Greece)

ARGENTINA: Lux, Ayala, Coloccini, Heinze (Rodriguez, 18) Mascherano, Cristian Gonzalez, D'Alessandro (Medina, 66), Luis Gonzalez, Delgado, Tevez, Rosales (Burdisso, 51).

COSTA RICA: Drummond, Salazar (Granados, 58), Umana, Myre, Villalobos, Diaz, Lopez, Brenes (Wilson, 77), Hernandez, Saborio, Arrieta (Scott, 46).

21st August 2004

Venue: *The Kaftanzoglio Stadium in Thessaloniki*

PARAGUAY 3 (Bareiro 19, 71, Cardozo 61)
SOUTH KOREA 2 (Chun Soo Lee 74, 79 pen)

Half-time: 1-0   Attendance: 4,080

Referee: Massimo DeSantis (Italy)

PARAGUAY: Diego Barreto, Martinez, Manzur, Gamarra, Torres, Edgar Barreto, Figueredo (Esquival, 46), Enciso, Diaz (Cristaldo, 76), Bareiro (Gimenez, 83), Cardozo.

SOUTH KOREA: Young Kwang Kim, Won Kwon Choi (Kyu Seon Park, 77), Chi Gon Kim, Yong Ho Park, Sang Chul Yoo, Do Heon Kim, Dong Jin Kim, Jung Woo Kim (Byung Kuk Cho, 60), Chun Soo Lee, Sung Kuk Choi (Kyung Ho Chung, 56), Jae Jin Cho.

Semi-Finals

24th August 2004

Venue: *The Karaiskaki Stadium in Athens.*

ITALY 0
ARGENTINA 3 (Tevez 16, Luis Gonzalez 69, Mariano Gonzalez 84)

Half-time: 0-1   Attendance: 30,910

Referee: Benito Archundia (Mexico)

ITALY: Pelizzoli, Moretti, Ferrari, Bonera, Bovo, de Rossi (Donadel, 46), Pinzi (Gasbarroni, 72), Palombo, Pirlo, Gilardino, Sculli (de Nero, 46).

ARGENTINA: Lux, Ayala, Coloccini (Medina, 69), Heinze, Mascherano, Cristian Gonzalez (Mariano Gonzalez, 84), D'Alessandro, Luis Gonzalez, Delgado (Rodriguez, 54), Tevez, Rosales.

24th August 2004

Venue: *The Kaftanzoglio Stadium in Thessaloniki.*

IRAQ 1 (Razzaq Fahran 83)
PARAGUAY 3 (Cardozo 17, 34, Bareiro 68)

Half-time: 0-2   Attendance: 6,213

Referee: Eric Poulat (France)

IRAQ: Nour Sabri, Bassim Abbas, Haidar Jabar, Haidar Abdul Razzaq (Mahdi Karim, 46), Haidar Abdul Amir, Nashat Akram (Salih Sadir, 46), Abdul Wahab Abu Al Hail (Razzaq Fahran, 73), Hawar Mulla Mohammed, Qusai Munir, Emad Mohammed, Younis Mahmoud.

PARAGUAY: Diego Barreto, Martinez, Manzur, Gamarra, Esquival, Torres,

Edgar Barreto, Enciso, Diaz (Figueredo, 63), Bareiro (Gonzalez, 78), Cardozo (Benitez, 75).

Bronze Medal Game

27th August 2004

Venue: The Kaftanzoglio Stadium in Thessaloniki.

ITALY 1 (Gilardino 8)
IRAQ 0

Half-time: 1-0   Attendance: 5,203

Referee: Jorge Larrionda (Uruguay)

ITALY: Pelizzoli, Moretti (Chiellini, 85), Ferrari, Pinzi (Mesto, 78), Palombo, Gilardino, Pirlo, Barzagli, Bovo, Donadel, del Nero.

IRAQ: Nour Sabri, Saad Attiya, Bassim Abbas, Haidar Jabar, Salih Sadir (Younis Mahmoud, 77), Abdul Wahab Abu Al Hail, Razzaq Farhan, Hawar Mull Mohammed (Ahmed Salah, 84), Qusai Munir, Haidar Abdul Amir, Mahdi Karim (Emad Mohammed, 57)

Final

28th August 2004

Venue: The Karaiskaki Stadium in Athens

ARGENTINA 1 (Tevez 18)
PARAGUAY 0

Half-time: 1-0   Attendance: 41,116

Referee: Kyros Vassaras (Greece)

ARGENTINA: Lux, Ayala, Coloccini, Mascherano, Heinze, Delgado (Rodriguez, 76), Tevez, Cristian Gonzalez, Rosales, D'Alessandro, Luis Gonzalez.

PARAGUAY: Diego Barreto, Martinez, Manzur, Gamarra, Esquival (Gonzalez, 76), Gimenez, Edgar Barreto (Cristaldo, 72), Bareiro, Figueredo, Torres, Enciso (Diaz, 63).

Women's Competition

The United States won its second goal medal in the women's competition defeating Brazil 2-1 after extra time. The Americans, who had won previously in the first competition for women played in Athens, Georgia, and were beaten Finalists in Sydney, struggled in a number of their games but triumphed in the end. In reaching the Final the Americans eliminated current World Champions Germany in the semi-final

In reaching the Final the Brazilians became a force to be reckoned with in the world game for the first time, and their play in the Final took the women's game to a new level. The U.S.A. took the lead in the first half, but Brazil dominated the second and hit the goalpost twice before they equalized. But in extra time the Americans regained the ascendancy and Abby Wambach scored the winner when she headed in a Kristine Lilly corner.

This game marked the end of an era for several members of the U.S.A. team who have been a key to the success of the women's game for many years. Mia Hamm, Julie Foudy and Joy Fawcett all indicated that they will retire from international competition following the gold medal win.

Group E

11th August 2004

Venue: The Panthessaliko Stadium in Volos.

SWEDEN 0
JAPAN 1   (Arakawa 24)

Half-time: 0-1   Attendance: 10,104

Referee: Fatou Gaye (Senegal)

SWEDEN: Jonsson, Westberg, Tornqvist, Marklund, Bengtsson, Mostrom, Ostberg, Andersson (Sjostrom, 57), Ljungberg (Oeqvist, 68), Svensson, Sjogran (Olsson, 84).

JAPAN: Yamago, Isozaki, Kawakami, Sakai, Miyamoto, Arakawa (Maruyama, 66), Sawa, Otani, Yamagishi, Shimokozuru, Kobayshi (Ando, 56, Yanagita, 85).

14th August 2004

Venue: The Karaiskaki Stadium in Athens

JAPAN 0
NIGERIA 1   (Okolo 55)

Half-time: 0-0   Attendance: 14,026

Referee: Diane Ferreira-James (Guyana)

JAPAN: Yamago, Isozaki, Kawakami, Sakai, Miyamoto (Yanagita, 20), Arakawa, Sawa, Otani, Yamagishi (Yamamoto, 84), Shimokozuru, Kobayashi (Maruyama, 60).

NIGERIA: Dede, Ekpo, Eze, Nkwocha, Ikidi (Sabi, 81), Mbachu, Akide (Ameh, 76), Okolo, Kudaisi, Mmadu, Nwosu.

17th August 2004

Venue: *The Panthessaliko Stadium in Volos.*

SWEDEN 2 (Marklund 68, Mostroem 73)
NIGERIA 1 (Akide 25)

Half-time: 0-1   Attendance: 21,597
Referee: Silvia De Oliveira (Brazil)
SWEDEN: Jonsson, Westberg, Marklund, Bengtsson, Larsson, Ostberg, Mostrom, Sjogran (Schelin, 46), Sjostrom (Oeqvist, 63), Ljungberg (Fagerstrom, 80), Svensson.
NIGERIA: Dede, Eze, Ikidi, Kudaisi, Nwosu (Sabi, 83), Ekpo, Mmadu, Nkwocha, Mbachu (Egbe, 78), Akide (Ameh, 70), Okolo.

	P	W	D	L	F	A	Pts
SWEDEN	2	1	0	1	2	2	3
NIGERIA	2	1	0	1	2	2	3
JAPAN	2	1	0	1	1	1	3

Group F

11th August 2004

Venue: *The Pampeloponnisiako Stadium in Patras.*

GERMANY 8 (Prinz 13, 21, 73, 88, Wunderlich 65, Lingor 76, Pohlers 81, Mueller 90)
CHINA 0

Half-time: 2-0   Attendance: 14,657
Referee: Kari Seitz (U.S.A.)
GERMANY: Rottenberg, Stegemann, Garefrekes, Jones, Odebrecht, Wunderlich (Pohlers, 83), Wimbersky (Mueller, 79), Prinz, Lingor, Fuss (Guenther, 58), Hingst.
CHINA: Xiao, Jin (Wang, 66), Li, Fan, Pu, Bi (Zhang, 69), Han (Bai, 60), Teng, Qu, Ren, Ji.

14th August 2004

Venue: *The Pampeloponnisiako Stadium in Patras.*

CHINA 1 (Ji 34)
MEXICO 1 (Dominguez 11)

Half-time: 1-1   Attendance: 5,112
Referee: Cristina Ionescu (Romania)
CHINA: Xiao, Li, Wang (Jin, 67), Fan, Pu, Zhang (Bai, 77), Bi (Han, 62) Teng, Qu, Ren, Ji.
MEXICO: Tajonar, Gomez, Sandoval, Gonzalez, Castillo, Vergara, Leyva (Lopez, 74), Dominguez, Mora, Perez (Saucedo, 36), Valderrama (Gutierrez, 46).

17th August 2004

Venue: *The Karaiskaki Stadium in Athens.*

GERMANY 2 (Wimbersky 20, Prinz 79)
MEXICO 0

Half-time: 1-0   Attendance: 26,338
Referee: Krystyna Szokolai (Australia)
GERMANY: Rottenberg, Stegemann, Jones, Guenther, Hingst, Garefrekes (Pohlers, 64), Lingor (Odebrecht, 46), Omilade, Wimbersky (Mueller, 46), Prinz, Bachlor.
MEXICO: Molina, Gomez, Sandoval, Gonzalez, Vergara (Gutierrez, 80), Leyva, Valderrama, Dominguez, Mora (Lopez, 76), Martinez, Worbis (Castillo, 67)

	P	W	D	L	F	A	Pts
GERMANY	2	2	0	0	10	0	6
MEXICO	2	0	1	1	1	3	1
CHINA	2	0	1	1	1	9	1

Group G

11th August 2004

Venue: *The Pankritio Stadium in Heraklio, Crete.*

GREECE 0
UNITED STATES 3 (Boxx 14, Wambach 30, Hamm 82)

Half-time: 0-2   Attendance: 15,757
Referee: Jenny Palmqvist (Sweden)
GREECE: Giatrakis, Stratakis, Katsaiti, Kavvada (Papadopoulou, 59), Benson, Lagoumtzi, Smith, Michailidou, Loseno, Kalyvas (Chatzgiannidou, 46), Panteleiadou (Soupiadou, 76).
U.S.A.: Scurry, Rampone, Reddick, Fawcett, Markgraf, Boxx, Wagner (Tarpley, 60), Foudy (Hucles, 71), Lilly, Hamm, Wambach (Parlow, 79).

11th August 2004

Venue: *The Kaftanzoglio Stadium in Thessaloniki.*

BRAZIL 1 (Marta 36)
AUSTRALIA 0

Half-time: 1-0   Attendance: 24,325
Referee: Christine Frai (Germany)
BRAZIL: Roseli, Aline, Tania, Juliana, Rosana (Andreia, 13, Daniela, 83)), Monica, Formiga, Elaine, Maycon, Renata Costa (Pretinha, 76), Kelly.
AUSTRALIA: Kell, Davies, Wainwright, Alagich, Salisbury, Shipard (Ledbrook, 83), Walsh (Kuralay, 71), Garriock, Peters, Foster (De Vanna, 57), Small.

14th August 2004

Venue: *The Pankritio Stadium in Heraklio, Crete.*

GREECE 0
AUSTRALIA 1 (Garriock 27)

Half-time: 0-1   Attendance: 8,857
Referee: Bentla Dcoth (India)
GREECE: Giatrakis, Lagoumtzi (Tefani, 73), Smith, Stratakis, Michailidou, Katsaiti, Chatzigiannidou (Soupiadou, 46) Panteleiadou (Lazarou, 46), Loseno, Papadopoulou, Benson.
AUSTRALIA: Kell, Davies (De Vann, 46), Wainwright, Alagich, Salisbury, Shipard, Walsh (Kuralay, 58), Garriock, Peters, Foster (Reuter, 74), Small.

14th August 2004

Venue: *The Kaftanzoglio Stadium in Thessaloniki.*

UNITED STATES 2 (Hamm 58 pen, Wambach 78)
BRAZIL 0

Half-time: 0-0   Attendance: 17,123
Referee: Dagmar Damkova (Czech Republic)
U.S.A.: Scurry, Rampone, Reddick (Mitts, 80), Fawcett, Markgraf, Boxx, Wagner (Tarpley, 57), Foudy, Lilly (O'Reilly, 69), Hamm, Wambach.
BRAZIL: Andreia, Monica, Tania, Juliana, Daniela, Rosana (Kelly, 72, Grazielle, 85), Formiga, Elaine, Pretinha, Marta, Cristiane (Maycon, 65).

17th August 2004

Venue: *The Pampeloponnisiako Stadium in Patras.*

GREECE 0
BRAZIL 7 (Pretinha 21, Cristiane 46, 55, 77, Grazielle 49, Marta 70, Daniela 72)

Half-time: 0-2   Attendance: 7,214
Referee: Christine Frei (Germany)
GREECE: Giatrakis (Moschos, 80), Stratakis, Katsaiti, Benson, Lagoumtzi, Smith, Michailidou, Loseno, Kalyvas, Panteleiadou (Pouridou, 69), Papadopoulou (Soupiadou, 46).
BRAZIL: Andreia, Tania (Grazielle, 25), Juliana, Daniela, Rosana (Maycon, 58), Aline, Formiga (Roseli, 54), Elaine, Pretinha, Marta, Cristiane.

17th August 2004

Venue: *The Kaftanzoglio Stadium in Thessaloniki.*

UNITED STATES 1 (Lilly 19)
AUSTRALIA 1 (Peters 82)

Half-time: 1-0   Attendance: 3,320
Referee: Cristina Ionescu (Romania)
U.S.A.: Scurry, Mitts, Reddick, Fawcett, Markgraf, Boxx (Tarpley, 67), Wagner (Hucles, 74), Foudy, Lilly, Hamm (O'Reilly, 67), Parlow.
AUSTRALIA: Kell, Davies, Wainwright, Alagich (De Vanna, 62), Salisbury, Slatyer (Reuter, 43), Shipard, Garriock, Peters, Small (Foster, 67), Walsh.

	P	W	D	L	F	A	Pts
U.S.A.	3	2	1	0	6	1	7
BRAZIL	3	2	0	1	8	2	6
AUSTRALIA	3	1	1	1	2	2	4
GREECE	3	0	0	3	0	11	0

Quarter-Finals

20th August 2004

Venue: *The Pampeloponnisiako Stadium in Patras*

GERMANY 2   (Jones 76, Pohlers 81)
NIGERIA 1   (Akide 49)

Half-time: 0-0   Attendance: 2,531
Referee: Bentla Dcoth (India)
GERMANY: Rottenberg, Stegemann, Garefrekes, Jones, Odebrecht, Wunderlich (Bachor, 55), Wimbersky (Pohlers, 46), Prinz, Lingor, Minnert (Fuss, 79), Hingst.
NIGERIA: Dede, Ekpo, Eze (Nwosu, 79), Nkwocha (Mbachu, 87), Ikidi, Nwadike (Igbojionu, 68), Akide, Okolo, Kudaisi, Sabi, Mmadu.

20th August 2004

Venue: *The Kartanzoglio Stadium in Thessaloniki*

UNITED STATES 2   (Lilly 43, Wambach 59)
JAPAN 1   (Yamamoto 48)

Half-time: 1-0   Attendance: 1,418
Referee: Silvia De Oliveira (Brazil)
U.S.A.: Scurry, Rampone, Tarpley, Chastain, Boxx, Hamm, Foudy, Lilly, Fawcett, Markgraf, Wambach.
JAPAN: Yamago, Yano, Isozaki, Kawakami, Sakai, Yamamoto, Miyamoto, Arakawa, Sawa, Otani, Shimokozuru.

20th August 2004

Venue: *The Pankritio Stadium in Heraklio*

MEXICO 0
BRAZIL 5   (Cristiane 25, 49, Formiga 29, 54, Marta 60)

Half-time: 0-2   Attendance: 3,012
Referee: Fatou Gaye (Senegal)
MEXICO: Tajonar, Gomez, Sandoval, Gonzalez, Castillo (Worbis, 65), Vergara (Lopez, 48), Leyva, Valderrama, Dominguez, Mora, Martinez (Gutierrez 48)
BRAZIL: Andreia, Monica, Tania (Aline, 56), Juliana, Daniela, Rosana, Formiga (Roseli, 77), Elaine, Pretinha (Renata Costa, 63), Marta, Cristiane.

20th August 2004

Venue: *The Panthessaliko Stadium in Volos*

SWEDEN 2   (Ljungberg 25, Larsson 30)
AUSTRALIA 1   (De Vanna 79)

Half-time: 2-0   Attendance: 4,811
Referee: Dagmar Damkova (Czech Republic)
SWEDEN: Jonsson, Westberg, Marklund, Bengtsson, Mostrom, Larsson, Ostberg, Ljungberg (Fagerstrom, 77), Svensson, Sjogran (Oqvist 71), Sjostrom (Olsson 87)
AUSTRALIA: Kell, Davies, Wainwright, Alagich, Salisbury, Shipard, Walsh, Garriock, Peters, Foster (Kuralay, 61), Small (De Vanna, 36)

Semi-Finals

23rd August 2004

Venue: The Pankritio Stadium in Heraklio.

UNITED STATES 2   (Lilly 33, O'Reilly 99)
GERMANY 1   (Bachor 92)

Half-time: 1-0   Attendance: 5,165

Referee: Krystyna Szokolai (Australia)

U.S.A.: Scurry, Rampone, Tarpley (O'Reilly, 75), Chastain (Reddick, 51) Boxx, Hamm, Foudy (Wagner, 65), Lilly, Fawcett, Markgraf, Wambach.

GERMANY: Rottenberg, Stegemann, Garefrekes, Jones, Odebrecht (Fuss, 71), Wunderlich (Bachor, 39), Prinz, Lingor, Minnert, Pohlers (Mueller, 58), Hingst.

23rd August 2004

Venue: The Pampeloponnisiako Stadium in Patras

SWEDEN 0
BRAZIL 1   (Pretinha 64)

Half-time: 0-0   Attendance: 1,511

Referee: Diane Ferreira-James (Guyana)

SWEDEN: Jonsson, Westberg, Marklund, Bengtsson (Oqvist, 86), Larsson, Ostberg, Mostrom, Sjogran (Schelin, 72), Sjostrom (Andersson, 78), Ljungberg, Svensson.

BRAZIL: Andreia, Monica, Tania, Juliana, Daniela, Rosana (Maycon, 79), Formiga, Elaine, Pretinha (Renata Costa, 87), Marta, Cristiane.

Bronze Medal Game

26th August 2004

Venue: The Karaiskaki Stadium, in Athens

GERMANY 1   (Lingor 17)
SWEDEN 0

Half-time: 1-0

Referee: Kari Seitz (U.S.A.)

GERMANY: Rottenberg, Stegemann, Garefrekes, Jones, Odebrecht (Guenther, 56), Wimbersky (Puss, 83), Prinz, Lingor, Minnert (Omilade, 56), Pohlers, Hingst.

SWEDEN: Jonsson, Tornqvist, Marklund, Bengtsson (Schelin, 76), Mostrom, Larsson, Ostberg, Andersson, Ljungberg, Svensson (Sjogran, 43), Sjostrom (Fagerstrom, 46).

Final

26th August 2004

Venue: The Karaiskaki Stadium, in Athens

UNITED STATES 2   (Tarpley, Wambach)
BRAZIL 1   (Pretinha 73)

Half-time: 1-0   Attendance: 10,416

Referee: Jenny Palqvist (Sweden)

U.S.A.: Scurry, Rampone, Tarpley (O'Reilly, 91), Chastain (Reddick, 61), Boxx, Hamm, Foudy, Lilly, Fawcett, Markgraf, Wambach.

BRAZIL: Andreia, Monica, Tania, Juliana, Formiga, Daniela, Pretinha, Marta, Rosana (Maycon, 111), Cristiane, Elaine (Renata Costa, 88).

Also available from Soccer Books Limited in the same series:

The Complete Results & Line-ups of the European Champion Clubs' Cup 1955-1991 – The Knockout Years
(ISBN 1-86223-089-7)   *Softback Price   £28.00*

The Complete Results & Line-ups of the European Champions League 1991-2004
(ISBN 1-86223-114-1)   *Softback Price   £27.50*

The Complete Results & Line-ups of the European Cup-Winners' Cup 1960-1999   (ISBN 1-86223-087-0)   *Softback Price   £29.50*

The Complete Results & Line-ups of the European Fairs Cup 1955-1971
(ISBN 1-86223-085-4)   *Softback Price   £22.50*

The Complete Results & Line-ups of the UEFA Cup 1971-1991
(ISBN 1-86223-109-5)   *Softback Price   £29.50*

The Complete Results & Line-ups of the UEFA Cup 1991-2004
(ISBN 1-86223-115-X)   *Softback Price   £29.50*

The Complete Results & Line-ups of the European Football Championships 1958-2004   (ISBN 1-86223-108-7)   *Softback Price   £24.50*